KRISHNA

From the same author:

The Mahabharata: A Modern Rendering

Devi: The Devi Bhagavatam Retold

Siva: The Siva Purana Retold

Srimad Bhagavad Gita
Bhagavata Purana

KRISHNA

Life and Song of the Blue God

Ramesh Menon

Rupa & Co

Typeset in 11.5 pts. Simoncini Garamond by
Mindways Design
1410 Chiranjiv Tower
43 Nehru Place
New Delhi 110 019

Printed in India by
Rekha Printers Pvt. Ltd.
A-102/1 Okhla Industrial Area, Phase-II
New Delhi-110 020

For my parents

ACKNOWLEDGEMENTS

The translation of the Bhagavata Purana that I used as my main source for Sri Krishna's life is the one by a board of scholars, edited by J.L. Shastri and published by Motilal Banarasidass. I am also indebted to Cornelia Dimmit and J.A. van Buitenen's reader in the Puranas, 'Classical Hindu Mythology', published by Rupa Books, for important sections from the Vishnu Purana.

I used two translations of the Bhagavad Gita as sources for my own rendering of the Holy Song: one is Dr. S. Radhakrishnan's, and the other by Christopher Isherwood and Swami Prabhavananda. I am aware that at times my own version is very close to their translations.

Katya Douglas edited this new edition of the book, and she transformed the text substantially.

I must also thank Saugato Mukherjee for proof reading *Krishna* and Moonis Ijlal for his inspired artwork for the covers of my books.

"I am neither deva nor gandharva, neither yaksha nor danava. I have been born into your family. This is the only way to look at it."

In the kali yuga, the age of evil, when virtue is impossible, only the name of Krishna sets you free.

– The Bhagavata Purana

This book is about the life and the Song of Sri Krishna, the last Avatara of Mahavishnu in the dwapara yuga.

A NOTE ON HINDU TIME

'365 human years make one year of the Devas and Pitrs, the Gods and the manes.

Four are the ages in the land of Bharata—the krita, the treta, the dwapara and the kali. The krita yuga lasts 4800 divine years, the treta 3600, the dwapara 2400, and the kali 1200; and then, another krita yuga begins.

The krita or satya yuga is the age of purity; it is sinless. Dharma, righteousness, is perfect and walks on four feet in the krita. But in the treta yuga, adharma, evil, enters the world and the very fabric of time begins to decay. Finally, the kali yuga, the fourth age, is almost entirely corrupt, with dharma barely surviving, hobbling on one foot.

A chaturyuga, a cycle of four ages, is 12,000 divine years, or 365 x 12,000 human years long. 71 chaturyugas make a manvantara; fourteen manvantaras, a kalpa. A kalpa of 1000 chaturyugas, 12 million divine years, is one day of Brahma, the Creator.

8,000 Brahma years make one Brahma yuga, 1,000 Brahma yugas make a savana, and Brahma's life is 3,003 savanas long.

One day of Mahavishnu is the lifetime of Brahma...'

PARIKSHIT AND SUKA

It was the early part of this kali yuga, four or five thousand years ago.

Great Yudhishtira's grandson, king Parikshit of the Kurus, had been cursed to die of snakebite in seven days. Pariskhit renounced his kingdom and came alone to the banks of the Ganga. Death was at hand and he had not found his peace. As the sun set, the king sat beside the murmuring river and his mind was restless.

Before long he saw a crowd of women and children coming towards him along the vivid water's edge: a motley, happy throng, full of laughter, they were lit by the last light of day.

As they came nearer, the king saw an unusual figure in their midst who spoke animatedly to them, stroking their faces and at times patting their heads. He looked a boy of sixteen, but Parikshit knew this was no ordinary youth but an ageless rishi.

He was handsome in a way both wild and serene. His body, clothed in just the wind, was sheathed in a lambency that owed nothing to the setting sun.

His hair was an unkempt mass of curls, hanging below his shoulders; his eyes were wide and luminous, and his slender arms hung down to his knees. Often he gesticulated with elegant hands to make some bright point to his rapt audience. He was dark, and his smile full of enchantment.

Suddenly Parikshit knew the youth had come here for his sake. He came smiling before the king and Parikshit bowed at the feet of Vyasa's illumined son, Suka.

Laying a hand on the king's head, blessing him, Suka sat down beside Parikshit. He waved the women and children away.

When they had gone, and a gilded moon rose over the trees, Suka turned to Parikshit. He said wistfully, "Do you know, O Kshatriya, that nothing brings peace as death approaches like hearing the Purana of Vishnu Narayana? I know you are a bhakta and I have come to you with the Lord's mystic Bhagavatam, which my father Vyasa taught me at the end of the dwapara yuga."

A wave of calm washed over the distraught Parikshit. He said, "Since I was cursed to die, every moment seems like a yawning life to me. Perfect Suka, I long to hear the Bhagavata Purana from you. I am desperate for its peace."

And there on the holy river's moonlit bank, invoking the Blue God who lies upon the sea of eternity, Suka began to narrate the immortal Bhagavatam in his voice that was at once so old and so young. Seven days and nights the deep telling lasted, while Parikshit forgot himself and even his imminent death in the wonder of the ancient lore. As he listened absorbed, his mind's vision turned inwards and his soul found its natural serenity, and the grace of Mahavishnu.

It was on the banks of the Ganga that the life of dark Krishna, the eighth Avatara of the Lord, was first told in the world.

And Krishna's song, the Bhagavad Gita, the song of God, was told by Suka's father Veda Vyasa, as part of the Mahabharata, which the elephant-headed God Ganapathy wrote with a tusk he drew from his own face while Vyasa recited the epic poem without pause, never allowing his great scribe to overtake his inspired narration.

BOOK ONE

ONE

Purusha *Dharmakshetre kurukshetre...*

"Look Arjuna, the Kuru armies!"

Once, as dawn flushed over the horizon, spilling on to a great battlefield, a Blue God reined in a brilliant chariot there, yoked to steeds like moonbeams. In it rode the finest warrior of that time. On the crack of two ages, between two matchless armies, he reined in the chariot that flew the crest of Hanuman flapping in an expectant wind.

On Kurukshetra, field of the Kurus, field of truth, he drove Arjuna in the Pandava's chariot on the brink of the war that would destroy the race of kings forever.

The God knew his loneliest hour had come. For this hour during the limbo, the yugasandhi between the dying and the unborn age, he, dark Lotus of the world, had been born. He knew this hour would transform the heart of the dreaming, myth-making earth; and it would change him as well in subtle, incalculable ways.

But now, at this critical hour, he saw his warrior of light tremble. Krishna drew in his horses. He saw anxiety coil round the Pandava, making him moan. Krishna said, "Look Arjuna, the Kuru armies!"

Suddenly Arjuna knew why he trembled. He did not see enemies before him, but his family. He saw fathers and grandfathers, masters, uncles, cousins, nephews and friends.

A sob of anguish came from him, "Krishna, my hands shake, my mouth is dry. My body trembles and my hair stands on end."

The Pandava swayed like a young tree in a storm.

"I cannot hold my bow straight, my skin burns as if it is on fire. My mind reels; I see evil omens in the sky. I have never known fear before but I shake with it now. I can't see how any good can come from killing one's kinsmen."

His own limbs barely still, Krishna composed himself against the terror that beset him at what Arjuna said. He knew his fateful time had come: time of wonder, when he could speak to dim generations of the future. He knew that, now, he could leave them something more lasting than memories of great battles, or even great loves.

He could leave a few magical words for those who are born, again and again, to suffer and grow in this deep and fleeting world—words of compassion, words of wisdom, of comfort and direction. But words failed him now and Krishna also trembled.

Arjuna cried, "I don't want victory. I don't want a kingdom, its power or pleasures. Of what use is a kingdom, of what use is life itself when my grandfather, my masters, my cousins and my nephews stand ready to fight us to the death? I can't bear it!"

Krishna felt forsaken by his Godhood. Lest Arjuna sense his fear, he climbed down from the chariot; his cousin's every word was a knife in his heart. He stood with his back turned to the Pandava, knowing he couldn't fail him *now*.

Prakriti

A life ago, it is the second week of spring in Mathura, capital of the Yadava kingdom. King Ugrasena's garden is in bloom. A breeze laden with the scent of flower, leaf, fruit, and with birdsong, blows through the asoka, bakula and punnaga trees planted both in arrow-straight rows and careful disarray by clever gardeners.

Scarlet and purple, cobalt and incandescent sunbirds hang in the air like miracles and sip the nectar brimming in the lush mouths of flowers.

They never notice the steaming pollen that cling to their fine legs whenever they rest on a petal's rim.

Koyals sing in the trees. Peacocks dance, tails unfurled to the heady rhythms of spring.

Ugrasena's young wife Pavanarekha is out for a walk in that royal garden. She has become queen just recently and, sauntering among the trees, she is impatient for the king to come to her. She is eager for his caress, his embrace.

Just then Dramila, a gandharva elf, crystal-eyed, a song on his lips, is flying over the palace on his carefree way, the wind blowing through him. Peering down, he sees the nubile queen. Spring-borne, her hot youth touches him.

Hovering unseen, a great sunbird over a luscious flower, he sees like pictures before his eyes—gandharvas have this faculty—the naked images in Pavanarekha's mind that fetch the colour to her face. And he lusts after her.

In a flash Dramila assumes the form of Ugrasena, as he observes him in his wife's reverie. He alights in a corner of the garden and strolls up to her, smiling for all the world like her husband. She gives a cry and runs into his arms.

That garden is made for the king's pleasure, and no one can see into it except from the sky. The gandharva loses no time in laying Pavanarekha down in the grass under a punnaga tree standing in crimson bloom like a wounded warrior. In a moment he has her clothes off, and begins making febrile love to her.

In the midst of the tumultuous coupling, as she gasps for the madness he brings to her blood, Pavanarekha opens her eyes. She screams. The gandharva has lost control of his disguise—now he labours above her with his face full of uncanny splendour!

She tries to push him away. But smiling radiantly, he holds her down without pause in his feverish movements. Until they are both consumed by a climax that wrings another helpless cry from her. He, too, moans and shudders, before he grows still.

"Who are you, wretched cheat?" wails Pavanarekha, panting.

Stroking her with unearthly fingers, he says, "You've been lucky today, my little flower. I am Dramila the gandharva."

But she is beside herself. "Vile immortal, you have defied the gods of the two twilights and violated me like an animal in rut. I was pure and you have ruined me."

Arching an arched brow, Dramila says, "You enjoyed yourself. Why are you crying now? Love is forbidden only between mortal men and apsaras, not between human women and gandharvas. I can love you again. Look, I am ready for it."

The queen thrusts him away and springs up. She covers herself, and breathes, "I could curse you, Gandharva."

Seeing the look in her eye he grows afraid. He knows a curse from a chaste woman can bind him to a mortal life in the world, even a bestial one. He flies up into the air and cries down to her, "My seed grows in you. My son will be king of Mathura one day. He will be daring, brilliant and powerful. He will have no equal in cunning or strength."

Pavanarekha wails louder. Before she can stop herself she cries in anger, "Your son will be a monster with no trace of mercy or goodness in him. He will never have the blessing of the Devas or the rishis."

He retorts, "My son will be the scourge of your arrogant clan," and vanishes before she can pronounce the curse welling up within her.

Kamsa, the gandharva's son, grows into a mortal enemy of his mother's people, the Yadavas. He is white as a ghost, pale-eyed, unnaturally tall after his elven father, cold, ruthless, supernaturally shrewd and strong.

Before he is sixteen Kamsa usurps the throne of Mathura and throws Ugrasena into prison. He then unleashes such a tyranny that many Yadavas flee their ancient home into exile: a fate worse than death for a proud people.

And the evil that comes to the city will be remembered for generations. It will bring nightmares to the grandchildren of those who stay and endure the rule of that satanic king.

TWO

Purusha *Yethanna hanthum ichchami...*

"Krishna, even if they want to kill me, *how can I think of harming them?* I don't want this terrible war if it were for the throne of the three worlds. How shall I fight my cousins for an earthly kingdom?

"How can I dream of being happy by killing Dhritarashtra's sons? They may be the most monstrous men. But if I kill them I shall be worse than they are, my sin worse than any of theirs. How can I dare spill the same blood that flows in their bodies and mine?

"Even if they are blind with greed and see no evil in murdering kinsmen, no crime in betraying childhood friends, shouldn't we who know the sin in this hideous thing, shun it?"

Arjuna's eyes burned with anxiety; he was carried away by the frenzy of what he was saying. Krishna tried to find strength to combat the evil that clutched at his heart. He reached into himself, deep within, but his divinity had deserted him.

Or perhaps, he had himself chosen at some unimaginable juncture to stand exactly thus, just a man now, alone and afraid on this battlefield at a crossroad of the fathomless universe; and face the other enemy within in a duel of the spirit. Krishna knew the price of defeat if he lost this hour.

Prakriti

The Yadavas are descended from Soma, the Moon God, and Brihaspati's wife Tara whom the Moon once seduced. Suka says one of the reasons for Krishna being born into the race of Soma Deva is to kill his demonic uncle Kamsa.

Another is that Mother Earth, Bhumidevi, Brahma himself and thirty Devas arrive in Vaikunta to meet Mahavishnu. They come to complain about the state of the world and to beg for help. The kshatriyas, who were once given power to establish dharma on earth, have become tyrants.

Kamsa, who is the Asura Kaalanemi, is the leader of the sinister conspiracy that has such sway.

A tide of terror and murder washes unopposed over the world; and strangely, the demons themselves long for deliverance. As if to attract their deliverer by the screams of those whom they torture, the innocents they murder, they are on the rampage towards the end of the age.

Bhumidevi came, ineffably soft and lovely, and implored Narayana in her voice of river, ocean, deep jungle and pale mountain, "I cannot bear my burden of evil any more. If it is not lightened quickly, I will plunge down into patala and the earth will be just another precinct of hell." She wept before Him.

Vishnu pulled two hairs from his head, one black and one white. He said, "These will travel down the mandalas and remove your burden. The Devas should also be born on earth, in amsa, to join this battle against the Asuras." And, smiling, "And the apsaras, as well, to comfort me below."

Though the reasons for his birth are innumerable, Krishna also comes to hold an unstable world steady, to protect it in a time of upheaval and transition—the yugantara between one age, a dwapara yuga, and the next, this vile kali. He comes to ensure that no power of darkness, nor indeed of grace, survives from a greater age to dominate a lesser one.

Most of all, he comes to attend a war on the crack of two ages, a war that will destroy the power of the arrogant race of kings, the kshatriyas, for ever.

THREE

Purusha *Dharme nashte kulam...*

Panic-stricken, Arjuna ranted. He was innocent of the deeper, deadlier war his quiet charioteer was already locked in: the intimate war that would decide the outcome of Arjuna's war, and a thousand others to be fought on the strangest fields, by unborn heroes in impossible futures. For primordial Evil now battled dark Krishna for the soul of Arjuna—that rarest man, an evolved disciple on the brink of final grace.

The Pandava said desperately, "When a family is divided, it is ruined. The old ways are forgotten along with the ancient truths and rituals. *When the laws perish, vice takes all the clan.* You know what happens then, Krishna. The women become loose, castes are mixed and the age turns dark."

Not knowing at all what Krishna saw clearly: that this Kurukshetra trembled on the verge between one yuga and another; both were now unsteady.

"It is straight to hell that family goes, and first of all those who began its ruin. The spirits of the manes in heaven fall, the timeless and sacred covenants are broken. All the generations of such a clan are doomed to hell. What a horrible sin you and I have plotted—to murder one's kin from greed for a kingdom. Instead, let Dhritarashtra's sons kill me, unarmed and unresisting."

Arjuna threw down his bow and buried his face in his hands. Krishna still sought some great strength within himself, and at first none came to help him. Evil gripped his heart in a vice.

Then, his human memories rose in a clear tide as they usually do only at the hour of death. His life as a man played itself out marvellously before his mind's eye. As he watched, he began to speak to Arjuna.

"From where comes this cowardly spirit at such a critical time? This fear is not for kshatriyas. It will not lead you to heaven, but to disgrace," said Krishna sweetly, turning back to the chariot, a familiar smile on his lips. "It is beneath you to give in to this womanliness. Cast it aside and arise, O Vijaya."

But dread was upon the Pandava, and he cried, "How will I attack Bheeshma and Drona with arrows in battle, when I should worship them instead? I would rather be a beggar in the world than kill my masters. How could I dream of enjoying a kingdom stained with my gurus' blood?

"Ah, when I see who our enemy is, I am not sure if I would rather win or lose this war. How can I live with myself after killing my cousins? Krishna, help me. My mind is roiled by confusion, my soul is weak with pity. Teach me, Lord. Tell me what to do, I am sick with sorrow."

Tears filled his eyes again and ran down his face. "Ah, nothing can drive out this terrible sorrow, which dries my senses and paralyzes me."

Arjuna said to Krishna, "I will not fight," and fell silent.

Krishna's memories flooded him with ecstasy—what a life it had been! Inspired now by the golden sanctuaries of his human years, the Blue God smiled at Arjuna.

Prakriti

If cold Kamsa of Mathura loves anyone it is his cousin Devaki. Even he is enchanted by his ethereal cousin.

It is on Devaki's wedding day that Kamsa first hears his doom foretold. He has chosen Vasudeva, prince of six powerful Yadava tribes, to be his brother-in-law. Though Vasudeva already has a wife, Rohini, he is a well-loved leader of his people and Kamsa hopes this marriage will assuage the growing resentment against his own tyranny. Vitally, the Yadava himself will then pose little threat to him.

Moreover, Kamsa has no children. He still wants an heir from his own near blood. He will raise Devaki's eldest son as his own and the boy will sit on his throne one day.

Kamsa builds Devaki and Vasudeva a fine palace and arranges a grand wedding. After the vows, the king leaps on to the bridal chariot and drives them himself through festive Mathura. Along the way his subjects pack the streets to fling flowers over the newlyweds. Devaki is as virtuous as her uncle Ugrasena whom Kamsa has imprisoned; the people love her as much as they fear and hate Kamsa.

Suddenly, a disembodied voice, an asariri, speaks out of the air, "Fool, this woman's eighth son will kill you."

Kamsa reins in his horses so harshly he almost breaks their necks.

"Who spoke?" he asks in his dangerous woman's voice, pale eyes flashing.

The crowd lapses into silence, but the people have heard the prophecy. The asariri repeats mockingly, "Fool, Devaki's eighth son will kill you." And laughs.

Kamsa leaps down from the chariot-head and seizes Devaki by her hair. He draws his sword.

"This is the gratitude I get for loving you," he hisses like some great serpent. He raises his arm to hew off his cousin's delicate head. But Vasudeva flings himself at his brother-in-law's feet.

"Great Kshatriya," he says, "don't let a mere voice deceive you."

"An asariri never lies!"

Devaki by now is in tears. Vasudeva cries to his terrible brother-in-law, "Wait my lord, before you stain your hands with a woman's blood, your sister's blood."

The demon of Mathura swivels round to gaze at Vasudeva with cobra's eyes.

"So what shall I do?" he asks in deadly quiet. Flinging Devaki down, Kamsa pulls his frail brother-in-law to his feet. "Mock my death? Ignore the warning given me by my fathers in heaven?"

"No sire," moans Vasudeva.

"Then?" Kamsa lifts the Yadava off the ground to be eye to eye with him.

Vasudeva gasps, "The voice never said the threat to you is from Devaki or me, but from our eighth son to be born. Why kill us, my lord? We will hand you every child we have, to do as you please with them."

"To finish them," rasps Kamsa, dropping Vasudeva back on his feet. "Very well. I won't stain my hands with the blood of a woman and a weakling. But I will have your children's lives."

A wail at this from Devaki.

"Silence! You will be my prisoners from now and we will see how any child of yours can harm me." Kamsa snaps white fingers at his guards. "Take them away."

In his silken way he remounts the chariot and drives off, lashing the horses. His soldiers lead Devaki and Vasudeva to a dungeon below the palace, which is now the monster's wedding gift to them.

And perhaps as befitting one who is destined to kill the king of the land into which he is born, Krishna is born in a prison cell.

FOUR

Purusha *Asochyaan anvasochas tvam...*

Those images of the past came to him, turning into mythic words: a river of wisdom pouring from timelessness into time. As he spoke the years seemed to fall away from Krishna, and he was enfolded in grace. His smile entered Arjuna's soul, a light—the heart of the Blue Lotus, sattvic and tremendous. A love transcending everything shone into the Pandava.

"*You sorrow for those you shouldn't grieve for*, Arjuna. Yet you tell me about wisdom. Wise men, Partha, don't grieve for the living or the dead."

His fingers kneaded the anxiety knotting his warrior's neck.

"You and I, and these kings of men, have always existed, and shall always exist. Just as the atman passes through childhood, youth and age in the body, after each human life the soul assumes another body, another life." He laughed, "The wise are not troubled by this, because the soul, which pervades all the living, the aging and the dying, never dies itself. It was never born or begun. It neither kills nor is killed. It is eternal, primeval, indestructible.

"In the body, we shed worn clothes. So, too, the soul that dwells in the body sheds worn bodies. And as the body puts on new clothes the soul puts on new bodies, as if they were the soul's clothes. But the atman isn't touched by fire or weapons, by wind or water. Inmost, subtlest element, always the being of beings, it is permanent, forever changeless."

Prakriti

In their prison Devaki will not lie with Vasudeva, nor say a word to him. She only sits as if graven from stone, staring ahead of her. And he, inflamed with a desire that sets their predicament at nothing, never stops importuning her. Until neither of them can bear it any more.

After a week she breaks her silence and cries, "If I lie with you I will become pregnant. And Kamsa will take our child and kill him."

She begins to sob, her face buried in fragrant hands. On that seventh night, gentle Vasudeva takes his bride in his arms. He turns her sculpted face up to him and all her resistance vanishes.

His lips find hers in the bronze moonlight flowing in through the window set high on a wall. Her lips seek his and dwell there; she, too, wants him more than he knows.

All at once, she is a grown woman. She surprises him with lust fierce as a star; she wakes him in his soul with a cry like an angel's. That cry, which to him is like the first cry of love in creation, and she locks him in legs of dark honey as if to keep him thus for ever.

Their rapture flows out through the bars of the window to fate-dictating constellations above.

The vigilant guard outside sends his boy off to tell Kamsa of his cousin's deflowering.

A black hair will travel down the chasmal mandalas, to be born a saviour from a woman who is like a Goddess. Another fair hair, Ananta, the serpent on whom Narayana sleeps, on the sea of foaming eternity whose spray is the galaxies, will come down into this world as well.

In a far and near place, which is everywhere and nowhere at once, where it is always both day and night, light and dark, Mahavishnu called the Devi Mahamaya to him: Maya, great Illusion, who deludes all of creation with ignorance.

"Plant the six embryos at the bottom of patala," said the *Sleeper on the waters of infinity, "in Devaki's womb, which Vasudeva unlocks each night with his loving."*

In seven years, six nephews are handed, one after the other, to Kamsa. He slaughters them like so many lambs, and in Satayaloka they become the liberated Hiranyakashyipu's sons.

Do not imagine Devaki does not suffer because she is the chosen mother-to-be. She remembers nothing of another life when she prayed to live once more on earth to become the mother of Vishnu himself. She knows only the torments of the days.

Vasudeva is full of prayer, full of fear of Kamsa, full of age and sorrow. The weight of it all is crushing in that prison. But mad and divine desire survives. Becoming time-travellers, dimension-crossers, they surrender themselves to a love that grows more ardent with the passing of each night, a love that is as inspired as their suffering is just bearable, just this side of death.

Only this keeps them alive—the obstinate grace on lip and skin, and in their hearts. As the screams of Kamsa's torturers and executioners' victims are wafted in past the round bars of midnight's prison windows, Devaki and Vasudeva make love as if to save the world with their loving.

Even Kamsa is amazed, and angry, each time he hears his cousin is pregnant. Though he has a thousand beautiful women in his harem to attend his every whim, the king no longer enjoys his soulless fornications. His bed of rut is stricken with foreboding. Not even the most bizarre orgies can arouse him any more.

Day and night, he is haunted by the voice he heard on Devaki's wedding day. He hears it in his dreams.

"Fool, this woman's eighth son will kill you."

The throaty laugh mocks him in the street before the rabble.

He is astonished by his fragile cousin's ardour. Shaking his lean head, he tells himself who would have believed it of Vasudeva the weakling? He bores a peephole and watches them into the small hours, never blinking. Not even he can understand such callousness...after six sons' death, such *love*.

Like a prisoner for his freedom, the king waits for the birth of the eighth son of his cousin Devaki, whom he has desired since they were children.

But what about the seventh?

The Lord God, Vishnu Narayana, called Mahamaya again. "Here is an embryo of Sesha," He said, conjuring the silver life around the white hair He plucked from his head. "Leave him in Devaki's womb tonight. But in six weeks remove him again and they will say the mother has miscarried. Then place him in Rohini's womb in Gokula."

Krishna's elder brother Balarama will be born from Vasudeva's first wife Rohini.

Even Kamsa is pleased his cousin has aborted. He won't have to stain his hands with another infant's blood. But is he at his peephole when the Goddess Maya removes Balarama from Devaki's womb? No. For this is the night Devaki conceives again and becomes luminously pregnant with Krishna.

That is why when he is born, they think it isn't time for his mother to have another child. Mahamaya herself enters Yasodha's womb across the Yamuna—the birth of God deserves some fanfare, surely.

The seasons sparkle, says Suka, when Vishnu enters Devaki as a holy child. Gandharvas sing in the spirit realms. Apsaras dance in the sky on insubstantial feet. Vasudeva finds it hard to look at her; in terror, Kamsa has his peephole sealed.

Devaki glows in the dark; the night lights up with her. Why, it seems the world is lit with the flame growing in this woman.

All Kamsa's soldiers want to stand guard outside Devaki's prison! Her aura can be seen across the Yamuna at nights, and incandescently in Devaloka.

FIVE

Purusha *Jaatasya hi dhruvo mrityu...*

Arjuna still looked downcast. Hearing Krishna's philosophy, he frowned as if unconvinced. Or as if the words that flowed by him were meant for a multitude of listeners other than himself: unborn yet avid listeners. It seemed the secretive future swelled around both of them, gazed on them with a billion eyes, brushed their souls with a billion spirit fingers.

Arjuna had the uncanny feeling of being on the bank of a timeless river flowing from Krishna; flowing for him, yes, but not just for him. He felt numberless presences gathered invisibly around, and the lustrous river beckoned to them, as well, to drink of its wonder.

The kshatriya looked at Krishna from the tail of his eye. But Krishna went on serenely, smiling with boundless compassion. He spoke as though he was playing on his precious flute.

"Even if you believe the soul is born again and again, and dies as well like that, you still should not grieve. For then, *death is certain for the living*, and life is equally certain, again, for the dead. Why grieve over the inevitable?

"You don't determine when any man, even yourself, is born into the world. Then how can you hope to decide when or not he will die?"

Krishna paused, the battle of the soul joined.

"You are a kshatriya. For you a dharma yuddha is the greatest good fortune. How can you be so full of doubt at a holy war? You should rejoice. This war is a door to heaven.

"But if you don't fight you will deny your own nature's glory, what you most are. Then you will sin, and for all time men will tell of your dishonour. Surely, you know that for a kshatriya dishonour is worse than death.

"They will say Arjuna was afraid on the great occasion and they will mock you. Even your friends will scoff. Just think, then, what will your enemies say? Will you be able to bear their scorn? So arise, Pandava. If you die in battle, you will go straight to heaven; if you triumph, you will enjoy the earth before you go."

Prakriti

There is uncanny grace the world over as the time of his birth draws near. It is as if the forces of evil are already in retreat. After years, the meek and the virtuous sleep peacefully, their dreams flowing into the deeper springs of their hearts. Hope returns to their lives and forgotten harmony.

Nature responds in rapture to Devaki's conception: Bhumidevi's thanksgiving to Vishnu that He had answered her prayers. Around the earth, after long ellipses of dissonance, the planets spin into symphonious orbit and syzygy.

Rivers flow crystalline. Abuzz with the rumour on the wind, forests grow swiftly, as if reaching for the stars. Rare plants, which bloom once in a thousand years, are ablossom.

Gaudily plumed birds of noble and ancient strains, which never came to this part of the earth, fly in dense migrations to the trees and lakes of Mathura.

Exceptional beasts flock to the woods outside the city. Rare fish are congregated in brilliant schools in the midnight-blue Yamuna, flowing past Kamsa's capital.

Then, quickly, it is a fateful night when not only zephyrs but brooks and rivers stand still, breezes and waters gathered in expectation. Devaki feels the first pain for her miraculous child to be born.

The seas sing hymns to the dusk, as the crimson sun sinks that evening. All the natural earth's heart is set around one prison cell in Mathura.

The forces of evil have no inkling of the great intuition that sweeps the world tonight. Even Kamsa on his vigilant throne is unsuspicious. Not knowing this is the night that was foretold, he gets drunk with two of his favourite women.

From their exalted cantons, the Devas rain down blooms of light that no eye of demon sees. Chitraratha, lord of the gandharvas, sings fervent praise. Apsaras dance filigree celebrations among clouds, stardust flying from their unearthly bodies.

As it draws on midnight a thunderstorm begins. Devaki knows she can no longer contain the child. But ah, how sweet the birth of him is, as he storms out of her!

The earth trembles to receive him; her celebration will last a hundred years.

Elsewhere, Kamsa also trembles in the arms of his nubile whore. Plucked roughly from him, his seed spills out thin as water. His eyes roll up and Kamsa swoons.

Vasudeva cradles his son in awe. He sees him with four arms, pure as a blue lotus, the Srivatsa whorl on his breast, and not a cry from his perfect lips.

"You have come, God of Gods!" breathes Vasudeva to his holy infant. "Be gracious, Narayana, abandon this four-armed form. If Kamsa knows you have been born, he will kill me."

At once two arms vanish, the intolerable brightness grows dim.

A space of wonder clears in that prison, between gross earth and quick heaven; or possibly, the prison is subsumed into another domain. Vishnu appears in a vision of light. He says to Devaki, "I have been born from you for the third time, Mother. The prophecy is fulfilled."

Moved by a compulsion he cannot resist, Vasudeva swaddles his dark infant in a shawl, takes him up in a wicker basket and goes out. Unknown powers open the heavy doors to the sheet-rain storm outside. The brutish guards are in a stupor.

Except Vasudeva with his precious bundle, nothing stirs in the night. Devaki stands peering at the downpour through the bars of her window, so sad to lose her son but consoled too, knowing that somehow all would be well from now.

Outside it is raining walls of water. Darting from shelter to shelter, Vasudeva scurries through the deserted streets. He comes past the last homes to the river risen beyond the motionless city. He stops there, full of terror and weighed down with a burden he can hardly bear. Drenched, he stands shivering in the momentous night.

Suddenly, a serpent's immense hood thrusts itself out of the raging water, a refulgent jewel at its throat. An awning with a hundred emerald segments shields Vasudeva from the solid torrents of the sky. Still, Krishna's father hesitates on the bank of the Yamuna.

The river, which paused earlier at the Avatara's birth, is now in spate, seething with whirlpools. His lantern in one hand, basket on the other arm, Vasudeva vacillates. The wind and the rain howl around him like spirits of darkness.

A voice speaks from the lightning-gashed night, "The river is a Goddess, Vasudeva, she will protect you."

But he still wavers. Then he sees another figure, full of light, rise out of the river: a shimmering female form. She walks on the current as if she trod on solid ground, and comes to him. He folds his palms to the apparition.

The river goddess takes his hand and now he shivers with the bliss of that touch, which leads him to the waters' edge. Clutching her barely material fingers, he sets foot after her into the hurtling flow. As she takes him on he finds the torrent is only around his ankles. In roaring midstream, the Yamuna hardly covers his knees.

On the other bank, by lamplight, Vasudeva sees the camp of the gypsy cowherds, Nanda and his people. Yasodha is asleep after her own labour to bring the infant Maya into the world. The wandering gopas have come with the taxes Kamsa levies from them. They are also here by fate.

As Vasudeva comes up to them he sees Maya has cast her illusion over the gypsies. They are all asleep, eyes open: figures in a picture into which Krishna's father steals. Moving in a trance he lays his son down in Yasodha's bed. Never knowing why, he picks up Yasodha's perfect baby girl, and turns back to the river swollen at the birth of God into the world.

Shielded again by the serpent's hood, the Devi takes him back across the Yamuna. She leaves him on the bank with a blessing, placing a fluid palm on his head when he kneels before her.

He sleepwalks back to Devaki through the empty streets of Mathura. Kamsa's guards are still asleep. Devaki has scarcely known what happened; she is also bemused by it all, also in the dream. Vasudeva sets the child down in his wife's bed and, exhausted, lies down beside her.

The baby cries at being set down. The night's miasma lifts and the world wakes up. The guards rush in to find the king's cousin has given birth again. Word flies to Kamsa in his insecure palace, but he is already up and preparing to visit Devaki. A dream told him she had given birth again tonight.

"The princess Devaki has delivered a baby girl, my lord!" cries the guard's boy to his sovereign.

"The asariri said her eighth child would be a son. Is there no mistake?"

"We have seen her, my lord."

"Perhaps the voice was wrong, after all," mutters Kamsa, clutching at sweet hope. But then, "Come! The child must not live, it is the eighth."

Devaki is trying to feed the baby, and Vasudeva is asleep, when the feline Kamsa stalks in and snatches her little one out of his cousin's arms.

For once this is more than Devaki can bear. She wrests the child back, crying, "She is a girl, Kamsa!"

But Kamsa lashes out with a kick and she falls in a heap. Vasudeva's protest is drowned by the king's thin roar. Kamsa snatches up the child and strides out, while she howls at the violence.

Swinging her by her little legs, he dashes her head against a rock in the yard, cutting off her scream.

But that child rises at once!

She is vast. Her streaming hair covers the sky and blazes with stars. The people, Devaki and Vasudeva fall down in worship. Kamsa cowers, whimpering, from the eight-armed vision.

The demon of Mathura is sure his death has come. But the lovely Devi only says to him in a dreadful voice, "Fool, he who has killed you before and will kill you again, has been born. And he lives."

With a look that roots him, she rises into heaven. Kamsa of Mathura has years of anguish to live through, before his death comes to free him.

The king limps back to his palace. He locks himself in his royal apartment and doesn't emerge for an hour. Then he staggers out, drunk.

"How foolish the girl was to tell me Devaki's son is alive! Fetch my generals."

When those soldiers come, roused from nightmare slumber, he orders his army to kill every newborn child in his kingdom.

"Leave not one alive, if you value your families and your lives."

The tramp of killers' boots on wet witness cobblestones, the midnight knock on the door, and murder stalks the streets of Mathura where Krishna was born, blue and wonderful, a few hours ago. He, of course, is safe across the Yamuna, but a tribute of a thousand babies' blood flows with storm-water through the city's gutters—as the blood of his birth.

The screams of the murdered, and more piteous, those of the mothers from whose arms the mites are wrenched, knife through a shocked dawn. Then, silence: the shallow, ominous silence of hell come to claim Kamsa's city.

At dawn, as the river flows tainted with innocent crimson, Kamsa decides he will hold a banquet to celebrate his triumph over God.

Across the joyful and sad Yamuna, Yasodha wakes at dawn and finds she has had a son dark as a blue lotus. He smiles at her; she is lost in his black eyes from the first moment.

SIX

Purusha *Neha abhikramanaaso asti...*

Lulled by Krishna's voice, entranced by his smile, his eyes, Arjuna began to float away upon his river of light that sprang between two ages.

Krishna now crooned to the warrior, touching his mind; softly, he chanted as much to himself as to his disciple, and at times he sang his wisdom: as if in prayer.

He sang in exorcism, "Along the infinite way *no effort*, even the smallest, *is in vain or lost*, and no obstacle prevails. This is the wisdom of yoga. Arjuna, be free from the fruits of your deeds, and from sloth as well.

"I am with you; make no anxious difference between success and failure. Act in perfect purity and calm. Even-mindedness is yoga, detachment is yoga, skill is yoga.

"For one who is determined, his understanding is single and lucid. But the thoughts of the undiscerning are many-branched, endless and endlessly confused."

Krishna laid an arm around Arjuna's shoulders. The sun had risen above the horizon; all around them the colours of the battlefield glowed.

The Avatara's river flowed through Arjuna, and he was part of its shining tide. His body was a miracle, its chakras made pure, pervaded by Krishna's song, mutating within the song's great rhythms.

Prakriti

The next morning, a paralysis of grief lies over Mathura. The king has forbidden any public mourning, on pain of death. Kamsa, too, is numbed by all the murdering of the night. His soul shrinks from him.

If a part of him doesn't for a moment believe in the monstrous self-deception that has snatched a thousand babies from their mothers, he does not want to hear its frenzied whispering any more or he will go mad.

He convinces himself, and his sycophantic court, that the carnage has saved his life and their positions of privilege; that whichever infant his killer-to-be was, it is now dead, and danger past.

The king is bland and cheerful, and uncommonly hospitable to his guests at his banquet.

He does not hear his people, the shattered common folk of Mathura, speaking quietly among themselves even as they mourn, about the salvation that is at hand. He doesn't hear the wonderful rumours begun by those who saw the vision of the Devi spring up from the stone against which Kamsa dashed her: the awesome Devi, who proclaimed his doom to the demon, "He who is all the Gods is born."

Later the same morning, Vasudeva crosses the Yamuna again, now in a ferry coracle, time frozen for him once more. He finds Nanda's wagon. Nanda, who has no inkling of the events of the previous night, welcomes his friend joyfully.

"We have a fabulous blue son, Vasudeva."

"You've fathered a son at your age!" laughs Vasudeva, strange light-headedness upon him. "But you have already paid Kamsa his taxes. What if there is another storm tonight? You shouldn't expose your baby to the elements. I think you should return to Gokula."

Nanda is a little puzzled at this advice. But he knows something of Vasudeva's circumstances. He has often wondered that the Yadava is not entirely deranged after everything he has endured. But Vasudeva plucks at the cowherd's sleeve.

"Nanda, I have a favour to ask you."

"Today, ask anything, my friend," cries Nanda.

"I, too, have a small son hardly a year old, by Rohini. I beg you, adopt him and raise him as your own."

"He shall be a fine brother to my boy," says Nanda without hesitation.

"Won't you come in and see my son, Vasudeva?" Nanda says, the joy of the Lotus' birth upon him again. Though he does not know, and neither does his wife yet, that their son is Vishnu incarnate.

Vasudeva climbs after the cowherd chieftain into Nanda's covered cart, where Yasodha sings softly to her dark baby, Devaki's son. Vasudeva sees the glow within the cart, the aura that streams from the child and enfolds Yasodha.

Nanda may have noticed the light as well, but he is too excited to pay it any mind. He only sees the baby with the shining black eyes and dark skin, surely bluish, who for him fills not just his cart but the world with light.

"Vasudeva, come near and bless my baby," calls Yasodha.

But Vasudeva is sad. He sits down, instead, and tells them how, last night in Mathura, Kamsa murdered his daughter. He doesn't mention that she was the tiny Goddess, or from where he had fetched her; nor how she rose when Kamsa dashed her against the stone, and what she said.

He does not speak of the night's massacre of infants. Very softly, Vasudeva says, "As for your son, it is I who should seek his blessing."

Nanda laughs. "Yes, a child's blessing is a great thing. And my son is such a pure baby, isn't he?" No pity for Vasudeva can dim Nanda's delight.

"Yes, such a marvellous child," agrees Vasudeva on his way out, after a lingering look at the infant in Yasodha's arms. Yasodha stares after him pityingly, thinking the poor man's fortitude has finally broken down, and sorrow unhinged him.

But then, as Vasudeva leaves the cart, and Nanda goes with him to make preparations to depart for Gokula, Yasodha forgets both of them as she turns back to her child. At once, she is lost in the wonder of him.

Vasudeva comes back to Devaki in her prison. She is consoled that her baby lives; if not near her, at least he lives. Vasudeva finds that he, too, can share her consolation. And it is their son's blessing to them, if they do not yet know it.

SEVEN

Purusha *Budhhyo yukto, Partha...*

Arjuna was a portal to unborn generations, as Krishna's resonant Gita spilled through him, each word a being alive: a bright host of masters!

They reached beyond him with fingers of wisdom. They reached into veiled times, down the mysterious labyrinths of another history, setting on fire the hearts of strange and visionary heroes, who would walk a very different world and make war again.

In his perfect passivity, while Krishna exhorted him to immaculate action, Arjuna became the Blue God's unwitting ally in an older war. He stood in a legendary universe and, listening absorbed, gave his astral body to become Krishna's subtle prophet.

It melted, melted down Arjuna's soul. A nuclear fire, it spread through the arteries of the earth, quick as devotion, swift as love. His charioteer held his soul in the huge mesmerism of his song, and breathed renewal into the Pandava—for a thousand generations of warriors.

"The wise, *who have yoked their intelligence*, are freed from the bonds of birth," said Krishna. "They reach Brahman, the sorrowless state.

"Arjuna, your mind is confused by all you have read and all you have heard. Your heart is bewildered. But when true insight dawns on you, your intelligence will see beyond bookish Vedic learning, and your spirit will be profound and unshakeable."

Ready to float away, Arjuna was restrained only by Krishna's immense love. Listening to the wisdom of his sarathy, the luminous being the Pandava had become, quivered in mystic emotion.

Prakriti

She is fair as a summer cloud, and ravishing. She has all the cowherd men turning to stare as, long braids wrapped in jasmine garlands, anklets tinkling, flared hips swaying wide below her wasp's waist, carrying like Lakshmi a lotus in her hand, she comes, with an innocent look in her eyes, asking the way to Yasodha's house.

It was not unusual for folk of every uncommon hue to arrive from distant parts, looking to catch a glimpse of Nanda's son as he lay in his cot sucking his big toe.

At first, it had only been gypsy cowherds who came in wild groups. They had heard of the child's unusual beauty and they knew from ancient prophecies that blue was the colour of the incarnations of the dwapara yuga.

But quickly more mysterious strangers found their way to Gokula: rishis with matted jata came from faraway forests, and solemn mountains.

In those earliest days, if any of Nanda's gopas felt the arrival of these holy ones was exceptional, no one made much of it. Not even when exotic birds, never seen in these parts before, infested the trees of Gokula in song-brimming swarms, especially around Nanda's house. Or when rare beasts walked boldly into Yasodha's yard; she could have sworn that a golden deer peered in at the window as she was changing her son's swaddling one day.

And what a fuss they all made of him, the little blue one, especially his kinsfolk, the cowherds.

"What a lovely face he has!"

"How handsome he is!"

"Such black eyes!"

"Look at the way he sucks his toe, as other children do their thumbs!"

They named him Krishna—*Dark One*—and he smiled back at them, his eyes shining, his face bursting with mischief.

She, Putana, has assumed such a beautiful guise with her sorcery that she enchants even Yasodha.

"Oh, what a beautiful boy, Yasodha. Let me look after him for you."

And she claims they are distant cousins, though she is more a cousin of the spirit of the monster in Mathura. But Krishna seems to take to her at once. He goes readily to her, smiling and gurgling.

Yasodha does need some spare time to cook, wash clothes, and make butter, curd and ghee. So she doesn't investigate Putana's antecedents and is happy to offer her a place to live, to look after Krishna part of the time and to help with the housework.

Putana ingratiates herself. She lives with Nanda and Yasodha for a month as a friendly, self-effacing helpmate. And of them all Krishna quickly grows the most attached to her.

Soon, Yasodha is also full of admiration for her 'cousin'; most of all, because unlike the other spirited wenches of the village, Putana is poised and reserved, and unmoved by the advances made to her by some of the cowherds. She even begins to go off inside the house as soon as she sees any young gopa coming along with a hopeful gleam in his eye.

A rare woman, thinks Yasodha, good at her work; and more important, Krishna adores her. No one has seen what Putana becomes at night.

Of course Krishna adores her. Only he knows, in his impenetrable way, why she is in Gokula. And one night of a full moon, past midnight, Putana steals from her bed, picks Krishna up, and carries him into her room.

Undoing her blouse, she bares breasts turned weirdly dark now, at dead of night, like her face and her hands. When suckled those black nipples yield milk laced with the deadly poison of her virulent body. Countless babies she has murdered by feeding them.

And one rakshasa lover died, thrashing in agony in a moon-soaked forest glade, as he spent his warm seed inside her.

Tonight, little Krishna eagerly takes the proffered nipple, hard with her evil excitement. He grasps it with a tiny blue thumb and forefinger, and guides it between toothless gums. He shuts his long eyes and, sighing, begins to feed.

Putana is relieved he hasn't made a sound at her midnight offering. She, too, shuts her eyes and settles back, waiting for the poison to work.

Krishna drinks thirstily at Putana's breast. And she has the strangest sensation of suckling not an infant, but a being whose dimensions she cannot begin to fathom.

Krishna feeds. Swiftly, he sucks all the milk and all the poison out of her. She finds his feeding so overpowering that suddenly Putana is afraid. As he drinks, she feels all her buried malignancy being sucked up into her body, her consciousness.

She experiences the fear of the countless infants she has murdered and devoured; terror assails her, karmic and inescapable. His fire licks through her, burning the sins of a hundred feral lives in a few searing moments, while she begins to scream in the agony of his purification.

She struggles to detach the awful child from her breast. But Krishna has not finished feeding. He drinks on, and try as she will to wrench him away, she can't get him off.

He drinks on, when the milk and poison run dry, and blood begins to flow. He drinks on while Putana's lovely body begins to metamorphose and she changes back into her true form: scaled, clawed and old as sin. He feeds calmly on at her life, without once opening his eyes, or heeding her ululating screams.

Nanda, Yasodha and, quickly, the rest of Gokula come running from their beds to find Putana dead on the floor, blood at her shrivelled breast, blood at her mouth.

Krishna still lies on her lap; he smiles at them, and gurgles with the satisfaction of his feed. The dead rakshasi's expression is contented, beautiful again.

A moment before life left her ravaged body to enter into his mystery, Krishna opened his eyes and gazed back at her. Then, she knew the true reason for her being with him and, all her evil exorcised, Putana was saved.

The cowherds stand astonished to see him lying on the fanged rakshasi's lap. But they still cannot bring themselves to believe he is anything more than Nanda and Yasodha's son, one of their own, a little gopa boy. Though he is blue all right, blue as the lotus that grows on pools deep in the jungle.

His own foster-father Nanda doesn't believe the Darkling is anyone extraordinary. He plucks his son up from the dead Putana's lap, rubs his head with cowdung, and waves a cow's tail over him to ward off evil's restless eye.

If anyone, only his mother Yasodha now wonders who her blue boy is; with a woman's instinct, she knows her Krishna had killed Putana. But even she does not for a moment imagine who her child truly is. Not when Nanda whispers a quickfire mantra:

May Hari protect you, who is the origin of all creatures, from whose navel the lotus sprang which is the source of creation. May Kesava protect you, who raised the earth on his tusks as the Varaha. May Janardhana protect you, who came as Narasimha to kill Hiranyakashyipu. May Vamana always watch over you, who bestrode the three worlds in a wink with weapons flashing!

He is beside himself.

May Govinda guard your head, Kesava your throat, Vishnu your belly and your loins, Janardhana your feet. May the imperishable Narayana watch over your face and arms, your mind and senses. May demons that attack you plunge to their doom, struck down by the blast of Vishnu's conch. May Vaikunta protect you in the principal quarters, Madhusudana in the intermediate directions, Hrishikesha in the sky and Mahendra on earth!

At his foster-father's anxious invocations, the dark child first smiles, then laughs, laughs aloud in delight.

EIGHT

Purusha *Sthitaprajnasya kaa bhasha...*

Krishna fell silent. He climbed down from the chariot, and walked a few paces away. Arjuna floated down the living silence in a lucid dream—watching himself, a small, fierce form of light returning to the zone of his body.

His back turned, Krishna stood gazing out over the two armies. He chuckled deep in his throat, as if nothing could be more amusing than these great forces of the world arrayed against each other. He loosened his clothes and made a sparkling bow in that place, between the legions of the Kauravas and the Pandavas.

Arjuna felt strange to be back from the spectral current of Krishna's Gita, in the cavern of the present. Such sights he had seen; he had trembled on the verge of such *Happenings*. How dull it was to be back in the opaque, enslaving body! How small was its scope!

He wanted to be sent off again down the current of unearthly song. He said, "Krishna, *who is this man who has steady wisdom*, what is he like? How does the man of Brahman speak, how does he sit or walk?"

Krishna threw back his beautiful head and laughed. "When a man knows the bliss of the atman, all the craving and torments of his heart vanish. When his spirit is absorbed in itself, perfectly satisfied, he is wise, illumined."

The Dark One exulted, eyes shining.

"The heaviest sorrow does not perturb him, the most pleasant desire does not move him. When lust, fear and rage have left him, he is a Brahmarishi. The bonds of his body are broken, he is enlightened."

The song invaded Arjuna once more; he was lost again in its profound currents.

"He who is beyond affection, who doesn't rejoice or grieve when he is fortunate or unfortunate, but is imperturbable, he is illumined.

"As the tortoise can withdraw its legs, so can the rishi his senses. Arjuna, the abstinent run away from what they desire, but desire doesn't leave them. Only the vision of God takes away desire itself," said Krishna.

Prakriti

One day, Nanda takes Krishna to the edge of the pasture. He sets him down in his little rope cot in the shade beneath an old cart and goes off with the herd. For a short while, Krishna lies sucking his toe. But then, a timely hunger seizes him.

Timely, because the cart, which wasn't here yesterday, is turning into a demon. Oozing slime, a hundred reptilian eyes suddenly agape everywhere on it, that cart is bearing down on the infant to crush life out of him.

But even as the macabre devil descends, a great hunger for Yasodha's breast grips Krishna. He begins to cry at the top of his magnificent little voice. Only a few children playing nearby see what happens next.

Wailing frantically, the blue child kicks his legs in annoyance at not getting the milk he wants. As it descends on him, the sinister cart receives one small foot at its base.

The playing children spin round at the crack of thunder. Breathless, they watch the cart break in two with a demon's shriek, and the halves being flung far and wide.

Krishna continues to wail like any hungry baby, his mouth puckered up, chubby legs threshing the air. The children see the fiendish form that rises out of the riven cart, grey hands folded, as it disappears into the sky with a howl.

Nanda and the other cowherds come flying at the commotion. Sent by the disturbed forces of evil that hold sway at the ends of the world, Sakatasura, the old cart-demon, had come from far away to kill Krishna. He had come even though he had heard the fate of Putana who was sent before him.

The other cowherd children, the eyewitnesses, stand gaping. One day they will all become inseparable companions of the Dark One, in his boyhood and youth. But this is the morning they first learn there is a blue child among them who is more than what he seems.

"Who broke the cart?" cries Nanda.

"That baby, that blue baby! And the rakshasa in it flew away."

Word reaches her from the scene of the violent miracle, and Yasodha comes running and snatches up her howling son. She gives him her breast at once; she can't bear her Krishna cry, not for a moment. He who broke the back of the fiend in the cart snuggles close, drinking hungrily, his eyes shut tight. He clutches his mother's finger in a plump dark fist and sighs.

Later the same evening, Yasodha returns to the broken cart and worships it in secret; lest it return with its demon to harm her baby.

She offers it ghee, palasa flowers, pears, oranges, bananas, and unhusked grain. She lights a lamp beside it: a mother's imploring diya. Her son sits on her hip, and watches what she does.

It is after this that Vasudeva goes to Garga, the brahmana, and asks him to perform life-passage rites for Balarama and Krishna, secretly, without the other cowherds knowing. For the gopas are neither brahmanas nor kshatriyas, but sudras.

But of course, Krishna's life is never destined to any long respite from the powers of darkness. All his years will be thick with the Putanas and the Sakatasuras of the world, tired of their own burdens of sin, seeking deliverance from him: they crave the touch of him, even if to get killed.

At an age's end there are so many demons in the world, who must not live to see the kali yuga. And why else has he, the dark saviour, come?

NINE

Purusha *Ya nisha sarvabhutanam* ...

He stood near the foam-white horses, and they nuzzled their slim faces against him, as he stroked them.

"Even a man who knows the way can be dragged from it, for the senses are powerful. But he who tames his senses, collects his mind in calm and fixes it on me, he is illumined.

"Desire springs from attachment to the objects of the senses; anger from desire, confusion from anger, and forgetfulness from confusion. When he forgets the lessons of experience, a man loses his discrimination; and he is destroyed.

"But when a man's mind is disciplined, his spirit is pure. In purity there is peace, and in peace sorrow ends. The intelligence of a quiet man is established in the peace of the atman, his immortal soul.

"*What is night for most beings* is when the quiet man is awake. When the world is awake and abustle, is night for the sage who sees."

Prakriti

He is the vision of his mother's eye. She sticks a peacock feather in his hair to be the sign of her love for him. But he, dark child, burns within himself. He has recently come in his human form, and is still afire with what he has always been otherwise: *with cosmic knowledge*, searing every cell of his mysterious blue body.

Putana's poison and Sakatasura's evil quench the blaze a little, as if he grew stronger by absorbing their darkness, and saving them. Yet, invisible flames lick at the child, and he desperately seeks something, anything, to cool the transcendent heat within.

And quite by accident one day, he finds that legendary something, when Yasodha gives him a first taste of what then becomes an obsession throughout his childhood: *butter.*

Yasodha buys golden bangles for her son, she hangs a golden chain around his waist. But neither she nor Balarama's mother Rohini can restrain the two boys. They crawl into the cattle-pen, romp among the cows, and are missing all day. Or they creep into the calf-pen, and pull the tails of calves born a few hours ago.

Once they begin to walk, especially once Krishna discovers butter, there is no controlling them at all.

He runs to the secret meeting-place of five- and six-year-olds. Black eyes flashing, peacock-feather fluttering, he scampers to the assignation under the old mango tree.

Yasodha in her kitchen hasn't seen him go. But then, what does she know of the fire that sears him? Fire of stars, pristine fire of dim beginnings and remoter conclusions: fire of many mysteries, cold fire that burns him blue.

"What's our plan?"

They chatter at him, his little conspirators under the smiling tree. Truthfully, they are terrified by what they already know is his single-minded scheme—butter-thievery. But Krishna raises a solemn finger at them and they fall silent, gravely awaiting their leader's dictate. He crooks the imperious finger, and tells them, "Follow me."

They arrive, tense, at the lane of the cowherds' kutilas, thatched huts on either side. Glancing back at his friends, Krishna raises the dark finger again. Silence, he commands. Bright eyes more than a little excited, and frightened, the others raise their fingers to their lips in chorus, echoing his gesture.

Signalling to them to wait a short way off, Krishna pads forward to the first hut. He darts his head round the door and sees the woman of the house sweeping her floor. He comes away; no hope here. As they move up the path there is none in the next two homes either. None of the women have yet taken their pitchers to the river.

But in the fourth kutila, as he creeps in stealthily, he hears noises: a bed creaking, a woman moaning. Intrigued, and precocious, he follows the sounds to the door. There he stands for a long moment, absorbed by what he sees on the broad bed. He stands unabashed, peacock-feather twitching, a smile spreading on his face.

Then he calls, "Lakshmi Matuli, didn't you go to the river today?"

The woman jumps up with a cry, pushing Motiya, the village idiot, off his awkward efforts. She tries to find some clothes to cover sweaty nakedness.

"Where's old Deva Matulan today, Lakshmi Matuli? Is Motiya trying to hurt you?"

"Oh no, Krishna! Motiya isn't hurting me. He isn't doing anything at all to me."

"He's doing something. Shall I go and fetch Deva Matulan?"

"No, my Krishna. Come into the kitchen, I'll give you some butter. That's what you've come for, isn't it?"

She finds her clothes and pulls them on. So does Motiya, the idiot grinning foolishly. But Krishna is not to be deflected.

"What is Motiya trying to hide, Matuli?"

Lakshmi bursts out laughing. Krishna runs out, chuckling, with her shouting after him, "Don't tell a soul, my sweet Krishna, please!"

"What happened, Krishna?" cry his friends.

"Oh, Motiya was in there."

When they insist on having details, he describes vividly for them what Lakshmi Matuli and the idiot had been doing inside. Then he warns them: if the story goes any further, there would be consequences from him.

"But let's hurry now, or all the women will be back from the river."

They run on to the next home. Krishna motions to the others to wait again, and glides up to the door. Silence greets him here. Nobody stirs; the place seems empty. He tiptoes inside to make sure. He is gone a few moments, then reappears in the doorway, signalling urgently. "Hurry!"

Hearts pounding in their chests, they follow their leader in to the scene of crime. His eyes round with what he has found in the kitchen, he points a plump finger at the ceiling, in a quite religious gesture.

"Look!" he whispers.

An earthen pot hangs from the rafters. The women have taken to hanging up their butter, hoping it will still be there when they return. Though Yasodha will not believe them, they know who the butter-thief is, who strikes like lightning when they are away. They have seen a peacock-feather blaze round the corners of their kutilas and fly gleaming out of their windows. And they have decided to hang their butter up as high as they can.

So now, Krishna cannot reach the butter, and the fire within scathes him. It is as if he suffers for sins that aren't his, crimes of generations, of entire races. But the crime at hand is hard to commit; the pot with the butter of salvation hangs out of reach.

Krishna has an inspiration. He orders his little legion to kneel, one on the other, and make a ladder up to the butter-pot. Last of all, he climbs gingerly up the swaying thing. It holds up miraculously. But not even from the top of the precarious edifice can he reach the butter.

Tears well in his eyes, his insides churn. Finally, on to his toes he gets, a small dancer, and his fingers just scrape the base of the pot.

"Raise yourself a little more," he calls to the hefty boy who is the base of the ladder.

With mysterious strength, he can't tell from where, that boy manages another inch. Krishna begins to swing the pot from side to side, as hard as he can. To no avail: he cannot swing it all the way to the ceiling to crack it open there.

Tears stream down his face. And then, with a cry, he looses a bolt of light from his fingers, a jagged streak that takes him as unawares as the others. It burns up the thick rope by which the pot hangs.

For a final moment, the pot of his dreams hangs by a thread, teetering. Then it comes crashing down, and there is butter all over the floor. With a squeal of triumph, the Blue God is down his ladder of friends in a flash, down on his hands and knees, and falling greedily to the feast.

The others follow more cautiously at first, but his enthusiasm is absolutely infectious. Soon, they are all gobbling the white stuff as keenly as Krishna, sharing in his primitive ceremony, fingers and faces covered in ambrosial butter.

Afterwards, sated, and Krishna magically free of the thing that burns him, they go down to the river shallows and wash each other clean. Then they bask in the golden sun, without a care in the world.

TEN

Purusha *Aapuryamanam achalaprathishtham...*

Carried by Krishna's spiralling song, Arjuna floated high above Kurukshetra. The currents of that song were the currents of time; the ages roared around him in legendary magnificence. Just the silver thread, umbilicus of the Gita, held him secure. Krishna, his eyes still full of the memories of his human life, sang on.

"When a man becomes like the sea, perfectly serene, when his desires come to him *like waters to the sea, and never move him,* he attains peace. When a man works in the world without any desire, he comes to calm.

"This peace is the fathomless ocean of the soul, the divine Brahman. Once a man enters it, he never returns to delusion. At the hour of his death he is alive in that eternal illumination. He attains the ecstasy of God."

One Krishna was adrift on the tide of his brimming memories. And another, a different Krishna, was the singer of the Gita that washed Arjuna on to unknown shores of vision, borne upon its perfection, its awesome detachment.

Prakriti

Krishna manages that the women, who are certain he is the culprit, are never able to catch him red-handed. They complain to his mother. He has found a new way into the pots hung on ceilings, an easier way to the butter than the ladder-and-tip, or the lightning bolt. For, the women begin to secure the pots with two and four ropes instead of one; and his friends demand he teach them the trick of the flash of light.

Krishna now has a long stick with which he breaks the thin pots open from below. And then he stands under them, dancing, as the stuff of heaven trickles into his open mouth, gob by unworldly gob.

The cowherd men take sides with Krishna and his friends, saying surely such small children can't reach such lofty pots. The real culprits must be older children, even thieving adults perhaps.

This only angers the women further, and they come daily with accusations to Krishna's mother. Her son has taken to leaving excrement behind in the pots—his way of cocking a snook at them, they say. Not without truth.

"He feeds the butter to monkeys, when the other children refuse it."

"But you have no proof it is my Krishna, and he denies it," says Yasodha. "What if I punish him and the culprit turns out to be someone else? Moreover, my son never lies."

What most infuriates the women who come to complain is the blue boy's brazenness.

"He will grow up to be a thief," warns one fat woman. Krishna shelters safely behind his mother, and sticks his tongue out at her.

"Look at him!" the woman howls.

"What happened now?" says Yasodha, who does not like her at the best of times.

"He stuck his tongue out at me."

Yasodha turns to find an angelic expression, so quickly assumed, on her son's face, as if butter wouldn't melt in his mouth. And she begins to giggle.

"It's you who encourage him," the woman fumes, and stalks out. Krishna and Yasodha dissolve in laughter.

"Tell me the truth, Krishna, did you steal the butter?"

He turns a solemn face to her, eyes wide and hurt.

"Would I lie to you, Amma?" A tear wells in those black depths. As usual, Yasodha is overcome with remorse and *such love*. She hugs him contritely. She kisses his tears away, drop by drop.

"No, of course not, my precious. I am so sorry," and she also begins to cry.

But the next day, the same woman flies in, shouting, "Thief! Little thief! This time I've caught you."

Just a skip ahead of her, Krishna darts behind his mother once more.

"What is it now?" Yasodha says testily. "Why do you bother me like this every day? Krishna has said he doesn't steal your butter. It must be a cat or a crow."

"What about my curd?"

"What of it?"

"Most of it is in your son's belly, but some is still on his face."

Yasodha looks down at her dark jewel, and he isn't quick enough to wipe away the tell-tale stains.

"Krishna!" she wails, "So it's true. Everything they say about you is true, wicked child."

She is hurt that he did not confide in her. She would not have punished him, she wouldn't even have scolded him. She would have been on his side; she would have protected him. If only he had told her.

But now she feels humiliated, and in front of this wretched woman. For the first time in his young life, she seizes Krishna up in anger and shakes him.

"Why did you lie to me?"

Krishna turns his perfect face up to her. He bats those black eyes. "But, Amma, I didn't lie to you ever."

"See!" squeals the fat woman. "Lies come easier to him than the truth. Under which asura nakshatra was he born?"

"He was born under the holy star of Rohini," snaps Yasodha. The woman snorts scornfully, but lumbers away. She sees Yasodha's ire risen, and dare not cross her. But she hides behind the hedge around Yasodha's yard, and peers through the leaves to watch the punishment to come. She wouldn't miss it for anything.

As soon as she believes the woman has gone, Yasodha bursts into tears. "Oh, Krishna, why do you steal?"

Krishna doesn't answer. Yasodha shakes him again. "I'll see how you steal any more butter or curd."

She picks him up and carries him into the yard, his eyes still sparkling with mischief. She sets him down next to the wooden pestle lying there. Fetching a rope, she ties him firmly to the pestle by his waist.

"Now let me see how you steal butter," she says, securing the knot. He sees how she avoids his eyes, and how tears escape her own. She bites her lip, still not daring to look into his face, lest she isn't able to leave him there.

Yasodha goes off into her kitchen. The woman behind the hedge pops up her head. She wags a triumphant finger at the trussed-up boy, "Now you've got what you deserve."

A job well done, she also turns home. But she hasn't gone ten paces when the child calls her back.

"Matuli," he chirrups after her. "Matuli, come and look."

She arrives bumbling back at the hedge, even as Yasodha comes to her kitchen window. Just in time to see the blue child crawl between two huge trees, a yamala and an arjuna. He drags the heavy pestle behind him, easily, till it is wedged across both trunks.

"Look, Matuli!" crows the Darkling, and with a tug brings the trees crashing to the ground. The fat woman faints.

Yasodha screams, comes tearing out of her house. Once more only the other children, Krishna's butter-army waiting for him at the end of the mud street, see the two ominous spirit-forms that rise into the sky out of the felled trees.

"Oh, my God! I've killed my son," wails his mother. "Krishna! Where are you? Answer me, Krishna."

But Krishna is not under branch or leaf. Called out by the crash of the falling trees and Yasodha's screams, the other cowherds and their women come running. Yasodha is sure her child has been crushed by one of the knotty trunks.

She is in a frenzy, snapping away branches, tearing at muddy roots, screaming at the others, "Don't just stand there, help me roll away these demons planted here to kill my son. Help me someone, or I die. Oh!"

She becomes dizzy and has to sit abruptly on the ground. Then, out of nowhere, a small hand rests on her shoulder, a soft mouth kisses her; a sweet voice lisps in her ear, "Amma, it's me," and the world spins right again.

With a cry, Yasodha gathers him in her arms, smothers him with kisses, laughing and sobbing.

ELEVEN

Purusha *Jyayasi chet karmanaste...*

Once more, darkness. The spring of Krishna's song dried on his lips, and evil, undefeated, fiercer than before, reached for him again.

His ship of light suddenly put out, Arjuna said in despair, "Krishna, you say *the way of the mind is finer than the way of action.* Then why do you goad me into this savagery? It is you who ,are bewildering me now. I am lost. Show me one straight path by which I can be free."

Krishna sat on the footstep of the chariot, gazing out to the horizon darkened by the armies and their blind intentions; and beyond it, to other horizons of inscrutable existence and purpose.

His body shook with another paroxysm of anxiety. No song welled within him any more. He was parched, a desert of fear, sands of infinity raging a simoom around his heart.

Krishna, abandoned, thought his death had come. Had it all been a huge joke then, an unthinkable cruelty? Great God's joke played on a vain blue pretender.

Who was he, anyway? An Avatara? Then why did he shake like a leaf on the step of the Pandava's chariot? A wave of panic rose before his eyes, eerie, flecked with golden foam.

'Mother!' he screamed in his cloven mind, as the thing that was surely his end bore down to finish him.

An age seemed to flash by that chariot stranded on waiting Kurukshetra, as evil took hold of him as dreadful paranoia.

Then, riding that crest she came to him, great and simple as the earth. Yasodha came to him, tall as the sky, full of love. She came from the past to contend on his part.

At once, the icy spell was broken, and a laugh of sheer joy burst out of him. So that Arjuna, floating away on a black tide, gave a start and looked up. Her task of love accomplished, Krishna watched his mother vanish in a haze of light.

Undammed, his song tumbled out of him again. Eddying around the chariot, it seized Arjuna in faith once more. But Krishna knew his battle on this historic field had just begun.

His Gita was his astra, parting sky and earth on its flight through time. Arjuna was his bow, taut with anxiety.

Prakriti

The next morning brings another complaint against Krishna. Today the accuser is his brother Balarama.

"Amma," he runs in and cries to Yasodha, "Krishna is out in the street eating mud again."

She rushes out, anxious that her son may become ill after his narrow escape from the falling trees. She seizes his hand and drags him up.

"Wicked boy, you eat mud as soon as I am not looking. You will be sick."

What does she know about the other fire that burns him? How does she know that without butter or curd, only earth—cool, raw clods—can quench it a little?

"No, I didn't eat mud," he cries. "Balarama is lying. They are all lying!"

But she snatches him up on to her hip.

"Open your mouth," she cries. "Open your mouth and show me if it's they who are lying."

Krishna grows agitated, then frantic. He is close to tears, his face crimson, a pounding in his chest. He feels something vast rise up in him.

He shakes his head and clamps his jaws shut. But his mother presses his cheeks with her thumb and forefinger, till she hurts him.

"Open. Krishna, open!"

Suddenly, he does. He lets his jaws go slack, he opens his mouth. And peering in, Yasodha sees:

Oh, she sees all the universe. The ethereal dome, the cardinal points, time, souls, nature, destiny, all the creatures, suns, moons, planets, the earth, the galaxies. The past, the present, the future. She sees Everything—ablaze!

in her son's mouth, and she faints away, her last thought whether the vision is because her Krishna is the Avatara. Then, next thing she knows, he strokes her cheek as she lies on the ground, with a dark hand he wakes her.

"What happened, Amma?"

"Oh, I can't remember, Krishna. I can't remember anything."

She picks him up and carries him inside, and the fire within him is quiet again.

BOOK TWO

TWELVE

Purusha *Lokesmin dvividha nishta puraa...*

K rishna said, "*The world has known the dual path taught in it, since its beginning*—the way of knowledge for men of contemplation; but for men of action, the way of deeds, of battles. You don't become free by doing nothing; you don't become perfect by abstaining from karma.

"He who does nothing, but only sits and broods over his desires, is no sage. He is a hypocrite. Do the work you are born to; without working you can't sustain even your own body. Let karma be your worship, Arjuna."

The dream closed around Arjuna. He was a time-traveller again, Krishna's song his vimana. His craft of words was rocked by the thunder of the ages, buffeted by distant mysteries of violence and terror, by such wonders; but the sphere of light was proof against them all.

Krishna's song withstood the uttermost tests of time, and it communed with Arjuna's soul.

"In the beginning, God made men, each with his nature and dharma. He said, 'By doing this you will prosper.' By doing your natural duty you worship the Gods, and they succour you. By working without attachment, you attain bliss. Such karma is the sacrifice that maintains the earth.

"Look at me, Arjuna. I tell you, I am not bound by any dharma in all the worlds, nor is there anything in them which isn't already mine. But I am always at work.

"Only the deluded think 'I am the doer'. Everything is done by the essences of nature, the gunas at eternal play. Those who go astray become attached to their work, they begin to take the gunas for the soul. Still, no one who is wise should unsettle the minds of those who do not see whole. Work must go on, always, or the worlds fall into ruin.

"Even the wisest man acts by his own nature. Every creature can only follow its innate nature. What can repression accomplish? It is always wiser to do one's own duty, however imperfectly, than the duty of another, even immaculately. It is better to die in one's own dharma; for to live by another's dharma is dangerous."

Krishna grew quiet and pensive; as though with these words he had not only delivered himself of wisdom, but also of a great burden.

Arjuna floated down his dream of light. He asked in quaint earnestness, "But what makes a man sin, even against his will, helplessly, Krishna?"

Krishna glanced sharply at him, as if to see if someone hidden mocked him in Arjuna's voice.

"Rage and lust, ravening, deadly: these are the enemies. Why, the intellect itself, deluded, feeds the flames of these two. Arjuna, lust veils the soul as smoke does a fire, as dust does a clear mirror. To pass beyond lust you must transcend the intellect.

"Powerful are the senses, greater than they is the mind, more potent than the mind is the intellect. But greater than intellect is the atman, who sets you free."

Prakriti

After Krishna pulls down the trees, the cowherd elders and his foster-father Nanda cannot pretend any more that there is nothing extraordinary about the blue child. But in the way of their kind, they still prefer to put it all down, Putana, Sakatasura, and the trees that came crashing down when a child tugged at them, to some wayward earth-spirits' powers in Gokula, rather than to their Krishna being an Avatara.

Divine Incarnation was a rare thing, and they are hardly prepared to believe a God has been born among them. And Krishna is happy to be just one of them, a cowherd child.

But one night, another gopa elder, Upananda, had a dream. Strange flying craft hung like jewels in a midnight sky above Gokula. Suddenly one of them, big as a full moon, shone with light. A voice like thunder rumbling spoke out of the mysterious vimana.

'Cowherds, though you are blind to the omens, the Avatara has been born among you. The time has come for you to leave Gokula, for there will always be danger here. Past four jungles' hearts there is a sacred forest on the banks of the Yamuna. Journey to that vana, Upananda; take all your gopas with you. There you will find sanctuary. Hurry, there is no time to lose.'

The light and all the fabulous craft in the sky vanished, and Upananda awoke.

The first thing next morning, he calls a council of the village elders, over which Nanda presides. Upananda relates his dream, and says, "Before some calamity follows the omens we have seen here since Krishna's birth, let us leave Gokula."

Nanda is about to agree, when one, two, and then, every one of the other cowherds speak all together. The first cries, "I also had a dream last night..."

Another interrupts before he can finish, "And I! There were pushpaka vimanas in my dream, the sky was full of them."

"Luminous ships of the sky. I saw them too."

"I saw the same dream. All of us stood together on the dark pasture, when the voice spoke out of the light."

They glance up nervously. But the sky is clear; not a wisp of cloud disturbs its serene vacancy.

Upananda says, "Since Krishna was born all sorts of strange things have happened."

"The holy men who came to see him."

"The birds and the golden deer."

"Putana."

"The cart."

"A child pulled down two trees."

Upananda, who remembers the night's dream better than the others, says slowly, "What if Krishna is the Avatara?"

Someone murmurs, "A butter-thief Avatara."

And they all laugh. But then Nanda, who has been silent so far, says decisively, "I saw the dream as well. We must leave here at once."

The next day, it is a week after Krishna brought down the trees—who were Kubera's sons once cursed to be born into the world for just this salvation from him—the cowherds load their possessions into their wagons and set out from Gokula, herding their cows and calves before them.

Wide-eyed and aquiver, Krishna rides with Yasodha, his peacock-feather erect and brilliant in the sun. He rides out in the first swaying cart while she sings to him in her husky voice.

All through the journey, she keeps him close beside her. And now, he is willing to sit quietly at her side, as if to make up for frightening her out of her wits the other day.

Four old forests they travel through, fording frothing rivers on rough rafts they lash together. They journey in wonder through valleys full of whispering winds and invisible woodland spirits where men have never set foot before. They cross hills, where tigers roar at night in numinous jungle hearts.

Making and striking many camps on their way, they go for weeks before they arrive on the fringes of the greatest forest of them all—virgin Vrindavana on the banks of the Yamuna, at the foot of a green mountain, Govardhana.

Here they hitch their wagons together in a crescent, its back to the forest, its tips opening on to fields that stretch away like velvet carpets. Though the rains are yet to arrive, the cowherds find the grasses taller and lusher than they have ever seen them anywhere. But nobody mentions this. They have come here to escape from miracles, and it is as if someone gently mocks them.

In their new home Balarama and his little brother, whom they now call Damodara, rope-belly, as much to tease Yasodha as anything else, are put in charge of the calves; chiefly to keep them out of mischief. So the cow-pens become the brothers' first enthralling domain in Vrindavana.

They make crowns of peacock-feathers gathered from the nearby forest—where they have been direly warned never to go—and earrings of forest flowers. They make crude flutes from cowherd's-reeds and play songs they make up themselves, on these and leaf-piccolos. Wearing crow-wing haircuts like two little princes, they extend their kingdom of wonder deep into the jungle.

Soon, they roam there at will, escorted by deer and jackal, elephant and tiger. They speak the wild tongues easily, talking to the denizens of the jungle who commune as much with silence as sounds. For, of course, they are no ordinary children and the beasts of the wild know them at once.

Meanwhile, their elders build huts with sloping roofs in the wide enclosure of moon-wagons. Nanda and the others, who have been nomads and gypsies till now, are convinced that this is where they are meant to settle for some years to come; and though no one speaks the thought aloud, that this is where the two little saviours of the earth are meant to grow: as the guardians of calves, and later of the grown herd, ranging free over field and forest and jade riverbank.

THIRTEEN

Purusha *Imam Vivasvate yogam..*

The blessed Lord said on the field of Kurukshetra, "*I taught this timeless yoga to Vivasat once.* Vivasat gave it to Manu, Manu taught it to Ikshvaku; and handed down the generations, the Rajarishis, the kings who were sages, all knew it. Until, the great yoga was lost in the world through the deep and forgotten ages, when darkness came. Arjuna, today upon this chosen field, hear the imperishable secret from me."

But Arjuna said, "Vivasat? He was dead long before you were born. How did you give this yoga to Vivasat?"

Krishna laughed gently, "My past lives, and yours as well, are more than you dream. Only, I remember them all, and you remember none. Yet I am never born into this world, but only seem to be; and I am master of my prakriti, my immortal nature, not its subject.

"Whenever there is a tide of evil on earth, Arjuna, I send myself forth into it: to protect the good, who else have they? To destroy the evil, who else will save them? To establish dharma I come, again and again, from age to age."

Prakriti

Krishna discovers a new passion. One morning he runs excitedly to his mother. He is nine summers old.

"I want a flute, Amma. One of the boys has one and what sweet notes he plays on it."

"But who will teach you to play?"

"I will teach myself."

She can never say no to him, and yields willingly to this harmless whim. So, the next day he goes off to the pasture with the cowherds and their animals, with a shiny new flute in his hand. He sits under the grandfather banyan tree that grows on the banks of the Yamuna.

All that first day he can't coax a note from the thick bamboo.

The next morning he dives into the river for a swim. With unerring instinct, fish from leagues around swim to the place where he does until they make a round pool with their congregational bodies. In teeming schools they swim to him, in silvery thousands, and the Yamuna spills over her banks. Laughing, as they rub against him in adoration, he lets them nibble his dark skin.

Then he climbs out of the river and picks up his flute. That second day he manages to squeeze out some quavering notes while the cows look up from their ruminative cropping.

A little tired, he falls asleep under the old banyan. In his dream the tree, transformed, appears before him as a gandharva, born here a hundred years ago just to teach him to play the bamboo flute.

"Golden Lord," the gandharva says, "let me teach you until you are ready to play your own song."

Krishna smiles at the wonderful minstrel, "Teach me."

The elf steps behind him, and with long fingers shows him how to hold the flute.

"Now blow, Dark One," says the gandharva.

Krishna blows a long, clear note, his first.

"More."

He blows a phrase, full of crystal resonance.

"More!" cries the elf.

Krishna begins to play in his dream, and he realises he has always known how. The gandharva says, "I have done what I came for. Now set me free, Lord."

Krishna blesses the unearthly spirit, laying a hand on his head. Bowing deeply, with a song of freedom brimming on his lips, the gandharva flies off in joy and vanishes from the earth.

Krishna wakes, raises his flute and effortlessly the first notes flow from his lips. The cows stop their grazing to listen. The birds in the trees and even the wind in the leaves are still, captive to the beginnings of his song.

Then on, the song swells in leaps and measures, until, in just days, turquoise river, green carpet-meadow and mysterious jungle all thrill to the Dark One's reverberating melodies.

And whenever he raises the bamboo to his lips, the village maidens, the gopis, come running. They hide in enraptured knots, ripe young bodies and souls straining to the music-maker.

FOURTEEN

Purusha *Tyaktva deham punarjanma...*

"*The man who knows me is never born again*; he comes to me when he leaves his body. Absorbed in me, he is delivered from lust, anger and fear. He is burnt pure in the fire of my being, I become his home. All men come to me, at last, and I take them all unto myself. Whatever path a man travels, it leads finally to me.

"I am not bound by karma and neither are those who know me. So, like the ancients who worked for moksha, you too must fight.

"The way of karma is not easy, and even the wise are perplexed about action and inaction. Only the realised yogin sees restlessness in inaction, and repose in deeds. When he acts, he remains poised in the serenity of the atman. He has abandoned lust for the fruits of his actions.

"Content always in the atman itself, he acts and is beyond karma. He is satisfied with whatever comes to him by chance. He is free from envy, unaffected by success and failure. He acts and is not bound by his deeds.

"All his work is a sacrifice, a ritual of worship. His enlightened heart beats as one with Brahman, the Holy Spirit. For him everything is Brahman. The sacrifice, the oblation, the sacrificer, and the fire are all one. They are Brahman.

"And he who offers no worship? This world is not for him; then how shall any other world be his, O best of the Kurus?"

When he heard the grave tone in which Krishna spoke, dread touched Arjuna, who had laid down his weapons and said he would not fight.

"Worship," the Dark One went on quietly, looking away from the Pandava, out at the armies, "is greater than any material sacrifice, and all karma ends inexorably in Brahman.

"Let the rishis of wisdom and vision be your masters. Learn from them by serving them with humility, by questioning and revering them.

"Like wood, the fire of wisdom burns karma to ashes. Nothing on earth is as pure as wisdom. On the ship of wisdom the worst sinner crosses the sea of evil. He who has seen the atman, slowly, but ineluctably, peace comes to him. Take up the sword of discrimination, Arjuna; cut away the doubt which lurks in your heart."

Arjuna looked at Krishna's face, and saw his eyes were moist.

Prakriti

One day, when he falls into a slumber under the great banyan, out past the emerald fields and within hearing of Krishna's song, Nanda has a dream.

Krishna was a baby again, lying on his father's chest. They had just been to the lotus pools between the river and the forest, to drink from spring draughts.

All at once, the sky grew dark with clouds. The woods were dim and forbidding, the wind whined ominously. Thunder and lightning rent the sky; and while mighty tree and yearning earth trembled, the rain came screaming down.

Nanda was afraid. "How will I leave my cows and run home? But what about Krishna if I stay out in this storm?"

At that moment there was a clap of thunder that threatened to break open the earth. With a cry Krishna clung to his father's neck. The Yamuna had risen angrily over her banks.

Hugging his child to him, Nanda fled towards the deeper forest for shelter. His cows lowed plaintively after him, but nothing would induce them to follow him into the jungle. Krishna howled at the storm.

When he found shelter, Nanda saw a marvellous light threading its way towards him. He gasped as she from whose hands the light shone drew nearer, and he saw who she was.

He saw her aglow under the brooding awning of the trees; she lit up the bleak forest. She came up to him. Full of awe, Nanda knew what she had come for.

Without a word, he handed his son to her, and folded his hands in worship, never raising his eyes to her face. The fair one laughed, so joyful as she took the child. The wailing infant grew quiet. Then, she spoke in a voice more beautiful than any the gopa could have imagined.

"You must tell no one, Nanda," she said. "It is your punya by which you see me like this. Go home now, and before you go choose a boon for yourself, whatever you want. Today I will give you anything, even what the Devas hold rare."

Nanda prostrated himself, and said, "Devi, mother of worlds, grant us love for both of you always, and nearness to you in every life."

"May your heart and your Yasodha's flower, Nanda. Illusion will never hold you, and on the day you leave your bodies, come straight to us forever."

She clutched the child, and turned back into the forest. But in his dream, Nanda still saw her as she made her way under the ancient trees, deep into the darkness.

At last she came to a clearing, and in it was a jewelled pavilion with a hundred golden and silver urns. There she saw an unearthly youth, blue as the heart of a rainbow. He lay waiting for her on a bed of flowers, smiling.

He wore robes of yellow silk, like molten gold. Around his neck was a vaijayanti, a wildflower garland of tulasi, kunda, mandara, parijata, delicate rainbow-orchids and an extravagance of lotuses.

With a start, she found the infant she had carried here had vanished from her arms. The youth in the pavilion called her with his eyes, his beauty, his immense serenity; he called her irresistibly.

On dancer's feet she went to him, anklets whispering, helpless, all her loveliness on fire. Yet again in eternal time she went to him, dazed, her soul lost to his smile. She went blindly to take the dark and languid hand he held out to her. She shivered at his first touch; she swooned to be so near him in this jungle of fathomless quiet.

Briefly she swooned, then woke again to his whispered endearments. But when she awoke the Father of the world was there with them; Brahma had come to their pavilion. They bowed to him, the four-faced Grandsire of Gods.

He initiated them into a secret ritual. This was a covenant they had sworn in a scintillant court of the Devas, on another world, in a time lost in the mists of ages: that the Blue One would marry her, his eternal love, once on earth.

Seven times around the sacred fire she followed him; Brahma was their priest. The seven mantras of the Veda Brahma made her intone. Shyly, her head bent down, she said them in the softest voice. He had her place her hand on the groom's chest, and his hand on her back, and she could barely contain her desire.

She recited the three mantras now. She draped the garland of parijatas around his neck and it hung to his knees. Krishna also draped a wild garland around her, and they sat on either side of the lotus-born priest.

Finally, with folded hands, they recited the five mantras of the Veda and bowed again to the original ritvik, who then, like any father, gave her away to the Dark One at the mystic wedding. The Devas rained murmuring petals of light down on them.

All this, and not once did their eyes meet. When it seemed an eternity had passed, Brahma blessed the couple and melted away like a mirage.

When they were alone, she looked up into his face. She smiled crookedly, in bashfulness and wanting him, and quickly turned her face away. She couldn't wait any longer. Wordlessly she bent and touched his feet with her lips, and then went to his bed of flowers.

When he came to her, she marked his forehead gravely with a tilaka of sandal, aloe, musk and saffron. She handed him a silver cup of amrita.

Now he anointed her limbs with the same ochre-gold paste with which she had touched his brow. He took her face in his hands and kissed her. Adroitly, he loosened her garment. She no longer knew night from day, this world from another; her very life was a dizzy thing.

But her hands were on him, with will of their own, stripping him first of his peacock-feather crown, then of his golden robe. Her vermilion bindi was smudged across her forehead, her lip-rouge rubbed away by his mouth. Her plait was undone as his hands seized her tresses that fell down to her knees. The silver bell she wore round her waist snapped its chain and tinkled to the ground.

She was beyond restraint now; her breath came in gasps. Suka says the Blue God took her tenderly, inexorably; like star-fire he came into her flower body, her thousand-petalled soul. With an echoing cry she was lost in his timelessness, and he in her.

AUM mani padme hum!

A small hand shakes him vigorously, and Nanda wakes with a start. The dream has left him in a state of tumultuous excitement, and guilt that he has ventured where no man is allowed.

"Matulan, Matulan!" the little girl cries. "Yasodha Matuli is waiting for you to come home so she can serve lunch. Will you go now?"

Nanda rubs his eyes and squints up at her. The sun is behind her head and in his eye. But in her face he sees the same perfect features from his dream. It is Vrishabhanu's little daughter Radha.

From somewhere within the forest the silence of the noontide is broken with a song like the music of the spheres. Krishna has taken up his flute again. Radha skips away to find him.

FIFTEEN

Purusha *Sannyaasam karmanaam Krishna...*

Arjuna said, "*Krishna*, first you say renunciation is the way, burning karma with wisdom. Then *you say that karma is sannyasa*. Tell me, which is the true path?"

"Both," said Krishna, "lead to freedom. But your path is the way of karma, of deeds. You are not greedy for a kingdom or its power. That is half your battle won already; you will be freed easily."

Krishna smiled, the crow's feet around his eyes cracking. "But, Arjuna, the wise don't speak of the ways of wisdom and action as being separate. Only the ignorant do."

His eyes twinkled at his cousin. Arjuna's mother Kunti was a Yadava; she was Vasudeva's sister. Krishna said, "You cannot renounce action anyway, without knowing what it is. Only he who is involved in karma knows its inner emptiness. Made pure, he realises the still and changeless Brahman. In detachment, he occupies the senses with the objects of sense. But not himself. He is like a lotus leaf, resting on water but not wetted by water. The yogin does not act out of desire but to make himself pure, to make himself wise."

Prakriti

One thirsty summer's day, Krishna and his friends follow the herd along the parched river's bank, downstream past the bend beside the vana. The river runs dry, just the merest silver trickle showing here and there. So Krishna climbs a flame-of-the-forest tree growing at the jungle's edge to look for water. He climbs almost to the very top and, pointing east from his kite's perch, calls down to his friends, "There. A pool of still water."

And a dark premonition stirs in him. But before he can climb down and join them, his friends, none more than twelve, have run off with the cows towards the forest pool of overhanging trees, which looks so inviting on this ferocious day. A little tired, or wistful, he climbs halfway down the tree and sits day-dreaming for a bit in a forked branch, gazing out over the jungle.

He has just dozed off into majestic dreams when shrill screams rend the air. He starts awake and, shading his eyes, stares out to the pool. He sees smoke hanging above the trees, and wonders where it came from. Then he hears the drumming of hooves, and sees the cloud of dust where the herd stampedes back to him, lowing in panic.

He is down the tree in a flash, flying across the browning pasture. As he nears the pool, he sees the trees of the forest are scorched where, blown on dry breezes, poison spray has splashed on trunk and branch, withering their leaves. The ground under his feet is burnt black and an evil aura hangs congealing over the acrid place.

His garland of flame-of-the-forest clutched in his hands, he runs to the edge of the pool. He sees his friends lying still on the earth, their skins turning blue. He bends to feel their faces. They are dead, all of them, their bodies cold.

With a huge parting of the water, Kaliya the serpent-king thrusts his hood high into the air. He glares down at Krishna from pouchy, baleful eyes.

"Won't the little gopa drink from my pool?" the great snake hisses, mocking. Spread in a hundred segments, his hood is a faded grey as its mark of Siva, the white death's-head, is all but burnt away by years of lying in his own venom.

"Are his friends asleep? Perhaps the heat has tired them? It is hot, isn't it? Have a drink, little gopa, the water is pure."

And at once the serpent's slimy pool is crystalline. All the steaming poison has vanished. Krishna gives a start. Kaliya laughs, and the water is opaque again, a black mirror smoking with the old monster's extrusions.

All around Kaliya his serpent-wives raise their hoods: a hundred emerald naginas, young and old, beautiful and enticing, with gemstones glimmering at their throats, and all given to evil. Krishna shins up a kadamba tree. Deep memory unfurls in him, unearthly flower.

"So you have forgotten me, Kaliya, and how I drove you from the sea. This evil age has made you forget, and you have become vain and stupid again. It seems I must teach you another lesson."

Krishna's voice is a God's, he hardly knows it himself. Kaliya cocks his hood, and sways when he hears the Dark One speak like that. His eyes gleam with malevolence.

"Come down from your perch, boy, and we shall see who will teach the lesson," rattles the serpent, a hundred forked tongues flickering from his mouths.

Krishna wishes Balarama had been with him, because Krishna's brother surely has his way with any snake. But Balarama has stayed home with Yasodha today.

"No one may pass this place safely, and you have poisoned the river for leagues around. The rain passes Vrindavana by since you came. Kaliya, I will teach you a lesson you will never forget."

Meanwhile, one companion of Krishna's who straggled some way behind the others runs back to Vraja. He arrives at Yasodha's door and cries, "Come quickly! Kaliya has killed Krishna and the others."

They race across pasture and woodland, the cowherds and their women close behind Yasodha, Nanda and Balarama, and arrive at Kaliya's pool. The serpent mocks them from his slime, "Have you come looking for someone, cowherds? Or have you lost a cow?"

He laughs. "Perhaps it is these boys you've come for? But they drank from my pool, and very pure it looked until they finished."

The gopas cry out seeing the bodies of Krishna's companions, their sons, turning blue beside the water. But not even the children's parents dare come closer, for fear of the looming beast of the pool.

Then, with a growl, Balarama starts forward and Kaliya hisses, "Or perhaps this is who you are looking for?"

He raises astounding coils above the water. Entwined in them, eyes shut and apparently dead, is Krishna.

"He fell into our pool," breathes the serpent. He lifts his tail tip like a finger and points bizarrely to the kadamba tree, "From there. Such a fall," says Kaliya, shaking all his heads in a travesty of grief.

Yasodha screams, and Krishna's eyes fly open. They are full of light. Balarama shouts, "Look, he's alive!"

The coils around the Dark One come loose. He bends one of the hundred shiny heads, and leaps on to the serpent's hood. To inaudible music Krishna begins a dance on his surreal platform. The cowherds watch, riveted, as he turns before their eyes from a gopa boy into a young God.

Krishna's laughter pierces the noon air like crystal lances. He dances on. Now, the serpent wriggles desperately, shakes himself in spasms. But he can't get his hood out from under the quicksilver feet.

Faster the dark feet fly, weaving a hypnotic taala, a hundred hands in the air. Grown immense now, his peacock-feather glittering in the gloom, the Blue God dances, his face in the sun.

The cowherds' wives, the gopis, cannot stanch the tears of mythic excitement that start in their eyes as they watch Krishna dance. The men fold their hands at the vision. Who can doubt any more that an Avatara has been born into their clan?

Krishna dances on, and, as he dances, the spell in that place is broken. The foetid vapours dissolve. In the dazzle of fresh sunlight, blood breaks at the king-snake's jaws, and the Dark One is a graceful blur on Kaliya's subject head. The serpent-wives rise around their husband and the burning dancer.

"Immortal Hari!" they cry, knowing him now. "Don't kill a lowly snake. Forgive him, Lord, don't make us widows."

But Krishna dances on. Then, his pride broken, Kaliya cries, "I give in, Lord! I will do anything you say. Spare me, I have wives and children. I did not know you in my vanity."

"So the wickedness leaves your foolish head."

The blur of the dance slows.

"Suck the venom from this pool. Then take your brood and slither back to the ocean from where you came," commands the Avatara in his God's voice.

The cowherds hardly believe what they see and hear, thinking this is a dream. And the gopis, their women, ah, they tremble. They have grown damp between their lissom legs to watch him dance.

"And out at sea, serpent, when your enemy Garuda sees my footprints on your head he will spare your life. Go."

Krishna's form dwindles to a gopa boy's. He leaps down, runs to his mother and hugs her. He kisses her again and again till she hugs him back and begins to laugh and cry at once, as she finds herself doing so often with her son.

Krishna runs to his dead companions. He kneels beside each one, and shutting his eyes, whispering some mantras he hardly knows himself, he passes his hand over their hearts. Instantly, colour flows back into the children's faces. A tumult of joy breaks out among the cowherds as their children sit up, rubbing their eyes as if they have woken from a deep sleep.

Dipping his hundred heads, Kaliya drains his poison from the lonely pool and leaves it like the purest crystal once more. In a hallucinatory moment, he comes in a human shape, naked and emerald, and lays his glossy head at Krishna's feet. Later, the gopas think they imagined this, and that Krishna blessed Kaliya with a twilight hand, as if in another dimension.

Then, Kaliya is a snake once more. He and his naginas bow their hoods to Krishna, and slide away into the jungle, on their way back to the ocean and fabulous patala below its bed.

This is the first time the cowherds see an open display of Krishna's powers. He shows them no more, and what they saw at the pool doesn't change the gypsies' ways with him.

But the young women, who saw him dance on Kaliya's hood, begin to lust after him to distraction.

That night, he lies in his bed, listening to the living jungle outside. Satin moonlight flows over him through the airy window.

For the first time, he realises starkly that much of his life is beyond his own control. He knows parts of it involve enactments of fate during which he becomes someone else, someone incredible. He thinks back on the astonishing happenings of the day, and how when he pointed his friends to the pool a vague uneasiness was his only warning of what was to come.

Swathed in silver light, he lies shivering in his bed. Knowing his first conscious terror of being both human and more, he leaves his childhood behind him that night. He slips across the threshold of a precocious youth.

Later, when he falls into an exhausted sleep, he dreams of a luminous glade, perfectly circular, in the depths of the hermetic jungle. At the heart of the enchanted place grows a tree that is surely not of these times, but a great plant from the beginning of the world. It is radiantly white, trunk, branch, root and leaf; its twigs brush the stars.

Every fair leaf on the shining tree whispers to him in a tongue of heaven, calling him, calling him, to a secret ceremony in the jungle's heart.

SIXTEEN

Purusha *Yo antahsukho antararama...*

In this city of nine gates, the body, only he who has mastered his nature by giving into it perfectly, without desire, renouncing whatever he does even as he does it, only he shall find peace.

"He knows the atman does not act, nor is it acted upon, but only nature's gunas. The sins of such a man are cut from him. He reaches the Brahman from where there is no return; his wisdom illumines the immortal self.

"When the soul's light puts out your darkness, that lustre shines forth from you: the Brahman revealed, splendid as a sun.

"The enlightened man sees all creation as equal. He knows pleasures that begin outside the self are fleeting, and they inevitably bring sorrow with them at the end. He has no use for these; he is a master of the rush in his blood of lust, of anger.

"*He finds his endless joy within himself, his light within himself*, in his own soul, and he comes to Brahmanirvana," said he who had come to cleanse the world and make it strong again, with the tender patience of eternity.

"Whose sins are put out, whose doubts are dispelled, to whom the welfare of every creature is his joy, he finds Brahmanirvana.

"The austere man, set free from lust, anger and fear, enlightened, comes to me, who enjoys all karma and all tapasya, who am the Lord of worlds, the friend of all men. And he finds Brahmanirvana," sang Krishna.

Prakriti

The gopa grandfathers say it is a hundred years since such a beautiful generation of girls has been born among them as the one that has recently come of age in Gokula. When the month is full, the ravishing young women come to the midnight-blue river to bathe.

Bright clothes festoon the river's bank, fulvous yellows, verdant greens, unworldly purples and crimsons. Jewellery sparkles in the noon sun. The breeze is drunk with their bodies' fragrances, and the sandal, aloe and musk they have rubbed on one another.

Today is the Devi's day and a full moon. So fruit, incense, polished lamps, vermilion and saffron also lend colour to the festive riverbank.

But the young women themselves are in the limpid Yamuna, bathing and singing. They are as naked as the fish; dark and dusky, with milky arms, breasts and backs glistening in the spring sun. Absorbed and merry, their voices echoing under a cloudless sky, they tell each other some very plain stories.

They share frank thoughts about what their ideal man will look like, and what they will do when they are alone with him. In ringing voices they tease each other about being big-breasted or flat-chested. Their laughter is raucous. Their descriptions of the positions of love are explicit, and which position each one prefers.

And they fail to notice that fourteen boys are hidden in the shrubbery, hanging on their every careless word, feasting their eyes on all the shining nakedness in the river.

The boys barely control themselves when, her eyes shut in simulated transport, one of the gopis shows how her imaginary lover would fondle her tear-drop breasts. Or when another describes, awkwardly in the eddying flow, an unusually contorted posture of love, which she cries will give her lover more pleasure than any other.

If anyone in the delirious spring place notices that each girl's fantasy lover bears an uncanny resemblance to all the others' it is the object of the young women's passion himself—blue Krishna in the bushes. And he, Dark One, has a plan for them.

The boys whisper together in some frenzy in the thickets. The calmest of them, Krishna says he can't see half as much as he would like to.

The young women's clothes lie beyond the bend in the river. So the boys, all in their puberty, old butter-thieves, crawl down to the water. They gather up the women's clothes, leaving only their jewellery and the offerings for the Devi. All fourteen have a good, vibrant armful, since there are thirty-three luscious wenches in the water.

Krishna climbs into a kadamba tree growing beside the Yamuna. The others hand the clothes up to him, their sport more innocent than his: Krishna knows all about the women's fantasies, since the day they saw him dance on Kaliya's hood. Though many of the gopis have followed him around in irresistible fascination once he began to play on his flute; and some even before that, since they were toddlers and little playmates in Gokula.

The gaudy clothes hoisted into the tree, and hidden from view, Krishna calls down to the girls, "Gopis, you shouldn't bathe naked. You never know where a water-snake will make his hole. And today is the full moon. Varuna will be angry, and send his servants to steal your clothes. Quickly, girls, see if your clothes are still where you left them."

He crawls out on a branch hanging out over the river and stares gravely down at them. They scream, and splash wildly to get deeper into the water, which is sparklingly transparent, and cover themselves with their hands.

He wags a finger at them, but keeps a solemn face. At the foot of the tree Balarama and the others are doubled up, covering their mouths so the gopis won't hear them laugh.

The young women see the green bank bare of their clothes, and they begin to plead.

"Krishna, give back our clothes. We must take our offerings to the Devi."

But they are all aroused to have him gaze down at them from his perch where they gambol naked as the fish that shimmer through the water. Even

Radha, who is the focus of Krishna's fantasies, flushes. But she turns her eyes from him and swims farther away with graceful strokes.

"To the Devi!" mocks the flute-player, subject of the gopis' insanest dreams, stretched mysterious as a young panther on his branch. "And you think the Devi will return your missing clothes? I fear not. If your Devi couldn't watch over them in the first place, how will she give them back now?"

Radha, the gopis' leader, cries, "Tie that cowherd up and bring him to me. Last week it was coloured water he threw on us, and today it's this. He wants a sound beating."

"I would be beaten by you, Radha my love," the Dark One whispers. "But you must catch me first. And for that you must come out of the river, mustn't they, boys?"

The boys in the bushes burst into loud laughter, and the young women gasp.

"Come out with folded hands, if you want your clothes back," commands Krishna, grinning on his branch.

"Will you give back our clothes if we do?"

"Look, here they are." He pushes a colourful bundle into view. "But, of course, if your mistress Radha would rather tie me up and beat me, then we can have the beating first and the clothes returned after. Anyway, you must come out so we can all see how beautiful you are. Otherwise you can walk back naked to the village."

Invaded by an undertow of serious intent in his voice, which subtly excludes his more naive companions, those gopis all tremble with a single thought—of being in his dark embrace!

One by one, some covering mossy maidenheads with their hands, others trying vainly to hide black-nippled breasts, and others only covering their own eyes, all the women except Radha wade out of the clear water. Some giggling, some blushing, they come quite bare on to the bank, the sun caressing them.

Krishna lies languidly on his branch, his chin resting on his hands, feasting his eyes, amused, and also so solemn at what he watches. Dripping, their long-legged bodies quivering with excitement, the women parade for him under his perch.

Krishna's friends, rowdy, pubescent boys in the bushes, are quite breathless, and speechless as well with what the gorgeous gopis display. The lot of them, women and boys, are absolutely taken with the moment's forbidden magic, and the unearthly desire of the Darkling on his tree.

Then, in a blink, Krishna is down the kadamba and running into the deeper forest with an armful of gopis' clothes. The throng of naked girls breaks into headlong pursuit, screaming, dying to lay hands on him, cover him with their aching bodies. Ah, to have him at once, all together!

Radha, who remais in the river, shuts her eyes. She begins to shiver all over her slender body, because suddenly she sees the chase coming straight for her: he does not run away any more, but towards her.

Her green spring world is filled with a rampant Krishna. It bursts open behind her eyelids with his mocking face.

Radha cries out. Her eyes fly open to find her companions still around her in the water. She blinks, and sees their clothes untouched on the bank, just as they left them when they took them off. But when she looks up into the kadamba tree, Radha sees no boy-God in the forked branch.

Her eyes brim over that it has all been just her reverie.

SEVENTEEN

Purusha *Anaasritah karmaphalam...*

The song of God flowed through Arjuna, and it purified him. Time's living prism, he refracted a shimmer of wisdom down this world's ages. But the river of light grew intolerably bright, and Arjuna shut his eyes.

Then, the whirling presence of the ages of men vanished from around him, and he had the sense of travelling back in time. Up a deep tunnel flashed Arjuna, flying on Krishna's holy song, until he came to an ancestral time before man walked the earth.

And he knew it was then part of a sacred island, this field of Kurukshetra. He stood on an interminable white beach with the ancient wind howling around him. Though the place was apparently deserted he knew he was not alone. A vast presence waited here with him, invisible and unhuman.

Far away, Krishna said, "He who works serenely, *with no desire for the fruit of what he does*, success or failure, he is the yogin, the sannyasin; not he who lights no lamp on this earth. Pandava, what men call yoga is sannyasa, no less. No man becomes a yogin before he renounces his selfishness."

A golden umbilicus, Krishna's words connected Arjuna to the primeval shore. He knew he must not turn to see what it was that waited behind him, awesome and sinister. The moon was full in the night sky, wisps of cloud hung across her face.

Arjuna glanced anxiously left and right. But he knew whoever the feral one behind him was waiting for would not arrive from either side.

Suddenly, a queer humming turned him back to watch the swollen sea. The humming grew until it filled the beach, and the sky in which the stars were still young. It was punctuated by a quaint, high clicking.

Arjuna felt the one behind him tense terribly and step forward, taut as lightning, towards the waterline. Then he realised that he himself was invisible, insubstantial, because the dreadful spirit stepped right through him. Arjuna felt him, *like an army.*

"Work is the way of the rishi who wants to attain to yoga, to yoke himself to the eternal. Once he achieves union, he is at peace."

Prakriti

With a fearful instinct about Krishna, who has come into the world for its liberation, evil sends its cruder creatures, demons that live in the open, to challenge him. They come ostensibly to kill him. But more deeply, they come to seek his violent deliverance; who else can free them from themselves? As Putana and Sakatasura, evil comes into Krishna's life, before the gopas move to Vrindavana, and as Trinavarta, master of the air, who comes as a whirlwind.

Out of the clear blue sky, one day, he envelops Vraja in a storm, while the men are out at pasture. The cowherd women gag at the stench of him, they are blinded by his sulphurous swirl. Yasodha runs to where she has last seen Krishna, her mother's instinct warning her of peril to her child. Dimly she sees him, already clasped in opaque coils.

As suddenly as it came the devil wind lifts away, carrying Krishna out of sight. Yasodha falls in a black faint. The other gopis rush to revive her and she wakes screaming. She chases after the spiralling monster, but he rises higher and higher, till he is small as a kite above Gokula.

Inside the demon storm, the fiend at its eye, airy Trinavarta, finds the blue child in his coils has grown mysteriously heavy. Krishna grows heavy as a planet, as if the earth was contained within his little body. He grows so dense that Trinavarta's whirlwind turns slower and slower, until it stops spinning.

Trinavarta struggles to escape, but the terrible child seizes him by the throat. The asura's ten slitted eyes bulge round; one by one, they fall out of their sockets, down to the ground below. The demon comes hurtling after them, blind and howling, and Krishna still clutching his throat.

Yasodha and the other women watch the fiend fall whistling from the sky on to an outcrop of rocks. They see his bloated body shatter like the city of Tripura cloven by Rudra's arrow, inhuman limbs flying off the hideous trunk. Then, Krishna rises blithely out of the mess and toddles towards them, not a scratch on him. He is covered in the asura's blood, and seems to have enjoyed his adventure no end.

That is when he has not yet begun speaking.

Later in Vrindavana, evil comes to the clear lotus pool just inside the jungle where the cowherd boys take their calves to drink. It arrives as the savage Bakasura, come to avenge his sister Putana's death.

Baka, master of bird forms, comes as a golden crane big as a hill. Blotting out the sky, he swoops down and, beak yawned like a valley, swallows Krishna. But the boy burns the bird's throat like a sunflare and, roaring, Baka vomits him out.

Krishna's friends stand petrified, as the crane attacks him again with a clatter of spindly legs, gilded feathers and rapier bill. Red eyes glittering, Baka flies at the young Avatara.

For a while Krishna seems to humour the macabre demon, dodging his awkward rushes, laughing, tormenting him by plucking out a few tail-feathers each time he blunders by. But when he sees how frightened his friends are, he takes the asura by the beak. One segment in each hand, he tears the golden bird in two, easily as a blade of grass.

Baka's black blood sprays over the rushes growing beside the breeze-swept pool, in great spouts splashing on to pastel lotus petals. Shrieking, the crane staggers in an ungainly dance of death, scattering his feathers over the water and the young Blue God.

When Krishna is older, there is Arishta, the humped monster, who comes as a bull bison, whom the Dark One dispatches effortlessly; and Dhenuka, the demon of the palm-orchards of Vrindavana.

How Krishna laughs when he sees Dhenuka, two-legged, but donkey-headed and donkey-loined, his mate with him. Then Balarama kills the bizarre, braying pair.

EIGHTEEN

Purusha *Atmyyva hyatmano, bandhuratmyyva...*

The waves rose, cloudy and foam-crested, before Arjuna. He felt a new presence in the water as vast and as gentle as the other, now a shadow before him, was menacing and implacable. Krishna's song swirled around the Pandava in protection, its caress of mythic words cocooning him.

"The warrior's way is his own will. *The will alone is the soul's dearest friend, and the will alone is the atman's enemy.* To the man of restraint, his will is his soul's friend. But the self-indulgent man's will is his atman's enemy."

Silver and green water rose surging from the horizon, like a mountain before Arjuna. Its peak of waves parted and a dazzling being stood up from it, her hair brushing the moon, her face was brighter than the moon. She was as naked as she was tall and lovely, as she stood basking in the moonlight; it was she who sang the humming, clicking song.

Now the Pandava felt the evil of the other one on the land, unbearably, like no evil he had ever known. Arjuna knew that except for Krishna's long protection that darkness would have destroyed him in a moment, before it became aware of him.

"The sage is absorbed in the atman. He is the master of his will, he is unchanging," chanted the Blue One, from another time.

A scream split the humming. The invisible Beast on the beach materialized, tall as the sky himself, taller than her, and armed with a weapon of night. With a rush of hooves he plunged into the water, his weapon raised, glinting in the moon. The thick tail behind his fiendish body drummed the sand.

A mild witness on the primeval beach, Arjuna stood petrified, a scream choked in his throat. She in the water saw the demon rushing at her. With a high clicking of alarm she tried to submerge and escape. But too late. With a sharp explosion, he discharged his weapon at her.

In a flash a hundred phosphorescent serpents held her helpless, her humming shrill with fear. With a massive claw he seized her hair and dragged her from the water. Arjuna saw she had scales too, but shining, innocent fish-scales, on her legs and her back.

She cried out piercingly, but the Evil One flung her down on the sand, beside the raging sea. He wrenched her legs apart and thrust himself into her with a knifing of his stumped back.

As Arjuna watched, the fiend began to lurch above the struggling female in paroxysms, his tail curling in lust. She screamed and screamed, but her sea-voice grew fainter and fainter. Until, she made no movement or sound any more. The Beast above her turned his horned face up to the moon and bayed his conquest.

In his time-bubble Arjuna heard Krishna again, and clutched at his voice for sanity.

"The light of a lamp does not flicker in a windless place. He who has realised the Brahman never wanders again from the inmost truth of his being," sang Krishna softly.

There were resonances in his song, echoing far beyond the realm of their everyday meaning, and calming Arjuna. Krishna's quiet Gita drowned the roar of the frenzied sea, out where she lay ravaged and lifeless once, the crimson stain on white sand under her spreading, as the sorrowing waves licked around her naked feet in compassion.

The demon had vanished through Arjuna, as he had come. But the shock of evil hung over that primitive scene of violation, seeping through the ages.

A tormented cry broke out of the Pandava, and he saw Krishna standing at his elbow, reaching out to embrace him in sanctuary. The place of death vanished and Arjuna sat sobbing like a frightened child in his chariot on Kurukshetra, knowing it had all begun long ago, long before there was man at all.

Still holding Arjuna tightly to him, as his warrior wept, Krishna said, "When his mind is yoked in the atman, set free from craving, the yogin is united with Brahman."

Prakriti

A peaceful month after the slaying of Dhenuka, there is trouble from another quarter, which Krishna brings upon himself. He does not want the cowherds to make their yearly offering to the lord of the Devas at an Indra yagna, as has been their custom since time immemorial, since before their fathers crossed into the land of Bharata.

"Why should you worship Indra when I am born among you? The Deva's head is swollen because the kin of Vishnu's Avatara still bring him offerings."

"Listen to me," he tells his confused cowherds, who are not yet used to him being the Incarnation. "It isn't right for you to make offerings to Indra, when it is Mount Govardhana that protects us. Your immortal souls suffer because you worship a lesser god.

"Indra feeds on your offerings and on your spirits. Snared by his lascivious dreams of Devaloka, you forget the direction of your lives. This is more dangerous than being attacked by rakshasas; it delays your moksha by a hundred births.

"Why don't you worship Govardhana instead?"

They puzzle over this novel philosophy, never expounded in the world before: that the worship of lesser gods is an impediment to salvation. But once they have examined his argument, they can't fault what he says. In their hearts they know they have become Indra's devout slaves; and the Deva does keep them fettered, childlike. Nor does he even deign to help them in their times of need and danger.

Nanda says to Krishna, "We are afraid to stop worshipping Indra. We fear his fury if we seek Govardhana's blessing instead."

Krishna smiles. "Indra is powerless to harm the least among the faithful. And you are the chosen. I will protect you from the Deva, and then perhaps you also will believe in me."

"But why worship a mountain?"

"The mountain is replete with the Brahman. Unlike Indra, the mountain wants no worship. It is an ancient master living on earth to show you the way to moksha."

Krishna senses his battle half won already, another knot coming loose in the sacred thread he has come to unravel. False worship may not be an obvious sin, but it is enshackling. The Avatara has come to set men free from the bonds of light, as much as those of evil. He has come to break all bonds.

"The mountain is beyond desire!" Krishna cries. "Make your offering to the mountain."

Thousand-eyed Indra is livid. He summons Samvartaka, his host of thunderclouds.

"*Bhoh! Bhoh!*" Indra roars at the belligerent thunderheads. The lord of Devaloka is frightened. What will he be reduced to if mortal men stop worshipping him, as that upstart is encouraging them to?

Even to the gods, Krishna is still much of a mystery. The Devas have always enjoyed ancient sway over mankind, and Krishna is only a human boy after all, of very transient flesh and blood. Of course, the ones of light know about the prophecy that Narayana himself shall be born as a man, at this conjunction of the ages. But what real proof was there that Krishna, who is no kshatriya as Rama was, but just a cowherd, is the Avatara?

"Arrogant Nanda has abandoned my yagna," cries Indra. "He thinks Krishna can save him from my wrath. The cowherds must be taught a lesson they will never forget.

"Fly to Vrindavana, my stormtroop; drown their miserable herd with a storm like they have never seen. Let them feel the anger of the king of the Devas. Go. I follow on Airavata."

Samvartaka descends on Vrindavana. The world goes dark around the jungle and the cowherd village, as bank upon bank of sinister cloud scud rumbling into the sky. It is the day after the cowherds had diverted their offerings from Indra to Mount Govardhana. It was easy enough for Krishna to talk, but how can mere gypsies stand up to the might of the king of the Devas?

The villagers flee home from the pasture when they see the omens. They huddle within their huts, herding as many of their cows and calves with them as they can squeeze indoors.

Once they fill the sky within the circle of the horizon, the clouds erupt in earthshaking thunder, and whiplashes of lightning which shred the darkness into shards of fear.

White cows low piteously in the gloom, women and children scream; and then the rain comes down in sheets. Earth and sky seem as one in that downpour. All creation seems to be made from just the element of water: deluge without beginning or end, *Pralaya!*

The herd panics. Lowing in fright, it dashes out from the frantic claustrophobia of the huts, where man and beast mill together in equal terror. The cattle would rather die, out in the familiar open.

Gopi women scream themselves unconscious. Children clutch their fathers' hands; their shrieks are drowned by the roar of the storm.

Outside, all is flood. The water swells angrily into the meagre huts. At first just calves are washed away by the current. But quickly, the Yamuna is in vicious spate, breaking her banks, flashing across pasture and forest.

Cows and bulls begin to perish as well, swept away by the cataract. The storm rages on in darkness, with heart-stopping cracks of thunder and gashes of blue lightning that connect heaven and earth.

Someone cries shrilly, "Where is Krishna?"

At that moment, a voice speaks from the sky, a God's voice.

"This is what you get for worshipping Indra for generations. It is only your offerings and your cringing that the Deva loves. But come and see how the mountain loves you."

The rain has stopped. Thunder still echoes, but weak and distant. Only Yasodha and Nanda venture from their hut to answer Krishna's call. When they do, standing knee-deep in the flow, faces turned skywards, they begin to laugh, at the sight which greets them outside, to laugh like children. Hearing them so full of joy, the others also emerge, and they too witness the miracle of Indra being thwarted in his revenge.

> *High above them, suspended between heaven and earth, Krishna holds aloft the mountain in his hand. He holds Govardhana inverted above Vrindavana—a living awning of earth, rock and forest.*

Grown into a God, Krishna with the mountain dominates the sky. As the cowherds watch, they see:

His body was no longer mere flesh and blood, but made of light, as he absorbed the lightning from Indra's storm. Krishna shone with the electric network coiled around him like writhing serpents, and his laughter echoed above the thunder, belittling it.

Then, the mountain in his hand began to glow within itself with a fabulous flame. Suddenly, it was no longer made of its earth, rock, tree, and forest, with mists and streams in its valleys; but of sheerest crystal. Govardhana had turned into an iridescent pyramid in the Avatara's hand: an archetypal pyramid of infinite faces, refracting spectral beams down whenever the lightning pierced it.

He too, Krishna vast beyond imagining, was made of the same lucent stuff; though he was flesh and blood as well, as was Govardhana in his hands. The cowherds stood transfixed.

That breathing pyramid, which covered the sky so no drop of rain fell down to the earth below, began to change colours. The mountain glowed virescent emerald first, then resonant turquoise, then breathtaking, lucific crimson; and quickly, every other fluorescent hue, changing faster and faster: a symphony of light.

The gopas saw that deep within it, at its blinding core, a heart pulsed. Krishna also glowed with that splendour, within and without his God's body.

Now, crystal pyramid and Blue God began to blaze brighter than suns, until at flashpoint the mountain and he were a single, coruscating Being out of purest fantasy. The God was the mountain and the mountain the God; both of them neither stone nor flesh, yet these too, and more: out of dreams.

Then Krishna's huge laughter, the living mountain's immense laughter, transformed itself into Pranava, a reverberant **AUM**. All the world and the sky with all its stars were just the precious syllable. At its immaculate end, its echo was the sublime point, holy Bindu which contained the galaxies within itself, their beginning and end.

Then, silence: perfect, complete. Earth, sky and stone were transported to another realm when time scarcely was. Within that chasmic, blissful silence the villagers stood spellbound, unaware of themselves.

At the very seed of the silence a song sprouted, a song which was that primeval silence—a lone flute song, plaintive, yet full of the gayest celebration. The mountain reappeared in the sky, now Govardhana again of great crags and forests, of waterfalls and clouds clinging to his peaks.

The heavenly pyramid was gone, and Krishna, too, had vanished from the air. He had grown human-sized again, and wandered among sky-floating Govardhana's green forests. They rang with his timeless song, drowning Indra's storm, lifting the cowherds out of their terror, and themselves entirely, on a tide of ecstasy.

The seven days of vision that the mountain and the God stay aloft, shutting out the storm, seem no more than some moments to the gopas. Until Indra, raging impotent on high, turns his white elephant home, his battle lost, his bonds on the minds of the cowherds broken forever.

Not unmoved, the king of the Devas swears, "This cowherd is the Brahman!"

The day after Indra's vengeful storm the world seems washed clean. Safe again under cerulean skies, the gopas are not certain whether Krishna's dazzling miracle was any more than a hallucination.

They, not Nanda but the others, say to Krishna, "You quelled Kaliya, you killed Dhenuka, and now you've lifted the mountain to save us. You are Nanda and Yasodha's boy, but your deeds are Godly. Why, you vanquished the king of the Devas before our eyes!

"Krishna, what are you? Are you a Deva, a danava, a yaksha, or a gandharva? We must know today."

Krishna grows very quiet; his sermonal aspect of the past few days has vanished. After all, he has taught not only the simple cowherds a lesson but the king of the Devas one. So now he pretends to be piqued by what they ask. Perhaps he is really annoyed that the people among whom he has grown find it so hard to accept him for what he is: a phenomenon, certainly, but all the same just their Krishna.

"If, gopas, you aren't ashamed to be related to me," says the Blue God to them, "why think of me in any other way? I am neither Deva nor gandharva, not yaksha or danava. If you love me and I deserve your love, you must think of me as your kinsman. I have been born in your clan, haven't I? Then, that is the only way to look at it."

He turns and walks out of their council. They sit in silence for a while, each wrapped in thoughts too deep to share.

Then from a way off they hear Krishna's flute. The birds of the jungle all burst into song in sympathy with him, and the sun breaks cover from behind the last straggles of Indra's storm.

NINETEEN

Purusha *Yam labdhva cha param laabham...*

He sent his calm to invade the Pandava; he sent his love in his song and by his embrace.

"When you gain the atman you know there is nothing left to gain. Then no sorrow shall move you. The yogin is disconnected from pain, he is united with Brahman.

"The body, the mind and the life are pure; the light shines through clearly. Eternal bliss is as natural as breathing to the yogin. The atman is plain to him in all beings, and all things."

Arjuna's tears fell on to Krishna's shoulder.

Krishna said, "He who sees me everywhere, I am with him and he is with me, forever. The perfect man sees all things equally, in the image of his own self."

But another image haunted Arjuna: the great, sweet face of her whose blood was spilt out on the white beach. And the face of the Beast.

"Krishna, how hard it is to see all things equally. The mind is fickle, impetuous, strong, willful, and prone to terror. It is simpler to tame the wind."

Krishna said, "Who said yoga is easy to achieve? *Remember it is the last achievement, beyond which there is no other.* Yet it is not impossible; I tell you, you can attain it."

Prakriti

Even the Devas of light often gather invisibly in the sky to watch Krishna and his friends at play in the vana.

Adorned by their doting mothers with glass beads, gunja seeds, precious stones and golden ornaments flashing in the beams of the sun that pierce the jungle's roof, the friends embellish themselves further with fruit, tender foliage, flowers, feathers and red earth, to be as colourful as the natural world around them.

They chase each other in excited games of catch. They play on reed-flutes and leaf-horns. They sing in high, unbroken voices. They strut, mimicking peacock, crane and royal swan.

They roam with the beasts of the wild, sing with the koyal, pull the monkeys' dangling tails, and swim naked in the streams and pools, lilies in their hair, and Krishna's grace always upon them.

Once, Krishna leads the cowherd boys to the white sandbanks of the Yamuna, circled with kadamba, hintala, neem and punnaga trees, humming with black bees enticed by the aroma of lotuses.

"Let's eat here today," says he.

They sit on the fresh sand around their leader, like petals around a tremendous blue pistil. Large leaves serve as plates, and clean slabs of flat rock as tables, as they share all the different food they have brought with them. Each boy praises his own mother's cooking to the cobalt sky; Krishna lies with his head propped on a long arm, eating, saying nothing about the food he picks at, only cracking jokes in the sun.

The Devas look down, envious of the gopa boys basking in the nearness of the Dark One. Then, before the meal is over, the calves stray into the forest and the boys grow anxious.

Krishna gets up, "I'll fetch them."

He washes his hands in the river, and sets off into the jungle after the calves. But though he walks a league or two, he doesn't find them. Instead he sees the trail of their hoof-prints vanish abruptly from the brown forest track.

He searches for them in caves and across streams. He comes back to the riverbank and discovers his playmates have all disappeared as well.

He sits down calmly on the shining sand. Untying it from his waist, he raises his flute to his lips. His song rings out in the sylvan place; it instructs him. He learns that Brahma has spirited away the boys and the calves. He wants another miracle from Krishna, to convince him he is indeed the Avatara.

Krishna plays on, and his song reaches beyond the heat of the noonday sun; it conjures with the rising mirages of the river. Those begin to take form in the mystic music. All his friends and their calves reappear, at first dreamlike around him, then becoming solid flesh and blood, laughing and chattering as if they had never disappeared.

Watching from his nearby hide, Brahma exults; he has not released calf or boy whom he took sweet captive. But how long can the blue boy keep this up? Can he deceive the cow-mothers of the calves and the women of Gokula? Now absolutely involved with his game, his test, Brahma turns back to Satyaloka where he has hidden the children and the calves.

The lotus-born Creator arrives in some excitement at his palace, but his own dwarapalakas bar his way.

"Let me pass, fools, don't you know me?" he cries.

"You are an impostor. We have just let the Lord Brahma into the palace. He sits inside, four-faced and four-armed, upon his throne."

"Krishna!" gasps Brahma. Turning to the children under his spell, he sees them all blue-skinned, clad in xanthic robes, flutes raised in a mocking song.

Meanwhile, a human year passes in the world below, as long as Brahma's brief journey back and forth from Satyaloka has taken him— a few cosmic moments. He flies back to Vraja on his swan.

Several boys and calves, who are not what they seem, but all made just of Krishna's song, frolic in Vrindavana at the year-end. Not the cows, nor the mothers of the children, not the young ones themselves have suspected a thing.

Overcome that the cowherd could delude him, master of worlds, Brahma reveals himself on the riverbank in glory, hoping to awe Krishna. With a smile, Krishna shows Brahma the Immanent One, the Parabrahman in the boys and the calves; and the Blue God himself Un-born and Primal.

Brahma stands rooted by that vision.

In a moment, Krishna reverts inscrutably to his gopa self, this world, and Vrindavana. Dazzled, Brahma bows to the Avatara. He restores Krishna's friends and their calves to him, and flies back to Satyaloka, chastened, well beaten at the great game of making illusions.

TWENTY

Purusha *Ayatih sraddhayopeto...*

"Krishna, where does he go *who believes but cannot control himself?* Is he destroyed like a torn cloud in the sky, with no support anywhere? Does he fall forever?" asked Arjuna, now desperate once more. "Ah, doubt grips my soul like a devil!"

He trembled again from conflict within.

But Krishna spoke like the sun now, radiating wise words. "A believer does not perish in this world or the next, Arjuna. A man who seeks Brahman never comes to a bad end."

The dead face of her on the beach rose again in Arjuna's mind. But Krishna went on calmly, ignoring the darkness that flitted across the Pandava's face.

"The believer who falls away from yoga is reborn in the homes of the pure and the prosperous, of kings, or into a family of yogins; the second birth is the rarer. From there the spirit treads the path towards enlightenment again. Inexorably, his belief takes him on.

"Arjuna, the man who worships me with faith, to me he is the brightest yogin, more precious than the tapasvin or the gyani or the man of karma. The man of bhakti is dearest to me."

Like temple bells calling him out of sorrow and futility, Krishna's words rang in the morning light. When Arjuna looked into his cousin's black eyes he saw such love in them. It was as if he had woken from a nightmare to find the sun risen and daylight in the world.

He smiled wanly at the Blue God.

Prakriti

It is autumn twilight, when Krishna looks up at the sky into which an amber full moon rises. He breathes the crisp air, redolent with lotuses blooming on the forest-pools. He hears the koyal's song, and decides it is time to satisfy the yearning of his gopis, all beautiful and older than him: his mistresses of love to be.

He knows how much they want him. He only has to set his flute to his lips and at just the first heady phrases, they appear from behind tree and bush as if by magic. They follow him everywhere, forgetting themselves, mad just to be near him.

Krishna has heard their men warn the women about him, sententiously. He knows they cannot turn the gopis' hearts. He sees the women's dreams by night and day; he sees himself there. He spies on them in light woods and beside the river. They laugh and call out to one another, each knowing the others' love intimately, aching from it herself.

"I am Krishna. Watch my hips sway, as I walk lordly by."

"No, I am Krishna. Listen to my song."

She sings in a man's voice, like his, a song set to the taala mandra. A song he often sang himself.

"Down Kaliya!" cries another. She begins a dance to mimic the day at the serpent-king's pool. Their laughter, he notices, is full of desire too long unfulfilled save in dreams and relentless fantasies.

"Don't fear the storm, cowherds," cries another gopi. "I have come with the mountain to save you."

Yet another has fashioned a thin flute of river-reed, on which she plays with inspiration. He spies on them all in secret, with love.

He watches them become him, turn by turn, in subtle roleplay. He watches the others then flock to that one, rub breast and back, face and thigh against her, lips parted, eyes shut.

He sees more in the woods. He sees them kiss and lie together, one upon the other, garments loosened, bodies grinding in pretence of making love to him.

Slowly, he woos them, on the riverbank and in fragile woods full of forest-spirits. Sometimes he meets them even within the darkest jungle. He goes with them in boats on the scented river on stolen evenings. He will let a hand brush against one or the other, leg or soft side, and watch how she shivers at his touch, and suppresses a moan. He hears them whisper brazenly about the damp in their clothes.

Often, he watches them from hiding, like a hunter, watches them yearn for him.

"I see his footprints: the marks of the lotus and the thunderbolt. And, look, smaller prints: one of ours. The wretch. He stood on tiptoe to pluck flowers for her from the tree."

"And he sat with someone else under this tree, and look at these flowers. They have the mark of string on their stems. Someone garlanded him here, and when he kissed her, these flowers fell."

"It was I," and a husky laugh.

The focus of his own desire is Radha. On her he spies night and day, invades her dreams with occult power. He finds himself at every corner of her mind; in her fantasies, he feels her petal hands and fragrant lips on his skin.

Yet, not once in the open day does he catch her, like the others, speaking of him or confessing her love. She is always cool and aloof. Not once does she try to sit next to him on the boat on the Yamuna, or to meet him alone in the forest. In fact, he has seldom found her even listening to his flute. If she does, which he knows she does, she makes sure it is from perfect concealment.

She is careful; not even her footmarks on soft ground betray her obsession with him. For her it is absolute, and she dare not give in to it yet. He realises she fears for her sanity.

She knows about his spying. She is so adept at leaving no clue of her love, he wonders if his vision of her daydreams isn't an illusion. How can anyone have such restraint, not betray a whisper of what she feels by the smallest, most inadvertent, word or sign? He knows she burns for him.

That autumn evening, says Suka, Krishna sees Radha and her companions out on the pasture, and he knows their time with him has almost come.

Leaving his friends, he saunters up to the young women and says, "In three months, on the night of spring's first full moon, you will dance with me in Vrindavana."

He pulls off his garland of wild jasmine and white butterfly orchids, which look as if they will fly away with the vanamala at any moment. Pushing past the other girls, he drapes it around Radha's neck. She stands silent, still not betraying anything of what she may have felt.

The gopis fancy they see another shadowy face, serene and mocking, beyond his dark one. A jewelled crown glows above it, from another world.

For three months after that day in autumn, he follows them restlessly. He woos them in and around the great forest and the river full of sighs for what he does: stealing embraces and kisses whenever he cares to.

But no more, and he keeps them and himself waiting, on fire.

TWENTY-ONE

Purusha

Krishna let his song taper into a silence, full of mercy that enveloped his warrior. Enfolded in this quiet—and the armies on either side seemed to him to be hushed as well, frozen in time—Arjuna forgot the vision on the primordial beach; as though he had never stood on that shore, with the wild wind screaming in his ears. As if he had never been a witness to evil in a time before man walked the world—man, so small and so important.

Krishna gathered himself within his reverberant stillness. His battles, as ever, were only beginning; and as always he was the eternal seeker. He knew that Arjuna he could save; with a song of light he could surely rescue his friend from folly. But who would redeem Krishna from his long aloneness, from himself?

At the end of another incarnation, and he was close to the end now, he was no nearer his own salvation. Except, perhaps, now he could remember this beautiful human life—his mothers, his lovers, his battles, his friends—all precious and fleeting against his other, immense transcendence.

"*Who are you, Krishna?*"

Prakriti

One day, at the end of three months, called by fate and instinct, Krishna comes alone into the forest. It is dusk, twilight of the thirteenth day of the first bright fortnight of spring. The moon is full, still low; the breeze is laced with the scents of mallika and madhavi. The silence of the forest is broken only by the noises of spring insects come to drink from the flowers, who carried golden pollen across the vana, end to end.

Every flower in the forest is fresh with spring, the koyal's song is rapturous with it. Krishna walks on, blindly following his intuition. He comes past lotus pools, on whose velvet moss-banks mushrooms with scarlet heads grow tall as men, and wild orchids bloom in phosphorescent colours.

The strange trees and exotic birds have no names in the tongues of men, because no man has been here before. Passing herds of tiny golden deer, like the one that came when he was a baby, he arrives in the inmost heart of the jungle, utterly quiet, awesome.

He suddenly finds himself at the edge of a perfectly circular glade, fragrant with incense, lit with firefly lamps: a glade that seems to have been cleared just for him by an unimaginable hand.

He recognizes it as the glade from his dreams. Bright garments to wear to the Raasalila, Krishna's dance, are strewn on the ground, and hang from trees. Made from unearthly fabric, soft and powdery as butterfly-wings, they are scented with sandal, aloe, musk and saffron. The circle is as colourful as a rainbow fallen to the earth. There are garlands everywhere, made with every wildflower of the spring.

The circle of dance is studded with violet pools, with goose, teal, swan and scarlet ibis floating on them. There are wonderful pavilions here, some provided with luscious fruit and gandharva delicacies; others are frankly inviting with soft couches, perfumed with sandal and musk, and heaped with champaka blossoms. Deer and lynx come, wide-eyed, to the edge of the magic circle and, standing still, gaze.

Krishna laughs aloud when he sees the circle of dream. A sense of *deja vu* stirs in him that—ages ago, and not only in dreams—he has been here. He walks in, stretches himself on a couch in a fragrant pavilion, and raises his flute to his lips. The song in Vasantam, a spring, seductive raga, trills out.

In dizzy spellbinding notes it flows off his fingers and his breath and flames through the spring forest, touching animals and insects, birds, flowers and trees. Tigers and elephants begin to rut helplessly in his song. Beetles and scorpions mount their mates in stiff, worshipful ritual. Hamadryads entwine, and the breeze, full of desire, wafts treasures of pollen from tree to tree.

All the forest in its thrall, the song races towards the crescent of huts at the jungle's edge. The cows and the dogs of the village don't hear that song; the cowherds of Gokula don't hear it. But, borne on moonbeams, it flashes through the night and pierces the minds of the gopikas.

When it finds Radha, first of all, she stiffens over her fire. She is filled by such a fine *lust*, which she cannot resist.

She remembers Krishna's promise of dance made that autumn evening, three months ago. She remembers, tonight is the night of spring's first full moon. She mumbles something to her sleepy husband about fetching water from the well, and runs out into the insane moonlight, which ignites her. The song pulls her along its path of notes into the waiting forest.

At the edge of the village she meets Lalitha, Sushila, Chandravali, Kanta, and Maithili, and soon enough all the others: thirty-three of them ravished by the music, out of their wits, flying to him. They pause only to arrange Radha's clothes, because she will be the first bride of this night.

Clutching one anothers' hands, they race along the moon-spangled path, when abruptly the music stops. They do not know which way to turn, but stop in their tracks, panting. The very jungle seems to still its heart around them. Deprived of the song's fervent temptation they shiver at the risk they ran being out here at this hour.

Then, softly, with a familiar, mocking smile in it, the flute takes up again, curling the night within itself, the moon, the jungle, the women, everything, transforming them at its potent will.

Once more the universe throbs with the urgency of his fever. Laughing, saved, the women plunge headlong after the song again, deeper into the forest, chasing the elemental magic to its source.

They arrive at the edge of the luminous glade. The music stops again.
The moon above the trees bathes the silent circle in light. Everything
is still.

There is no sign of he for whom they have come. But at the heart
of the glade, there grows a tree, its trunk and branches, roots and leaves,
all white. Its bole is as wide as twenty trees of the forest, and its high
twigs brush the face of the moon.

After their careen through the forest, in that silence of primitive
desire, they hear their own breathing like seas. They hear their hearts
beat like tribal drums in the pregnant jungle.

It is Radha who first steps into the circle of dance, she who first takes
her life in her hands and offers it, pulsing, entirely vulnerable, to the Blue
God. With complete dignity, that this is where she is meant to be, she
steps forward regally and takes her place beside the white tree, whose
leaves are full of heaven's whispering.

But the others are too dazed by all the colour and miracle, and by
the coursing of their own blood, to follow her. Until Radha calls them,
and they come to her like sleepwalkers, and holding hands, form a ring
around the tree out of timeless dream.

When they are all inside the circle, the tree grows quiet; Krishna
steps fluidly out of it. There is no more white tree there brushing moon
and stars, but only the Dark One, and he comes among them. Lost in
this dream, the women reach out to him, oh, just to touch him, leaf and
root!

He takes each one by the hand and leads her to a new place within
the circle. To Radha he gives a tiny lotus, thousand-petalled: the mark
of the soul. He caresses her face for the first time. She shuts her eyes
and will swoon; when he takes away his touch, which for her already
lasts forever.

He begins to hum and then, to sing softly; and he plays the song on
his flute. As the music flows again, the dance begins. Slowly, they sway
from side to side, in a circle around him. Beside themselves, they cry
in the ecstasy that seizes them, "Sadhu, Krishna! Sadhu, sadhu."

As the song quickens, he also dances. Such a dancer! He is
everywhere, spinning first to one woman, then weaving back to his

central place; then taking another partner, and then another. Round and round they dance, and time becomes a charmed stream, bearing them far from themselves.

Faster and faster dances Krishna. He moves so quickly that he dances with them all, at once; so quickly that, somewhere along the dance, like a child's bright wind-wheel, time's flow is reversed and they dance, fascinated by him, into another dimension...

Where Radha found herself alone with him, even as she danced, and bare as birth on a bed of down in a love-pavilion, her legs garlanded around his neck. He was miraculous at the moment he parted her like a sacred sea, moment of her sweetest tide. She cries out...

Sushila found herself alone with him, even as she danced, her back bare against the bark of the ancient tree, full of whispering again. He bent gracefully but pierced her with exquisite, delirious pain, and she cries out...

Lalitha found herself alone with him as she danced, she saw the reflection of his face like a deep blue sea above her, as she peered into the mirror of a forest pool, kneeling on its green bank. She cries out for her sudden, unendurable joy, as he broke into her from the night like a galaxy...

Visaka found herself alone with him, even as she danced. She saw the moon reflected in his black eyes, just before she bore down, biting her lip. With a cry, she was absorbed in his serene and tumultuary blueness...

As dark youth and cosmic spirit he engulfs them all in the same, undying instant, even as they dance. After their long, fantasy-filled wait for him, they can hardly bear him now for the rapture he thrusts on them. With a lovely outcry, they collapse on the soft earth in his arms around the mystic circle.

And the bliss of the Brahman sweeps the world.

But the music stops only for a moment, and only for a moment does he pause in his lila, his whirling wheel of love. Then the flute-song thrills out again from somewhere upon the edge of all the world's forests, and he is alive in them once more, inexorable, oceanic. He leaves his mark on silver breast and naked moon-limb, as their breath heaves and their hearts lurch.

Ineffably he loves them—singly, and together, within the blue fire of the circle of dance, and in thirty-three forests of wonder, for as many days, in as many forms: as man and beast beneath the old trees, as painted tortoise and shining fish in the forest-pools and streams, as glimmering snake and scorpion under the rocks of the earth, as insect and dragonfly on the leaves and on the wing, as twinned stars fusing in the caverns of the sky, in myriad mandalas, forever and ever.

Yet, they are not satisfied; like a yagna fire fed with butter, they only burn more fiercely for his holy loving. And he loves them mad, loves them until they cannot bear him. He loves them past dying.

And Krishna's fire within him? It isn't quenched, but surely cooled a little with the womens' love, with Radha's measureless love. Every night, for the thirty-three nights he dances with them, the Devas come and hide among the leaves of the white tree to watch the unearthly spectacle. And watching, they tremble in their immortal bodies of light.

TWENTY-TWO

Purusha

The images of his life as a man faded once more. The Gita that had streamed through the Pandava, through the ages of men in this world, paused. The river of soul-lights was still: the tide of mutating generations, mysterious hordes, billion upon billion of eddying lives, forms of the surface, intricate forms of himself lost in the night of the deluge, the cosmic night so dark and blind. They had come in a rush, bright as stars; and so they faded, as suddenly.

Krishna thought, "Whom do I seek here, standing between these armies, one of darkness, the other of light? Whom do I seek again, but my own self? Un-born, unknown.

"I have come as a man before, as beast, fish, tortoise and manticore; and again, in the malignant darkness I must be born a pale avenger. But this is the finest incarnation of all, straddling two ages as not even perfect Rama did."

Krishna was aware that though he and Rama were one, they weren't only that. On the cusp of these ages now, when momentous constellations crossed deep in the sky, he was just Krishna, and no one else. He was greater than Sri Rama, less than him, and him as well; but another too.

Just as the prince of Ayodhya had become someone else when in the end he banished Sita, though it was as if he had cut his heart from him:

by this deep Gita, Krishna became himself. He had come for this; yes, to pierce the core of his own isolation.

He felt himself reborn in this knowledge. As if the other, the First One, was made complete, and all the legends of starry time—because a blue sarathy sang words of wisdom between two armies to a lost warrior, one day on earth. As if from this hour, morning of the charioteer, the epic of mankind began again, *mutant*.

Through Arjuna his song percolated into the seeds of unborn generations, waiting to metamorphose, to change the very nature of mythic time, the earth's dreaming heart.

From there, his Gita defined the paths of freedom anew, the images of the future: the races, their bodies of legend, intricate lives, nations, wars, pain and, more than anything else, death and dying.

Prakriti

Once he imprisons his father Ugrasena and usurps the throne of Mathura, Kamsa's evil grows apace. After the slaughter of the thousand babies on the night Krishna was born, Kamsa will stop at nothing to keep his power. For nothing else makes him feel secure.

Just as little else gives him pleasure any more, except inflicting pain; he depends on torture and murder for arousal. As for gratification, it is beyond him now, an impossible, ceaseless quest.

But Kamsa can never forget the Goddess' warning on that fateful night. Every night since, her face glowing in his sleep, she mocks him in his dreams, "The one who will kill you is alive, Kamsa, your kingship is a fool's paradise."

The rule of pale-eyed Kamsa, son of Dramila the gandharva, is a brutal tyranny for his people. Mathura has become the heart of Evil on earth, and Kamsa is its grand demon.

Once a month, the princes of darkness meet in Kamsa's palace: Jarasandha, Sishupala, Paundraka, Salva, Dantavakra and the rest. Kamsa is the prime mover of the sleek confederacy. Not even his father-in-law, Jarasandha of Magadha, can match his ambition or dedicated ruthlessness.

These kings meet during the nights of the new moon to offer macabre worship to the powers of chaos. It is whispered by those who still dare, for fear of his secret police, that on such nights Kamsa and his allies worship nameless Evil with human sacrifices. Frequently, the life offered up is that of a virgin, after she has been violated by the fiends who congregate in the palace at Mathura.

And Evil, glad at its burgeoning influence on earth, gives them whatever they want. Wealth and power it gives them, and in return they purge the earth of the enemies of darkness.

The verminous prisons of Mathura are filled to bursting. The slightest indiscretion of speech on the streets is enough to cost a man a slow death at the hands of Kamsa's torturers.

The people have grown suspicious of their neighbours; the seeds of mistrust the king has sown through the years have sprouted in deceit and betrayal. These are heartless years of oppression and dreadful poverty. The demon has sucked the land dry with insane taxes.

It is known that Kamsa handsomely rewards in gold and kind anyone who betrays a rebel who speaks against his rule.

The years weigh as heavy as centuries in Mathura. The king outlaws the worship of Vishnu in his city, on pain of death. The children of the city are raised in schools run by the secret police, where they are taught Godlessness and pure rationalism. But the brighter pupils are spotted early and brought to the palace for special education. Here, they are initiated into the mysteries of Evil and its empire on earth.

If they pass the trials of horror in Kamsa's dungeons, they become commanders of his elite secret service—experts in psychological warfare and torture, soulless, blindly obedient, minions of power.

They are the king's eyes and ears, his terrible hands out in the dim alleyways of Mathura: young men who will betray their mothers to him without a thought, or procure their sisters for him. And they enjoy wealth and privilege beyond the dreams of any other citizens.

Those boys of exceptional intelligence who do not succumb to Kamsa, and beyond him to the powers that are his masters, disappear without trace from the palace school. A generation of the best minds has been secretly slaughtered, even after Krishna was taken across the Yamuna to safety on the night of the thousand infants.

Kamsa fears the young most of all; they represent the passage of time and the terror of death to him. They remind him of the prophecy on Devaki's wedding day, and also of the Goddess who rose from the stone. He either claims them or kills them.

Some moonless nights, creatures of this world who are neither kings nor men come to Kamsa's conclaves, creatures whom not even his soldiers dare address. They come from far and wide with news of the condition of their other empire on earth. Silently they come and as quietly depart, their inhuman faces shrouded.

But in the sanctum below the level of the dungeons in Kamsa's palace, there is a golden throne set around a great table for every visitor. Here, the heart of the night and the soul's dark are laid bare in bloody rituals.

The screams of those whose throats are slit, or whose genitals are severed in that room, the screams of those whose blood is offered in golden goblets to unseen drinkers, those whose flesh is eaten, the screams of those who are ritually raped and killed even in the act of lust by silver knife or strangling, or who die of sheer terror: these screams are not heard beyond the stone walls and heavy doors of that chamber.

The sinister voices of devils from the pit, risen with gifts of power for Kamsa and his associates, are not heard outside. They remain locked away in the hearts of the fiends who enter there.

Kamsa pours potions into the drinking water of Mathura that keep his people in a permanent stupor; so that over the long years of their suffering they cease to even think of revolt. Not when their wives, their sisters and daughters, are taken by force to serve Kamsa's monstrous guests; not when a secret policeman takes mindless objection to a brother or father's less than servile manner, casually murders him in the street and leaves his body to rot in the gutter; not even when the younger children are taken to the king's palace to satisfy the bestial appetites of a perverted court, and often enough the king himself, who is now beyond any pleasure that is remotely natural.

Not under any circumstances do the people of Mathura plan a rebellion against their demonic sovereign.

Rather, in the way of their ancient race, they wait in profound patience, believing that everything they now endure is retribution for their own sins of past lives. They comfort each other in suffering shared, in the compassion of helplessness; and there is no family in the degenerate city that has not, in one form or other, tasted Kamsa's tyranny.

And their king pours sedative potions into their drinking water and exhorts them to harder labour, because the threat of conquest from neighbouring kingdoms is always imminent.

Eternal vigilance, he tells them, is the price of the rare freedom they enjoy in Mathura. For that they must work harder, with more discipline and self-denial, and pay him more taxes so he can keep their proud army stocked with the most devastating weapons. So the enemies of Mathura will think twice before attacking her.

The people of Mathura, the Yadavas who have not fled, work slavishly and pay him extortionist taxes, while they subsist at the edge of starvation. Not because they believe in the manic nationalism Kamsa and his agents preach, but because he will torture them or kill them if they do not pay.

Fear has become their most important instinct for survival; it is like breathing to them. Also work, like worship, helps them forget their plight.

But no tyranny is absolute. From across the Yamuna stories filter into dismal Mathura about the blue-skinned saviour with a face like the sea at twilight, who is growing up in Vrindavana; his exploits are already a legend throughout the land. Though they seldom dare mention his name, the people of Mathura install an image of Krishna—who will come one day from the wilderness to deliver them from Evil—in the temples of their hearts.

Though their lives could be forfeit by this, they worship him in secret as Vishnu's Avatara. And they wait for their saviour, every day. They dream of him, and in their collective sleep he comes to them, like a sun, promising deliverance. Their situation is so desperate that if Krishna did not exist they would invent him.

Kamsa is a master of potions. There is one that confers inhuman virility, another excites lust in the chastest woman, yet another elicits babbling confessions from the most stubborn prisoner. There is a potion for inflicting extreme pain, while keeping a man conscious, another that bestows superhuman strength. But none is as complex as the one that will conquer time.

Kamsa now devotes his attention to the new potion he is concocting with instructions from his masters of the night. The one that will restore youth to his body, make him immortal, and his rule on earth permanent. The rule of hell.

TWENTY-THREE

Purusha *Bhumir apo analo...*

His song flowed again, unknown, irresistible. "In yoga, with your mind devoted to me, you will know me. And then there will be nothing left to know.

"Among a million men, perhaps one seeks perfection. Of a million such who do, each by his chosen path, perhaps one truly knows me. And you know me, don't you, Arjuna?"

Otherwise they wouldn't be out here together.

"My nature is made of *earth, water, air,* fire, ether, mind, intellect, and ego: eight aspects."

He spoke almost helplessly; a God upon the edge, mastering his final weakness.

"But this is only my lower nature. My other aspect is the Soul, and the world is founded in it. It is the seed and the end of all things. I am the cause of everything, no other.

"Like pearls on a string the worlds are strung on me. Kaunteya, I am the essence of the waters, the light of the sun and the moon.

"I am AUM and the Vedas, the sruti of the cosmos, and the manhood in men; I am the sacred smell of the earth, and the brightness of fire.

"I am the life of all lives, the purity of the sage, the wisdom of the wise, the lustre of the lustrous, the strength of the strong. And all creatures am I, of sattva, rajas and tamas."

Krishna's head was now white, no streak of black remained; lank strands worn to his shoulders, shone in the sun, whenever the sun penetrated through the thick clouds.

Prakriti

One day, the itinerant Narada, Brahma's son, the brilliant rishi, arrives in Kamsa's court. He comes by magic skyway as the holy ones did quite openly in those times, stepping out of thin air in a flash of light.

Narada comes posing if not as an open ally of Evil, at least as a warm sympathizer; and he is full of the cleverest flattery to be found on any of the three worlds. His reputation as a meddler and mischief-maker provides him with excellent camouflage. When Narada is spoken of it is invariably in these terms, and seldom as one of the greatest bhaktas, which he is.

Kamsa welcomes him. After all, it was Narada who once told him that he was not a Yadava at all, and Ugrasena wasn't his father. It was Narada who told him about Dramila the gandharva, who one spring day flew down into the palace garden. King Kamsa considers Narada Muni his friend.

"Kamsa," begins the old campaigner, when he has settled into a red silk couch, "have you grown so complacent?"

"You forget I am a king, Muni. Sagest among sages, you are like the breeze, with no burden on your back. But I carry a kingdom upon mine. I cannot afford a moment's complacency."

Narada studies his slim hands in silence.

Kamsa laughs, "I can see through you, my friend. You have something to tell me."

Narada does not reply at once. He looks around, apparently admiring the garish palace. He smiles at one of the nubile young women who wait on the king and his guest. Then, selecting a purple grape from a bunch on the table, the rishi says, "It was a foolish thing to do."

"Don't talk in riddles!" Kamsa's suavity is deserting him.

"You know very well what I mean, old friend," says Narada.

"I do not. And since you have come all the way to Mathura to tell me, I presume you will before you leave."

"Killing Devaki's first seven children was a foolish thing to do!" hisses Narada, leaning forward suddenly, so his face is close to Kamsa's. The muni's bright eyes confront the king's pale green ones.

He doesn't pause a moment, but goes on briskly, "A foolish mistake, because it diverted your attention from the eighth child. And he lives."

"Impossible!" scoffs Kamsa, but with a start of fear.

"Impossible, you say? Yet, every child in the streets of Mathura has Krishna's name on his lips. Why, even your soldiers dream of dark Krishna, and none of them dares tell you about him."

A silence falls.

"Krishna," the king rolls the name on his tongue. "But tell me, wisest, how did this Krishna, if he really is my sister's son, escape that night when every newborn in my city was put to the sword?"

"So you want to hear about Krishna, after all," Narada smiles. "Then listen."

He tells Kamsa about Krishna's boyhood and youth. Some of the details he knows came from Indra and the Devas, who are the witnesses of the world, and some from Brahma himself.

He tells of the exchange of babies between Devaki and Yasodha; of the slaying of Putana and Sakatasura; of Dhenuka and Kaliya; of the lifting of Mount Govardhana; of Bakasura the golden crane; and the bull bison Arishta; of Aghasura, who came as a monstrous python and was also killed.

Kamsa sits very still and hears him out.

When Narada finishes, the king blinks his serpent's eyes. He claps his hands to summon a servant. Now he knows why he has not had a night's restful sleep in sixteen years.

"Fetch Vasudeva, and call my sabha to sit," says Kamsa softly.

His work done, Narada sighs and putting a last grape into his mouth, says, "I think I will leave you now, but with a word of advice. Don't wait any longer before you kill him, Kamsa. And don't forget Rohini's son Balarama. Once they grow into men, you will be helpless against them. Strike now, quickly."

Narada melts back into the mysterious world from where he came.

In the court of the Yadavas, Kamsa speaks in his woman's voice. He reviles Vasudeva.

"With no thought for honour or family, this coward broke his word to me. I am ashamed this traitor is married to my cousin. I am ashamed of myself that I did not see him for what he really is."

It is some years since the night when Krishna was born. Kamsa likes to think that no one else remembers that night. But no one has forgotten it.

The king proclaims, "I have just heard that our nephew Krishna is alive, and being raised in Vrindavana as the cowherd Nanda's son. Imagine. Our own blood, our prince, is growing up as a gypsy.

"Yadava lords, I will bring Krishna back to Mathura. And, after he has been taught the ways of the kshatriya, I swear my nephew will sit upon this ancient throne one day. Long live Mathura!"

The king is taken aback when the Yadava nobles, all seasoned courtiers, applaud like schoolboys. Do they really believe him, or is it that they so want to? He wonders, but it suits him at this moment to allow them their fantasy; at least until Krishna is brought to Mathura and got rid of.

Kamsa can ill afford the open enmity of the Yadava nobility. They could even rouse the people against him. But his hooded eyes note who the leaders were in the applause; he will deal with them later, after the black cowherd.

"Akrura," Kamsa calls. "Lord of gifts, you must go to Vrindavana and bring our nephew home. The festival of Siva's bow is in fourteen days. Let the two boys Krishna and Balarama be here for it. I hear they are keen wrestlers. Tell them they will have a chance to show their skills to the people. Hurry, dear Akrura, I can't wait to see my nephew."

Shrewdly, Kamsa sends this messenger. Akrura is an honest man and Krishna will trust him. His heart fluttering, Akrura bows and goes to prepare for his journey. Kamsa dismisses the sabha, except for a handful who are part of his other, sinister order.

"Go after Akrura," he tells one of them. "The old demon Kesin prowls Vrindavana. Tell him to kill Krishna and Balarama.

"Lest he fail, get the elephant Kuvalayapida ready for Siva's festival. Let Chanura and Mustika be prepared too. I have a potion for them to drink before they wrestle on that day, and another one for the beast.

"It is time we are rid of these paltry annoyances. It is time for greater dominance. The simpering Vasudeva must die, and Devaki. They shall be brought to the chamber one night, soon." He moistens his snake's mouth at the thought.

"Nanda must die, and the old dotard Ugrasena, whose cowardly spirit still haunts this palace. And all these primped Yadava lords who dare clap for the cowherd in my sabha—I will put an end to all the traitors. As soon as I put an end to this Krishna, this…*cowherd*."

He and his comrades in evil begin to laugh to think that a cowherd is the one meant to overthrow them.

"They would find a cow-grazer to worship," cries Kamsa, holding his lean sides. "Because we have made cows of them all, while we are the only bulls left in Mathura."

But memory can be a wicked thing. Suddenly, Kamsa remembers Narada's story of Arishta, the bull bison, and how Krishna killed him. The demon of Mathura falls silent, his face twitching.

Green eyes full of fear, he waves his confederates away from his presence.

TWENTY-FOUR

Purusha *Tribhirguna mayai...*

It would rain today on Kurukshetra. Kshatriya's blood and common soldier's blood would mingle with rainwater and flow in red streams, before the earth drank it down, and what remained was dried by wind and sun in stains of violent remembrance: if the Avatara had his way.

Krishna looked out to the Kaurava army, knowing his own kin were among its legions, fighting this last battle against their prince of grace. Catching the sentimentality in himself, he thought perhaps if Arjuna hadn't broken down, he, Krishna, might have done so. And then who would have freed him from his sorrow?

"*It is the three gunas that delude*, Arjuna; all this maya of life and death is theirs. Who makes me his sanctuary crosses the ocean of the world, the sea of samsara. Demons, evil ones, do not seek refuge in me yet."

Now Krishna smiled, "The virtuous who worship me are of four kinds: the man in trouble, the seeker after knowledge, the seeker after happiness, and the man of discernment.

"The discerning man is dearest to me. Why, he and I are one. Unlike the others, he comes to me after many lives, having realised that I am all there is. He is the rarest of the rare, the mahatman, the great soul," said the Dark One pointedly.

"Those whose minds are full of lust worship the Devas with rituals. And yes, I grant them their hearts' desires, make their faith fruitful, whatever form it takes. Those who worship the Devas, go to the Devas; but my bhaktas come to me.

"Those who are confused think of me as my manifestations. They don't know my transcendent nature, Un-born, changeless, supreme.

"Arjuna, I know all the beings, those alive now, those of the past and all those yet to be. All. But who knows me? Only the enlightened who have overcome sin, who are set free from duality's delusions, who find sanctuary in me and are saved from old age and death.

"They know the atman and Brahman and all about karma. They know that I rule both this world and the next, and they come to me when they die."

Prakriti

On the thirty-fourth day of Krishna's mystic lovemaking with the gopis in the circle of dance, Akrura, the master of gifts from Mathura, arrives in Vrindavana as evening grows into night. When the last rays of the sun mantle the forest and the village, he arrives in his elegant chariot, and asks some surprised cowherds where he can find Krishna.

Akrura is a Vishnubhakta, a cloistered midnight student of the holy Shastras, and he knows all about the prophecy. He has also heard the whispered, legendary rumours in Mathura, and his heart is in his mouth with anticipation at the thought of meeting the Avatara.

After his month with the Raasakridha, the Dark One is more aware than ever of his own destiny. He knows his manhood has come, a deeper phase in his life. It is time for him to leave the environs of his idyllic boyhood, they cannot contain him any more.

Yasodha catches him staring at her as if he was trying to imprint her every feature on his mind. But when she asks him why he stares, he only smiles and moves away. He tells Balarama he feels sure it is almost time for them to leave Vrindavana. Though he doesn't know yet for what destination.

"You will come back here, but not I."

He ranges the forest and the riverbank, gazing around him, while all the memories in familiar tree, cool water and charmed glade assemble before him, and his eyes brim over. More often than usual these days, the cowherds hear his flute; but now a song full of sorrow, and they wonder what the matter is with Krishna.

And the gopis? And Radha? Radha feels him withdrawing into himself as the days and the forbidden nights flash by like moments. His loving is as awesome as ever, but in the lull, when the dance grows languorous, she sees something in his sea-eyes that contains yawning vistas of time and place.

Akrura first sees Krishna among the calves at milking-time. He is the colour of a full-blown blue lotus, swathed in golden light, as if all the last rays of the sun fell in yearning just on him. As Krishna turns slowly to face his future, the nobleman from Mathura sees his great, petalled eyes, full of vast intelligence, set in a face truly like a dark sea; a face so powerful it is more than merely handsome; a warrior's face already, yet compassionate more than fierce, and still young.

The Srivatsa is twirled on his bare chest; his arms hang down to his knees. He wears flowing pitambara robes, electric yellow, and is adorned with forest blooms. He has a white lotus for an earring, his nails are long, and his feet red with forest earth. Above it all the peacock-feather gleams.

Balarama appears at Krishna's side, white as wave-froth and jasmines, wearing robes as blue as his brother's skin. They stand facing Akrura in the dying light, their grace and presence startling: two young cowherds and so much more.

Stirred more than he can bear, with a cry Akrura falls at their feet. Bending his head in ecstasy he worships the twin vision, not knowing that he is the first to do so.

Moved, Krishna crosses quickly to the prostrate Yadava. But he hesitates. He bends and touches Akrura's head in baptism with his palm marked with the thunderbolt and the conch.

Then, reverting at once to his earthy gopa self, Krishna pulls the messenger to his feet and embraces him, crying, "Welcome to Gokula!"

Later, Akrura eats with them in their home. The brothers now share a kutila of their own in the moon-crescent, a small way from Nanda and Yasodha. And instead of being Kamsa's faithful messenger, Akrura tells them all about the monster in Mathura: his persecution of the Yadavas, his secret police, and his sinister tyranny. He tells them about Kamsa's plan to have them killed at the wrestling.

"Powers greater than himself, to whom he has given his life, guide his destiny. And he worships Siva, who forgives his bhaktas any sin at all. But, Krishna, there is something else I must tell you today which might change your lives."

Akrura knows he must take Krishna with him. He draws a deep breath, "Yasodha is not your mother, nor Nanda your father."

In the lamplight, shock leaps in the Avatara's eyes. Balarama puts a hand on his brother's shoulder. Krishna sits very still. Softly as the dark breeze in the trees outside, he says, "My lord, I know you speak the truth because I see your heart is clear. But though Yasodha did not give birth to me, nor Nanda sire me, they will always be my mother and father."

Krishna's voice fails him. Rising quickly, he strides out into the night under the streaming moon. Through the window they can see him in silver light. He bends his body, buries his face in his hands, and sobs tear their way out of him. Akrura gets up to go out to Krishna, but Balarama restrains him.

"Let him be. It is done now, and he must face the truth."

Outside, visions beset the young God. As if learning that Yasodha and Nanda are not his natural parents has released a flood of other memories—of fathomless pasts and strangest times yet to be: a kaleidoscope of soul-lives. And this small life of his is, somehow, at the heart of this web of fate, transforming all the rest.

Out under the blinding moon, he sees Kamsa also as part of the quivering web, in this life and in countless others. He clearly sees the demon's purposes; he learns his deepest affiliations.

Yet the tears of simple grief for a mother and father snatched from him, course down his face and a new resolve steals over its beauty. Gradually the tremors subside. Wiping his eyes, he turns back to the hut.

"Who then, good Akrura, are my mother and father?" asks Krishna, returning to his wooden stool beside Balarama.

"Kamsa's sister Devaki and her husband Vasudeva, whom the king holds his prisoners." Akrura stares at his hands for a moment. "Vasudeva is your father also, my lord," he says quickly to Balarama. "But why am I telling you all this? Surely, you must know, you are incarnations."

Balarama has frozen, but now Krishna cracks a smile, "My lord, we didn't know these things. I am afraid you do not properly understand what you call incarnation!"

All of a sudden his golden laughter fills the night in that simple hut.

"But grant us one boon tonight, O Akrura, though I suspect you have come to take us from our home for good."

"What is that, Lord?"

"Though you sever every other tie, at least let Rama and me remain brothers," Krishna laughs again. But his laughter has grown hollow; a shadow crosses his face. He hugs his brother fiercely, and Balarama strokes his hair.

Krishna rises. "It is late, and you must be exhausted from your journey. Sleep well, dear Akrura. And be assured," an edge is in his voice, "that we will go back to Mathura with you tomorrow. We must leave early. Yes, we will be pleased to come and wrestle in your great city."

He leaves them and glides out into the night, for it draws on time for the dance; the glade in the forest waits for him.

Still in a daze, he walks through the vana. Suddenly a figure in a white robe appears like a vision to accost him. Keeping pace at his side, its head bent, the figure speaks in a tongue older than the world, which Krishna somehow knows.

"Remember the curse of Sudaman," says Brahma. "Your manhood has come, and for a hundred years you must be parted from Radha. A hundred brief, mortal years, Krishna, there is much to do."

"But why?" cries the young God in anguish, turning to the ancient one. But Brahma has vanished.

Then, a woman's voice, an asariri, speaks out of the night, "Kill Kamsa, he deserves to die. Free your mother and father, they have suffered too long in Mathura; and remove the rest of the burden of evil from the earth. Compelled by the demon's tapasya of another life, Siva has blessed Kamsa. Who will tame his overweening power but you?"

That night's loving is fiercer than any other, even the first. Radha is alone with him, because tonight his song had called only her; he frightens her with his intensity. In the throes of her efflorescent climax, she reaches out a slender hand to wipe a tear from her lover's eye. The dance having ended in sweet tumult, they fall asleep in each other's arms.

An hour before daybreak, Krishna rises softly. For the last time, he kisses her eyelids, tremulous with dreams, he kisses her lips and her naked breasts. Drinking deeply of that final sight of her, clothed only in a veil of dew, he steals away while he can still bear to. By her side he leaves his lotus, like a precious child.

But Krishna cannot bear to see Yasodha before he leaves Vrindavana.

BOOK THREE

TWENTY-FIVE

Purusha *Kim tad Brahmam*

Arjuna asked, "*What is Brahman?* What is the atman? What is karma, sublime Krishna? What is the domain of the elements and that of the Gods? How can a man know you, as he dies?"

Krishna answered, "Brahman is the imperishable. Brahman alive in the individual being is the atman, the soul; and karma is the force of creation. And he who thinks of me, as he dies, he certainly comes to me. Whatever a man thinks of as he dies, to that he attains, absorbed in his final thought forever.

"He who says **AUM** as he dies, thinking of me, he attains the absolute, the Brahman: the seer, the ancient, the subtlest, the supporter beyond darkness.

Those who come to me, Arjuna, never return to impermanence, the places of sorrow. They are not born again. They have reached perfection. From Brahmaloka down, all the worlds and their creatures die and are reborn. But the one who reaches me never comes back."

Prakriti

Just within the limits of the dark city, still on the king's high road, they see a hunchbacked young woman. Her face is fresh as spring, and

Krishna leaps down from Akrura's chariot. A palpable aura of evil hangs over Mathura like a curse. Balarama shudders.

"This is a change from Vrindavana," he says wryly.

"Tell me, darling," cries Krishna to the bright hunchback, "whose oil are you carrying in that jar, lotus-eyes?"

She is smitten, she is aquiver. The beautiful stranger appears like someone from another life, a lover from a dream; and her heart is seized with yearning. She has never seen eyes like his, certainly not in emasculated Mathura. She feels naked in that gaze, so known and so wanted, hunch and all.

But her wits have been sharpened by her deformity. She flashes him a tart smile and says, "Don't you recognize me, my love? I am Naikavakra."

Hers is a fearless voice in those repressed streets. Some townsfolk gather round at once, attracted first by her ringing tones, and then by the striking appearance of the two youths who ride in Akrura's chariot. Wild, those boys seem, dangerous looking. Already, the people's hearts skip a beat when they see Balarama and Krishna.

"I am Kubja, if you want the name my mother gave me. And as everyone here knows, pretty stranger, I am Kamsa's masseuse. He isn't happy with the oil ground by anyone else."

She grinds her bent hips, winking at him. "He rewards me well, stranger, for I am the best at my trade, and my king knows it."

Krishna throws back his head and laughs, as perhaps no one has laughed here for years. Like bees drawn by honey, more and more people collect around Balarama, Kubja, and the holy Darkling. Krishna signals to Akrura and the lord of gifts leaves, unnoticed.

The brothers' attraction is hypnotic. They are radiant in their garlands, with hair down to their shoulders, come fresh from the forest to this forlorn street of crippled spirits. But if Kubja's back is bent, her spirit is straight as a sunbeam. Krishna swaggers up and throws a saucy arm around her.

"Tell me, darling, are my brother and I fit for your scented oil? Or aren't we royal enough?"

He winks at her too, slipping a flagrant hand under her clothes, bold as cowherds, fondling her soft breast. She is briefly taken aback. Then she flashes her stunning smile again.

"Come, sit on the pavement and let me anoint you. Let these others see what they might have been like, except that they have let Kamsa take their manhood from them, and turn their lives into a nightmare."

By now, the street corner is thronging with curious townsfolk. This is the day before the festival of Siva's bow, and the secret police have instructions to handle the people carefully. Travellers from other lands will come to Mathura and the city shouldn't appear to be repressive.

At the farther reaches of his self-deception, Kamsa even sees himself as a benevolent ruler. Then again, he is confident nothing untoward will happen in his city when Siva protects it, as proclaimed by His bow that stands tall in the palace. Moreover, Kamsa knows that after being cowed for so long by his brutality, his people no longer have the spirit to rise against him.

Kubja kneads the young strangers with expert hands. She is enjoying herself. A fair crowd gathers there by now. The brothers shine in her rainbow oils in that defeated place, the paranoiac street of the city of darkness. Krishna moans in contentment. Brazen as money, he lies on the pavement with his head in Kubja's lap as she tends to him.

"At last there are some men in this city," says Kubja when she has finished. Krishna rises, glowing in the twilight.

"And perhaps they will come home with me?" she asks now, hopefully. But also playfully, never able to forget her deformity.

"And why not?" Krishna cries merrily.

He takes her chin in his palm and turns her face up to his. "I will surely go to the house of such a beautiful girl if she asks me. But first, dear Kubja, *be straight!*"

Even Balarama's mouth falls open when, as in a wish, covering her feet with his own, and with a clicking of her spine, *Krishna pulls her hunched back straight as an arrow.* In the wish he sets her down, kissing her lightly, laughing.

Such a hush falls. Someone from the back of the crowd whispers, "Who are you, stranger?"

"I am no stranger, friend. I am Krishna."

"Sadhu, sadhu!" they breathe, and mill round to touch the brothers' feet, to prostrate themselves abjectly. Feeling sorry for them, broken and pathetic as they are, Balarama and Krishna raise them up and embrace them.

Kubja pulls Krishna's hand to her breast in unabashed gratitude. She cries, "Can't you come home with me, beautiful one? You shall have my virginity, which not even Kamsa has broken. And I will make love to you as no one ever has. Come, my lord, heal my heart as you have my body."

Krishna throws back his head and roars with laughter. He allows her to take his hand and lead him away, Balarama following disconsolately. But a short way off, taking directions to her house and making sweet promises to her for the night, the brothers slip away towards the palace and the enclosure of Siva's bow.

They go strutting through the crowded, shop-lined streets of the vaisyas. The vaisya women stop whatever they are doing, overcome by the sight of the two of them. They stand motionless at doorway, window and balcony, like women in a painting.

TWENTY-SIX

Purusha *Sahasrayugaparyantam...*

"He who knows that the day of Brahma is *a thousand ages*, and a thousand ages is his night, knows day and night.

"At daybreak all the lives that are hidden come forth to be born. At twilight, they are dissolved again into the dormant seed of life. Helplessly, the same lives stream forth once more at dawn of Brahma's next day.

"But beyond this being and return, beyond the day and the night, there is another unmanifest, eternal Being who does not perish when all existences do. He is not born with Brahma's day, nor dies with Brahma's night. Those who reach Him, do not return. He is my supreme abode. He pervades all this birth and death, and he can be attained by bhakti.

"Fire, light, day, the bright half of the moon, the six months of the northern sun: these are the times when the yogins of illumination go to the Brahman.

"Smoke, night, the dark half of the moon, the six months of the southern sun: these are the times when the yogins find the lunar light of Pitriloka, and they return to birth.

"Light and dark are the ancient and enduring paths of this world. By one the yogin goes and never comes back; by the other he returns."

Krishna waited for his words to pass through his entranced warrior. Stormclouds obscured the sun above Kurukshetra.

Prakriti

It is late evening when, exotic with garlands hung around their necks by the worshipful people of Mathura, Krishna and Balarama arrive at the enclosure of Siva's bow. Their limbs shine in Kubja's oils, as if to dispel the evil that hangs so heavily in the air.

They saunter up to the guards of the immense bow: Siva's blessing to Mathura and its despot, who once worshipped Him with an unflinching tapasya. A prophecy tells that only he who breaks Siva's bow can kill the demon of the city.

"It's not for boys to play with," mock the guards, seeing them and growing unaccountably disturbed. "The strongest men in the land haven't moved this bow."

"Whose bow is it?" asks Krishna, innocently. "You see, sirs, we are poor cowherds come from Vrindavana to admire the great city and people of Mathura."

"It is the bow of Siva, fool, which is why not twenty men, not an army, why, not the Devas of Indra can lift it."

By now, just as Krishna intends, the people have gathered thickly around the bow. After the straightening of Kubja in the open street, word of his arrival has spread through Mathura like light. No one will miss any more miracles, not for their lives. A small crowd throngs the cold palace, and the haughty enclosure.

"Sir," Balarama petitions one of the surly guards, who apparently have not yet heard of Krishna's coming, "my brother is a Sivabhakta, let him touch the bow."

The guards stare in some confusion at the crowd around the cowherds. They squint at the gopa youth, who seems to be actually blue-skinned. But it must be the twilight playing tricks with their eyes.

"Very well, boy, you may approach the bow. But then move on quickly, it's nearly time to shut the gates."

Krishna grows very quiet, and steps towards the bow. The crowd falls silent and moves back. Krishna bends at the waist; with one hand he lifts Siva's bow from its pedestal like a toy. As the guards' mouths fall open and they step away from this terrible cowherd, he bends Siva's bow as easily as an elephant would a stick of cane. With a report that shakes the walls of Mathura, the bow snaps.

Kamsa at his window drops the mirror in which he is combing his wiry hair. It shatters in a hundred fragments.

When they recover from their shock, the palace guards rush roaring at Krishna and Balarama. But the brothers strike them down with the broken halves of the bow, with speed and strength that aren't merely human. And they vanish from the palace, leaving the enclosure corpse-strewn and bloody.

Krishna and Balarama wander back beyond the city-walls, to the gypsy camp of Nanda's cowherds just arrived from Vrindavana; while the streets of Mathura are ablaze with the news of the advent of the Avatara.

In his palace, Kamsa trembles.

TWENTY-SEVEN

Purusha *Idam tu te guhyatamam...*

Out on Kurukshetra, now dark as twilight under morning clouds, Krishna said, "Listen to my song, Arjuna, now that you do not cavil. *It has the secrets of wisdom* and knowledge; it will set you free. This is the highest knowledge, easy and immortal, and it is known directly. It is my way, the way of the Avatara.

"I pervade all the universe with my unmanifest spirit; but all things dwell in me, and not I in them. This is my mystery. As the free air that moves everywhere dwells in the ether, in akasa, so too all existence abides in me.

"When the ages have made their round, all the creatures are gathered back into the seed that I am. When the next creation dawns I send them forth again, bound in my maya. I, the lord of maya, send the multitudes forth and gather them back into my being.

"The ignorant pass by this human shape of mine; of me, they know nothing. The illumined, the mahatmans who know me, worship me with a steady heart, and with the ritual of wisdom. They know who I am, that I am the source undying.

"I am the ritual, I am the sacrifice. I am the ancestral oblation, I am the herb that heals. I am the holy mantra, I am the melted butter. I am the fire, I am the offering.

"I am this world's father, its mother, its supporter and its grandsire too. I am the end of knowledge, the purifier. I am **AUM**, I am Rik, Sama and Yajus," whispered Krishna, humming to a spellbound Arjuna.

Prakriti

Through his window king Kamsa watches the sun rise on the morning of Siva's bow festival, and is filled with dread. He thinks back inevitably to his childhood, to the gandharva father he has never seen, and he is on the verge of tears; on the verge, in fact, of everything, as first light spills over the world.

His secret policemen have reported Krishna's arrival in his city. And he feels besieged in his own palace, though its opulent chambers are full of kshatriyas from friendly kingdoms, their queens and entourages come for the festival.

Akrura comes to his king, and, eyes averted, tells him that the youths from Vrindavana have arrived in Mathura.

Then, late in the evening, Kamsa hears the thunderclap of Siva's bow being broken in his courtyard. In panic, he calls for Chanura and Mustika. The king cannot sleep. Lying pale and naked, ministered to by two recently favored girls from his endless harem, one of whom is twelve years old, Kamsa repeats his earlier instructions to his minions, as if they haven't understood him.

To underline what he says, he now adds, "You both shall share in my kingdom if you kill the gopa boys tomorrow. Only, remember, the cowherds are being called Vishnu's Avataras."

When Chanura and Mustika have gone, he sends for the master of elephants, also for the third time that night.

"Is Kuvalayapida prepared?"

"He is in musth, my lord, and we have kept him away from the cow-elephants," the man says, he also for the third time.

"Yes, I hear him trumpet in the lonely nights."

As if the elephant is aware of his mention, a scream of his frustration wafts in on the breeze. Kamsa shivers. He produces a small vial, steaming with a potion.

"Make sure he has a few drops of this before you let him loose."

The man bows. Taking the vial, he withdraws without turning his back on his sovereign. Left alone with their tyrant, the girls begin their intimate attentions on his person once more. But anxiety locks the demon's loins, and he is impotent tonight. But he dare not be alone with his fears, so he keeps the girls with him. Soon, they curl up like the children they almost are, and fall asleep in his bed of so much sin.

The king pours himself tumbler after tumbler of strong wine, but the night assails him with visions of doom. His reflection in wine-glass and mirror is headless, as is his shadow when he paces the floor. The hairs on his arms stand on end.

Outside the window, the trees of the hallucinatory night seem to be made of gold. When he dozes fitfully, he dreams of himself copulating with the dead and with goblins, in agony, his loins bloody. He dreams that he sat stark naked on his throne in the crowded arena, and the people all pointed at him and laughed.

It is a long night for Kamsa, before the first light of dawn softens the sky above his palace. Obeying a deep impulse of childhood, the king kneels at his window and folds his hands to the sun. He bows his head in supplication to Surya, God of day and light.

As Kamsa watches the sun rise, he knows that all is lost and the hour of retribution has come. He is not sure if he is afraid or relieved as he prepares to meet death. But then, once again unquenchable hope clutches at his heart. Perhaps the elephant in rut, perhaps Chanura and Mustika would kill the cowherd? But as if in response to his thought, he hears an unearthly melody, sprouted from nowhere.

Above the noises of the crowd below, thronging early into the arena, a flute song echoes in his ears, calling him, calling him to be free.

He can't bear its haunting sweetness, and runs out of his apartment, covering his ears with his hands.

TWENTY-EIGHT

Purusha *Gatir bhartaa prabhu sakshi...*

"*The goal, the upholder, the Lord, the witness, the abode, the sanctuary and the friend am I. I am the origin and the dissolution, the ground, the refuge and the undying seed.*"

Thunder and lightning cracked the sky, silencing the conch-blowers and drummers of both armies, eager for battle. The Pandavas waited for Arjuna; Yudhishtira and Bheema waited, and the Kauravas, Duryodhana and his brothers.

Krishna said quietly, "Worship me. I am the heat of the sun; I withhold and pour down the rain. I am deathlessness and death; manifest am I, and the hidden germ of life."

Prakriti

From daybreak, the people of Mathura pack the tiered platforms around the wrestling arena. Nobody stays home today; the crippled crawl here; the old and the infirm are carried in.

An hour after sunrise, the visiting kings and their queens have taken their places in the royal enclosure. Finally, to loud fanfare from the palace guard, Kamsa himself mounts his ornate throne set on the highest dais. Below him sit the colourful women of the harem.

In the open area reserved for visitors from outside are Nanda and his gopas. Among the common people of Mathura today, Devaki and Vasudeva sit, anxious to catch a glimpse of their son. Devaki insisted that they come.

"I must see my child," and Kamsa had readily given his consent for his cousin to watch her son die.

It is a restless, anxious crowd which waits for Krishna, one that knows its own future hangs in time's balance this fateful morning. As the people sit nervous and fidgeting, pandemonium breaks out at the entrance to the arena.

Krishna and Balarama have arrived, and the drug-crazed, rut-maddened elephant Kuvalayapida is loosed on them. It thunders trumpeting at the brothers. Its mahout hangs on its neck, prodding it with his goad, crying to the beast to trample the strangers.

Nimbly side-stepping the first charge, the brothers turn on the leviathan. Krishna lets out a roar that silences the crowd, paralyses the elephant: *the roar of an angry God*! He seizes the beast's trunk, and in a flash twists it to its knees. Easily, as taking a dry twig from a tree, he snaps off one of the creature's tusks, and it screams now in pain and fear.

The mahout scrambles off the animal's neck and tries to flee, but Krishna catches him. There is a gasp from the crowd, which sees through the lofty archway into the arena. With a blow of the elephant's tusk the young God smashes the mahout's head into pulp, and is sprayed with the man's blood.

Balarama wrenches out the other tusk. In a gory moment, quick as seeing, he beats the elephant's side-guards dead. Kuvalayapida still screams. He struggles to get to his feet, blood streaming down his trunk from the holes where his tusks were.

But launching himself from among the dead guards, flying through the air like a dancer, Balarama kicks the beast on its great temples. The grey giant crumples as if it has been struck by Indra's vajra. It doesn't stir, its skull smashed like an egg-shell, brains dribbling through the rupture.

Splattered with blood and ichor from Kuvalayapida, Krishna and Balarama stalk into the arena like two young lions. A miracle awakening in their spirit, unmindful any more of Kamsa above, or his spies among them, the crowd yells out its heroes' names.

"Krishna!" they roar.

"Sadhu! Krishna!"

"Rama!" they shout. "Jaya! Jaya!"

And so Devaki first sees her son, after all these years, and Vasudeva, his children. And now they hear of them from the whispering, tumultuous crowd.

"Krishna killed Putana."

"He broke Sakatasura's back."

"He toppled the Yamala and Arjuna trees."

"He danced on Kaliya's hood and sent him slithering off to the sea like a worm."

"He killed Arista, Dhenuka, and Kesin. Look at him."

"He held Govardhana aloft for seven days. And he has come to set us free."

"The fair one is Balarama, who makes the women glad."

"He is the older. How beautiful he is."

"They are Vishnu's Avataras. Look at them and be saved."

Suka says that Devaki's breasts are suddenly full of mother's milk as she listens to her son being praised. The milk seeps into her clothes with love for her dark boy. Her eyes well blind at seeing him. The years fall away from Vasudeva like rainwater when he sees his sons. He seems to regain his youth before his wife's eyes.

The women of the harem cannot restrain themselves.

"His face is like a great lotus."

"Oh, just seeing him makes me wet, sisters."

"And me."

"And me," they chorus, in unearthly joy.

"Look at his rippling body."

"So young."

"See the Srivatsa on his chest."

"Oh, I would press myself against it."

"The Blue Lotus."

"And the fair one, how handsome Rama is!"

"He killed Dhenuka."

The legends are confused at times, for in Mathura they have heard them told only in whispers from wild wanderers and gypsies passing through the city.

The queens in the royal enclosure are not immune.

"They aren't even full-grown."

"Though grown enough for me," breathes another.

"And they must wrestle Chanura and Mustika."

"Hard as diamonds."

"Huge."

"Demonic."

"Are there no impartial judges here? Boys can't wrestle grown men."

"I would wrestle with these boys myself. I am dizzy just looking at them."

"I would love to grow them up."

"Surely, the gopis of Vrindavana have seen to that."

Kamsa hears this chatter, venom in his ears. Growling, hooded eyes flashing, he raises his hand for the wrestling to begin.

Bigger than a sumo-giant, Chanura lumbers towards the slight Blue God, and immense Mustika at Balarama. But the brothers are quicksilver. They toy with their titanic opponents, butting them with lowered heads and darting back out of reach, as the wrestlers try to clinch with them. Round and round they circle. Krishna allows Chanura to lock him about the waist with massive arms, and the women in the crowd cry out: some delicate ones faint. Kamsa is on the edge of his throne, thinking it is all over, for all his anxiety.

In a lone, effeminate voice of encouragement, he cries to his wrestler, "Finish him, Chanura! Remember, a share in the kingdom."

But Krishna silences Kamsa with a terrible smile. He shrugs off the wrestler's death-lock as he might a child's grip. Chanura stumbles, nearly falls, his arms aching where Krishna flexed himself against them. The oil on the wrestler's glistening body mingles with his sweat, which forms its film of fear on his skin.

Fear grips Kamsa's demon by the throat when, moving into another clinch, Krishna whispers, "Your master's potion won't help you today,

Chanura. But it was written before you were born that I would kill you. Come."

Krishna falls on one knee; effortlessly he lifts the wrestler into the air. Standing, he whirls him round and flings Chanura down. With inhuman force, he bursts the giant apart so his limbs and head fly off his trunk in an explosion of gore. Chanura's scream echoes within the awed silence of the crowd.

In a flash, Balarama wrestles Mustika to the ground. Kneeling on his chest, his fists a blur, he beats Kamsa's wrestler's head into a mess of blood and brains.

With a shout the strongest of Mathura's wrestlers, Kosalaka, bigger than Chanura, charges Krishna. But the Avatara has no patience for any more wrestling. A back-handed blow severs Kosalaka's head from his neck, and he falls without a whimper. The other wrestlers run.

His arms raised in victory, Krishna shouts up to his cowherd friends, butter-thieves of old, to come and join him in the arena. When they demur, he clambers up the stands and pulls them down to share in his triumph.

The crowd is delirious. They know the hour of freedom has come. They know in their hearts, in every fibre of their miserable flesh, that the prophecy is being fulfilled. Their bodies are flowering in subtle song: this for them is salvation.

But Kamsa is on his feet, his face a mask. He screeches at his guards, "Seize them! Seize all the cowherds. Seize Nanda. Kill Vasudeva."

That voice freezes the jubilation; the crowd reverts to its habitual terror.

"Seize anyone who celebrates the cowherd's victory! Seize..."

But the thin voice chokes. With a growl, Krishna lopes up the platform-steps. He takes the demon, his uncle, by his throat, and with a wrench of his wrists, breaks Kamsa's neck. With a primeval cry of some deeper, more mysterious victory, Krishna lifts the king of Mathura's pale corpse above his head and hurls it down into the arena below.

Leaping after it himself, he begins to drag the long carcass in the dirt, dancing in ritual celebration until the soft ground is furrowed in a trench. Round and round the wrestling pit, the Dark One dances his triumph.

Seeing their tormentor dead, believing they were indeed liberated at last, the people of Mathura erupt in joy. They weep, they sing, and cry out their delight. They jump down into the arena and dance with Krishna, and the sky echoes their joy.

When Devaki first approaches her blue son, it is with folded hands. She comes as one of the grateful crowd, lined up for his blessing, even if she doesn't chant and sob his name like the others. He stands there, borne on the tide of destiny, blessing them all.

She comes to him in her turn, her eyes shining. He stares at her for a long moment; slowly he reaches a hand out to touch her face, as if to make sure she is real. Then with a cry he falls at her feet.

"Forgive me! Forgive me for taking so long. But I never knew."

A little awed by her incredible child, Devaki blesses him shyly, laying her palm on his head.

TWENTY-NINE

Purusha *Trividya mam somapah...*

"Worshippers of the three Vedas, drinkers of the Soma rasa, stray from the path. They reach Indra's realm, and enjoy the pleasures of the Devas. But when their punya is exhausted, they are born again into the world of men. They are transients in heaven.

"But those who worship me, I secure what they have, and bring them what they do not. Anyway, the worshippers of the Vedas and the Devas worship only me. For I am all the Gods and the Vedas, too.

"Those who worship the Devas, go to them. Those who worship the manes, go to the pitrs; to spirits go those who worship bhutas and pretas. And my bhaktas surely come to me.

"Every offering made with love, I accept with joy: a leaf, a flower, a fruit, a palmful of water. Whatever you eat or sacrifice, whatever you do, offer it to me, son of Kunti.

"I dwell in all creatures. None is hateful to me, none especially beloved. But those who worship me, they are in me, surely, and I in them. Even the most evil man, let him worship me and I will be with him; and swiftly he will become a sage and come to peace.

"Arjuna, know one thing for certain, those who worship me will never perish. Let them be rich or poor, men or women, let them be anyone; my bhaktas reach the ultimate goal."

Krishna's eyes twinkled at his friend, "How much more a devout kshatriya should worship me in this impermanent, sorrowful world."

Arjuna was startled in his dream; the words of peace snatched at his soul. But Krishna shone at him in the gloom, as it began to drizzle with a drop or two that fell on their faces, and on Kurukshetra, as if to purify it for the ceremony of blood that was to follow.

Arjuna hung on Krishna's every word now, resolution to fight grown overwhelming within him. His heart was set on battle again, and he did not know if he would see the light of another day.

"Fix your heart on me," sang Krishna, "be devoted to me, love me; and to me you shall come, in life and in death."

Prakriti

Krishna frees Ugrasena and sets him once more on the throne of Mathura as king of the Yadavas. News of Kamsa's death goes abroad, and the people who fled in the time of tyranny flock back to the city. The Yadavas return to the home of their ancestors; the Vrishnis, Andhakas, Dasarhas, and Kukuras, all the tribes return.

Krishna compensates them for their exile, which has indeed been like death for a noble people. He gives them generous wealth out of Kamsa's overflowing coffers to begin their lives afresh.

He comes to Nanda, "Father, it is time you returned to Gokula. I must stay, but I will come back to you soon. I shall miss you all as much as you will miss me. Tell Yasodha that I will come sooner than she expects. I left without telling her only because I could not bear to see the tears in her eyes. She will understand, she knows me better than anyone."

Wordlessly, bowing his head to ineluctable destiny, Nanda embraces Krishna, then turns away quickly because tears start in his eyes and he does not want Krishna to see them. It is the first time he has been parted from his blue son, since the night Vasudeva crossed a swollen river and smuggled an infant saviour into a gypsy cowherder's cart.

Nanda leaves Mathura the same day with his gopas, and Vasudeva's gift of a thousand cows and their calves, draped in golden garlands and ornaments and covered in silk: tokens of a well-nigh inexpressible gratitude.

In Mathura, Vasudeva has the upanayanam, the investiture of the sacred thread, performed on his sons for the second time, by the brahmana Garga. Then the boys enter Guru Sandipani's asrama for a formal education of which they have known nothing so far. They study the Vedas with the master, and the Upanishads; with deep humility, they submit to the discipline of the hermitage. Their divinity and wild natures firmly restrained, the brothers are the model students of the asrama from the moment they enter it.

Alongside princes and sons of poor brahmanas, the Avatara sweeps the simple dwellings. He chops firewood and gathers fruit and roots from the forest. In class he is absolutely attentive to the Guru, the quietest sishya of all.

Avidly he imbibes grammar and astrology, sacred etymology and Vedic ritual. He learns military theory with the others, and the mantras for the unearthly astras. Logic and political science Krishna masters, the techniques of peace treaties, sedition, and war.

The brothers finish the course of five years in three months. No one has ever done it before in less than four years; but the time of the incarnates is short. Sandipani never has to repeat a word of instruction to the brothers.

Often, profound master though he is, he feels that they, his disciples, know so much more than he does. He feels gently mocked in all his learning; though only by his wise heart, never in the least way by Krishna or Balarama, humblest and most loving of his pupils.

Krishna makes a special friend at the asrama: Sudama, a brahmana boy with a long face, soulful eyes and a great quietness and simplicity about him. They arrange to do their sweeping and wood-chopping together, and begin to love each other like brothers.

In the forest, one day, Sudama says, "Krishna, will you remember me once we leave the asrama? I, a poor brahmana, and you will live in a palace."

Krishna begins to laugh; he embraces his friend. "Dear Sudama! How do poverty or riches affect our friendship? I will always love you as I do now."

But Sudama smiles sadly to himself. He doesn't quite believe his friend, whom he adores.

"Come, Krishna, lay your axe down and tell me some stories of Vrindavana. Tell me again about Kamsa's death. How I love to listen to your adventures."

So, yet again, Krishna recounts the legends of Vrindavana; once more, he tells how Siva's bow was broken and of the wrestling in Mathura.

Sudama says, "Before we go back, play me a song on your flute."

Krishna takes up his flute. But the song from it is melancholic, because suddenly he remembers Radha and the gopis. He thinks of Nanda, and sees Yasodha crying for him.

When they return to the asrama, they find some men come from Mathura to call Krishna back to the city.

"Jarasandha of Magadha is amassing an army to attack our city. You must return at once."

THIRTY

Purusha *Na me viduh suraganah...*

It rained then on Kurukshetra, and the rhythms of Krishna's song were woven into those of the rain. "Arjuna, listen, now that you have a mind to: *not the Devas*, not the maharishis *know my beginning*. I am their source.

"The Saptarishi and the four Manus came from me, and from them all these generations of men in the world. I am the origin, and so the wise worship me. I give them fixity of understanding. I light the lamps of their wisdom, and dispel the ignorant dark."

Arjuna said, "Krishna, you are the Brahman, first of Gods, Un-born, pervasive. Narada, Asita, Devala, Vyasa, all the rishis say as much, and now I hear it from your own lips. And I believe it all.

"Not the Devas, not the Asuras know your manifestations. Only you know yourself. So, tell me, on which of your forms shall I meditate? What are they? Tell me, Krishna, your song is amrita to me."

Smiling, Krishna said, "Listen to my divine forms. But only some which are main, for to all my forms there is no end. I am the atman in all beings; I am the beginning, the middle and the end of all that ever is.

"Of adityas I am Vishnu, of lamps I am the sun; of planets the moon, Maricha of the maruts.

"Of the Vedas I am the Sama, Indra of the Devas; of senses I am mind, consciousness in the living.

"Of rudras I am Sankara, Kubera of the yakshas; of vasus I am Agni, Meru of the mountain peaks.

"Of priests I am Brihaspati, Skanda of the generals; of waters I am ocean, Bhrigu among the rishis. Of speech I am **AUM**, japam of the offerings, and of ranges the Himalaya.

"Of trees I am the aswattha, Narada of the munis; of gandharvas I am Chitraratha, Kapila among the siddhas.

"Of horses I am Ucchaisravas, nectar-born, Airavatha of elephants; of weapons I am the vajra, Kamadhenu among cows. Of lovers I am Kama, Vasuki among serpents.

"Of the nagas I am Ananta, Varuna among marine beings; of the manes I am Aryaman, Yama among judges.

"Of titans I am Prahlada, time am I of measures; of beasts I am the lion, Garuda among birds."

Prakriti

Krishna goes back to Mathura; but Jarasandha does not come immediately. Krishna sends his cousin Uddhava with a message to Nanda and Yasodha, the gopis and Radha. He sends his love, but says he himself cannot go yet to see them because of the Magadhan threat.

And one night, when the skies open above the city, he remembers another unredeemed promise made on a street-corner.

Late that night, above the lash of the rain, there is an urgent knocking at Kubja's door. Her mouth falls open when she unlocks it and finds him on her step, shivering, drenched in the storm.

He says laconically, "I hope you were serious when you invited me to your home. Because I have accepted your invitation."

She cannot speak, but nods her head, her eyes full of incredulous joy. She stands aside for him to come in.

Her pastel walls bear explicit paintings from the Kamashastras; seductive incenses hang in the air, and other scents: sensuous musks. Garlands are strewn everywhere; Kubja runs a house of pleasure. Her girls stand smiling behind curtains of tinkling beads.

At her invitation, he sits down with a sigh.

"We have only a short time," he tells her quietly, thinking he will faint from the other storm raging inside him if he doesn't take her in his arms. "Why don't you send your girls away?"

This she does, though he can see she is afraid of him, or of what she feels for him, now they are alone together. This is no street-corner.

Kubja brings him food. She brings him strong wine that calms him a little, and he stops shivering. She goes in to bathe, embellish herself, make herself perfect for him. She comes back, breathtaking, and he draws her to him.

Three nights he stays in Kubja's house, and he redeems every moment of her years of being deformed. But then, the world calls him back. He is rested by her, soothed in her arms, the womanly scents of her lush body, her fine skin. He is calmed by her wild love-making, stilled in her husky cries.

He goes back to the battleground of politics: the grim realities of evil and tyranny, war and killing. His destiny.

As he leaves her house, Kubja says, "Visit me again, Krishna. I will never take another lover. And if I must be crooked in a hundred lives for you to spend another night with me, so be it. Don't forget me, Krishna, I will wait for you."

Krishna and Balarama come to Akrura's house.

Krishna says, "I have a favour to ask you. You came to Vrindavana as Kamsa's reluctant messenger. Now go as my willing envoy to Hastinapura. I hear that, after their father Pandu's death, our cousins the Pandavas and their mother Kunti have come to the city of elephants from the forest. Their blind uncle, the Kuru king Dhritarashtra, keeps them in his palace; somehow, I don't think they are welcome there."

Akrura stays in Hastinapura for a month. Krishna has a shrewd instinct of the destiny of the Pandavas and the Kauravas. To make war as much as love, the Blue God has come: to precipitate the greatest war of his times, and to break the power of the race of kings forever.

In the palace at Hastinapura, Vasudeva's sister Kunti comes to meet Akrura. "Gentle Akrura, does anyone in Mathura remember me still?

Does my family think of me at all? Does my nephew Krishna ever speak of me? I think not. I think even he who is said to know all things has forgotten my suffering here, among these," she pauses, "*enemies.*"

Dhritarashtra does not treat Kunti and the Pandavas fairly. He wants to give the throne of the Kurus to his own son, Duryodhana, while it belongs justly to Kunti and dead Pandu's eldest son Yudhishtira. His design has twisted the blind king's mind, for he dotes on his son, who is a devil.

Akrura says to Dhritarashtra, "My lord, some day you will be judged for the injustice you are planning. Better you give it up while you still can."

He carries Dhritarashtra's reply back to Krishna: "If my mind is partial towards my own son, it is the will of God and there is purpose in it."

Before the year is out, Duryodhana and his brothers try to burn the Pandavas and Kunti alive in a house of lac. They escape through a tunnel, and flee into hiding.

Krishna watches over them in the wilderness.

THIRTY-ONE

Purusha *Pavanah pavataam asmi..*

"*Of purifiers I am the wind*, Rama among warriors; of fish I am the whale, Ganga of rivers.

"Of creations I am the beginning, the end, and the middle; of sciences I am the science of the soul, the dialectic for debaters.

"I am death, who devours everything, and the source of all, all that is yet to come. Fame am I among the feminine beings, and prosperity, speech, memory, intelligence, firmness and patience, too.

"Of hymns I am the Brihatsaman, the Gayatri of mantras; Margasirsa of the months, of seasons I am spring.

"I am the dice-play of deceivers, I am the splendour of the splendid; karma am I, and the punya of the good."

Krishna smiled.

"Of the Vrishnis I am Krishna, Arjuna of the Pandavas; of the sages I am Vyasa, Sukra among poets.

"Of kings I am the scepter, the policy of conquerors; of secrets I am the silence, their wisdom of those who know.

"And more, I am the seed of all being; nothing which is, exists without me.

"But what do you want to know all this for? There is no end to me, precious friend, I support the universe with an atom of myself."

Prakriti

When Jarasandha's daughters, Arti and Prapti, both widowed when Krishna killed Kamsa, go back in mourning to their father's house, the powerful emperor of Magadha swears he will wipe the Dark One and his Yadavas from the face of the earth.

A week after Akrura's return from Hastinapura, Jarasandha lays siege to Mathura with an army of twenty-three aksauhinis. Footsoldiers, cavalry, chariots and elephants surround the city.

Krishna sits up in the highest tower above the palace, alone, waiting for a sign. He orders the city-gates sealed, but he does not order an attack yet. He waits, a lion in his den, hearing the jackals howl outside. He waits unmoved, in dhyana.

They beat on kettledrums, blow on crude horns and conches, and cry up to him, mocking. Still he waits; this will be his first great battle. The forces of night have gathered again under Jarasandha's banner. The game is out in the open and the enemy is at his door: since he dared challenge them by killing Kamsa.

Salva blockades the eastern gate of Mathura. Vinda, Anuvinda and Paundraka, and the king of the land of five rivers, the southern gate. Rukmi, Druma and Sudakshina threaten the western gate. At the main northern gate is the invincible Jarasandha himself, with Sakuni, Trigarta and Somadatha.

The jackals howl up at him, taunting, but Krishna makes no move. He sits still as a stone in his lonely tower, immaculate.

Balarama brings news of the deployment of the small force of Mathura—Vasudeva, Uddhava and Kritavarman at the east gate; Ugrasena, Prithu and Sudaman at the south; Akrura, Satyaki and Gada at the west, and Prasena and Balarama himself at the northern gate.

Krishna says quietly to his brother, "Down there is a burden of the earth, calling itself Jarasandha's army. It is a congregation of evil."

"Your last day on earth has come, cowherd!" someone yells from below.

"Evil massed at our gates, and we locked within," whispers Balarama, but his eyes glow in anticipation of battle.

Krishna gazes out below him at the sea of demoniacal men, knowing their darkness intimately. All night he sits huddled in a shawl, lost within himself, in unremembered times and antique, fathomless causes.

An hour before dawn, he uncoils and rises softly, a shining beast of prey ready for the hunt. He says, "It is time to leave our youth behind us. Come, we must be armed for battle, it promises excitement."

His smile in the dim tower room is like the rising sun. It lights the final yaama of the night; it lights his brother's heart.

Krishna comes out on to the open battlement. With unusual solemnity, he raises his hands above his head in an occult mudra. Jarasandha's army falls hushed, for the sky above them is suddenly lit up. Two chariots descend like white eagles, shimmering on Mathura.

They are rare; they are unearthly. The enemy below can't be sure if they are silver flying disks, smooth as mirrors, or brilliant chariots drawn by steeds of light. They seem to be both, each mimicking the other.

Four-armed, as he was born, Krishna stands before his brother, with his ancient wheel, conch, mace and bow. And Balarama has his ploughshare weapon, the Halayudha of many blades, potent and mysterious.

Krishna says softly, "It is time for war."

At crack of dawn the gates of Mathura fly open, and its army streams forth with first light. Their enemies, rootless, murderous mercenaries, many of them warriors from beyond the borders of Bharatavarsha—these are the days of their savage migrations—laugh when they see the size of the defending force.

But then, like two storms in their chariots, flying banners with an eagle and a golden palm, Krishna and Balarama ride out of the northern gate of Mathura.

Krishna's clarion blast on his sea-conch, the Panchajanya, freezes barbarians' blood. Demons tremble to see him four-armed and effulgent, the Sudarshana Chakra spinning silent over his finger. With a roar as shattering as the thunder of his brother's conch, Balarama is among them too.

Holding their breath the women of Mathura, Kubja prayerful among them, climb the ramparts to watch the battle, even as Jarasandha's hordes cover Balarama and Krishna with arrows like rain.

Seeing his men beset by mercenaries' shafts, Krishna raises the Saringa, his fabled longbow. In a blur enemy elephants fall, their temples split open, and horses pierced through. Chariots collapse smashed by his supernal volleys out of twin quivers that sprout arrows like a mind its thoughts. Columns of foot soldiers are mown down like blades of grass, or torched like lacquered hayricks.

And then, it seems Yama himself comes hunting on that field: Krishna looses the Sudarshana Chakra at the enemy. The blazing wheel cuts a path of death before the Blue One and, terrible in his ambiguous chariot, he rides this path through the legions of Evil, his peacock-feather a green flame above him.

Krishna makes a sea of blood with his fire-tide of arrows and his humming Chakra. His chariot, ship of light, shines in the crimson flood; now flashing through the air as an unearthly disk, then flying along the ground as a silver chariot, its horses' hooves and its wheels crushing severed heads that paddle like tortoises among arms like serpents, severed hands and feet, fish-like, riven bows of war like wavelets, and hair like weird moss floating.

Krishna flings back his blessed head and roars above the waves and islets of that sea of death: from his bottomless, divine heart he roars great and holy victory. He roars in thunder like the Avatara he is, his chariot and his body drenched in scarlet; he roars and roars above the clash of metal and the screams of the dying.

Across the battlefield, Balarama kills thousands with beams of fire and flying blades from his eerie Halayudha. Some fall dead with no mark on their bodies, while others are sliced in shreds, or incinerated.

When the day's battle is over, and the fell army has been annihilated by the brothers who are saviours, Balarama pulls Jarasandha from his broken chariot. But Krishna cries that he shouldn't kill him. Ruefully, Balarama lets the vanquished king go free. His shame worse than death, vowing to come back, Jarasandha staggers away through the sludge of the blood and bodies of his decimated legions.

Krishna frees all the other humbled kshatriyas as well: Rukmi and Sishupala, Salva and Paundraka, and the rest. He says, "Their time to die hasn't yet come. They have more armies to muster and bring to our gates. Let them go."

He is obeyed without question. He has turned the destiny of the Yadavas around; he alone is its master now.

The roads of Mathura are festive that night, when the Blue God rides back victorious into his city. Throbbing drums and the torrid music of celebration erupt into the air; and the Yadava women dance for him in abandon in the lamplit streets.

They rain flowers over him from the rooftops and mark his brow with a hundred crimson tilakas. Altogether forgotten, like some nightmare from which they have woken, are the years of misery under Kamsa the monster. The people of Mathura are free now, and they celebrate their freedom ecstatically.

Radiant with victory, the brothers ride, side by side in triumph, through the thronged streets to the palace, followed by a thousand chariots bearing the spoils of war. They bring the jewellery, the bloody armour, and the weapons of the dead.

There is to be a feast at Kamsa's old palace from where Ugrasena now rules Mathura again.

Past midnight, Krishna slips away from the revelry in the king's halls. Shrouded once more in the dark cloak, he comes to Kubja's house, his sanctuary in the still strange city he has just defended so magnificently.

In her stranger's bed he tries to rediscover himself, after what he had become during the day's battle: what he had become to his own terror. After a remote paroxysm he lies still in her arms of unstinting tenderness.

Now his Godhood of the day leaves him and he is wracked with sobs. Just a man again, young and afraid, sleepless he mourns the slain.

THIRTY-TWO

Purusha *Bhaktaas tvam paryuaasate...*

Knowing clearly that Krishna's Gita was more vital than the war before him, Arjuna said to his divine cousin, "*Of those who worship you, Krishna, and those who worship the Parabrahman, who has the greater yoga?*"

With no hesitation, Krishna replied, "Those who worship me are perfect yogins. Those who restrain their senses, who are serene, compassionate to all beings, and worship the Parabrahman, they, too, come to me. But the task of these is harder, because the Unmanifest Brahman is difficult for embodied beings to attain.

"Have no doubt, Arjuna, that my bhaktas I swiftly deliver from the ocean of sorrow. Fix your mind on me, let your thoughts come to me, and in me you will live forever.

"If your mind wanders at first, meditate slowly on me, by stages. If you can't do this, act in my name. If this is also impossible, just offer your life to me, whatever it is. Better than gyana is dhyana, but better than dhyana is bhakti. With bhakti, comes peace."

Prakriti

Once, Syala called the brahmana Gargya a eunuch before the Yadava court, and they laughed scornfully. In fury, the brahmana went to the deep south where he sat in a fervid tapasya to Hara, praying for a son who would avenge the insult.

After twelve years of penance, Siva blessed him with a son, black and hirsute as a bee, hard as a diamond, strong as an immortal, who couldn't be killed by any Yadava!

The boy Kalayavana, 'Black Greek', was adopted by the Yavanas, whose incursions into the land of Bharata had begun. In time, being easily the bravest and most powerful among them, he was crowned the invaders' ambitious, invincible king.

Always subtly helpful to Krishna's causes, the itinerant Narada whispers in the Black Greek's ear, "Your only equals in battle are Krishna's warriors, the Vrishnis of Mathura. Defeat them, and you will truly be as your father intended—the undisputed master of the world."

Kalayavana musters an army of mlechchas, alien mercenaries, a rootless army of thousands, and marches on Mathura.

Seeing the tide of barbarians pour over the horizon with their chariots, elephants, and legions, Krishna says to Balarama, "Jarasandha is gathering another army to lay siege to us again, and this Black Greek comes to seek war. If they attack together, they will slaughter our men and savage our women. We must leave Mathura at once; fly through the back gate."

"And go where, Krishna?" asks Balarama, dismayed.

"Come with me. Call everyone to leave their homes and follow us. I have a surprise for my people."

After eighteen wars against Jarasandha, the Yadavas are indeed his people.

Kalayavana camps outside the southern gate of Mathura. Under cover of darkness every man, woman and child in the city follows Krishna blindly into the night. They go through the northern gate, and travel west, unseen.

Though they aren't aware of it, the land slips away under their feet by more than just their own effort: by his power as well. As the sun rises the next morning, they find themselves already on the shore of the western sea.

As they stand on an empty beach, where only gulls wheel and call overhead, they see rising out of the very waves—*a great city-fortress of smooth marble walls, ethereally radiant, a miracle in the dawn sun.*

"Dwaraka!" exults Krishna, flinging his arms wide. "Your home from today. My city, which even our women can defend. Dwaraka, home of Yadavas."

Wading into the water he leads them through schools of feisty dolphins, gathered like waylights in the warm shallows, into marvellous Dwaraka. The marine city has been created for him by the worshipful Devas, who are finally convinced he is the Avatara. They have had Viswakarman raise the miracle in the sea.

Dwaraka is twelve leagues square; its mansions have crystal towers and terraces, jewelled domes, floors of beaten gold studded with pearl and amethyst, coral and emerald; its barns are made of silver and brass, there are shrines in each home for the worship of the Gods.

Dwaraka reminds many of the Yadavas mystically of another ancestry, of how on another world Mahavishnu asked them be born on earth to fight at his side against a terrestrial tide of evil. This is like a fleeting enchantment in their minds, and the luminous memory subsides.

After the Dark One's displays against the Magadhan forces, Indra has sent his own sabha, the glittering Sudharma, in homage, to adorn Krishna's palace in Dwaraka. Varuna gives him foam-white horses, black-eared, fleet as thoughts, a thousand of them. Kubera fills the coffers of Dwaraka with the eight precious treasures from the deep stars. All the thirty Devas bring the most unique gifts.

In a daze now, a waking dream, the Yadavas wander the tree-lined streets, the sprawling parks set with glimmering pools with fountains plashing in them. But Krishna steals back to Mathura.

Approaching noon, the Black Greek sees a lone blue figure emerge from a side-gate of the deserted city—four-armed, long arms down to its knees, carrying no weapon, clad in molten yellow silk, wearing a garland of lotuses, and bright as a full moon. The Srivatsa adorns the chest, with Vishnu's ruby, the Kaustubha, gleaming above it.

In quaint honour Kalayavana says to himself, "I will fight him alone and unarmed, too."

Throwing down his own weapons, the Black Greek follows the Darkling under the noonday sun. Dodging through grove and thicket, Krishna sets a searing pace, uphill and down, fording streams and weaving through dense woods.

He shows himself only to be spotted, to be sure the Greek is on his trail: big as a bear, lumbering along with clumsy strides, shouting, "Ho, Yadava! Stop and fight like a man."

Kalayavana is uncomfortable with the dazzle of the pace. Short of breath and red in the face, he yells taunts at Krishna, trying to provoke him to turn and fight. The Black Greek knows he is invincible against any Yadava, even Krishna: he knows about Siva's boon to his austere father. But then, so does the Blue God.

High above them in a mountain-cave lies a great king from another epoch. In his time, an age gone by, Muchukunda had been a guardian of the rishis of the jungle against marauding asuras.

When Muchukunda grew old, Siva's son Karttikeya came to watch over the munis. Muchukunda had sacrificed all his years to protect the holy ones, and Indra had prolonged his life to that end. Now his queens and sons, all his family, were long dead.

Indra granted him a boon, anything other than moksha, which only Vishnu can give. The king asked for sleep, undisturbed slumber, of which he never had enough while he was a guardian of the jungles.

Indra had blessed him, "He who wakes you from your dreams will be ashes."

Along the chase secret memory unfurls again in Krishna: shining bloom! Like an arrow to its mark he flies straight to Muchukunda's cave. Darting in, he hides himself in a tunnel behind the olden king who lies asleep on a slab of rock.

In hot, swearing pursuit, Kalayavana arrives panting at the cave-mouth. A hand raised to shade his eyes, the Black Greek peers into the darkness within. He sees Muchukunda lying there and he thinks that king is Krishna.

"Get up and fight, Yadava coward!" roars Kalayavana.

Nothing stirs inside the cave. Kalayavana takes a step into the dimness and kicks the sleeping Muchukunda. The ancient one has slept for an age, thousands of dreaming years. At the Yavana's kick his eyes fly open.

Shaking his head, his lips moving, he slowly comes awake. When he sees the Black Greek at his side a fire springs from Muchukunda's body. Kalayavana is burned into a mound of ashes, which a breeze begins to blow out of the cave on eddying gusts.

Krishna emerges from the back of the cave. His body is alight, illumining that dimness. Muchukunda, who belongs to an older and wiser time, knows him at once. He prostrates himself at the Avatara's feet.

Krishna lays a hand on his head, and says, "I have come to grant you a boon, Kshatriya! Ask me for whatever you want, and it shall be yours."

"Lord," says the king, "I will ask for what all the other Gods couldn't give me. Bless me with moksha, Dark One."

Krishna says, "First go and enjoy all the pleasures of heaven and earth that you have foregone. Then you will be born as a brahmana and attain moksha in that final life. I bless you, noble Muchukunda."

Krishna vanishes, back to Dwaraka.

Muchukunda, scion of Ikshvaku, House of the Sun into which Rama was born, comes out from his cave, blinking. As he goes along, titanic himself as all those of his time had been, he sees how men of this age have grown puny. He sees how their natural glory has waned and their faces have turned base and sly. He can hardly believe they are descended from the great races of old.

He realises that the kali yuga is at hand, and that the Blue One he saw within the cave is the Avatara born in the House of Yadu, at the end of the twenty-eighth dwapara yuga. He knows that there is scant pleasure left in the world.

Avoiding the dwarfish and, to his mind, bestial men he sees on his way, Muchukunda walks slowly towards Gandhamadana, fragrant mountain, the gatekeeper to Devaloka, realm of Gods.

THIRTY-THREE

Purusha *Adveshta sarvabhutanam...*

Arjuna gazed at Krishna with such absorption that the Lord ruffled his hair as one does a child's.

"*Who has no malice to any creature*, who is compassionate and friendly, free of egoism, always calm, he is my bhakta, dear to me. Who does not shrink from the world, and from whom the world doesn't shrink, who is no slave of joy or sorrow, anger, fear or agitation, he is dear to me.

"He that is pure, with no expectations, skilled, imperturbable, who has surrendered to me, he is my bhakta, precious to me. He who is devoted, who does not rejoice or grieve, does not hate or lust, who has passed beyond good and evil, he is dear to me.

"He who is the same with an enemy or a friend, who is indifferent to slander and fame, to pain and pleasure, cold and heat, whose spirit is unattached, to whom praise and blame are one, who is contented and tranquil, his speech controlled, his mind steady, who has no permanent dwelling, he is my bhakta, and dear to me.

"And dearest of all is he who surrenders to me in faith, with all his heart."

Thus spoke Krishna.

Prakriti

The eventful years of war pass, and some of welcome calm as well. Then, Krishna is in love again. One day he sits in his palace in Dwaraka, high above the murmuring waves. He has a letter in his hand, which he reads over and over again.

The brahmana who has brought the missive sits beaming beside him. Krishna reads aloud, "'Krishna, if Sishupala takes me for his wife, he will be the jackal who stole the lion's prey.'"

He laughs. "Look at the fierceness of her spirit."

He reads on, "'So be there on the day of my kalyana, most beautiful among men. Come with your army, vanquish the others, and take me as your spoil of war. If I cannot have you to be my husband in this birth, I will kill myself for another hundred, until you are mine.'

"Do you know, O Brahmana, how humbly I asked Rukmi of Vidarbha for his sister's hand? But he has promised her to Sishupala, my young cousin of Chedi."

Krishna scoffs, "Sishupala, whom I have beaten time and again at Mathura's gates whenever he came under Jarasandha's banner. Sishupala whose life I have spared so often. And now the princess of Vidarbha sends you to me with this message."

Balarama comes into the room, and Krishna hands him the letter. Rama reads it and, a broad smile on his face, cries, "It is time Dwaraka had a proper queen. All the others who come and go from your bed are well enough in their place. Krishna, this is the girl you must marry. She is a match for you."

"The day after tomorrow Sishupala is meant to marry Rukmini in Kundina. But he shall not have what is already mine."

"No, he will not!" cries Balarama, embracing his brother. Better than anyone else, he knows the Dark One's torments: the loneliness, the abysmal doubts that ravage him. Balarama knows a little of what it is to be man and God at once.

The streets of Kundina, the capital of Vidarbha, have been washed clean for the wedding. The houses have been perfumed with the smoke of frankincense, the street-corners set out with arches and banners. And the kings of the earth loyal to Jarasandha and Sishupala have gathered here in strength, because Rukmi is one of them.

They know Krishna had asked for Rukmini's hand, and Rukmi turned him down. It is to be a wedding of honour. For Jarasandha's allies, crushed so often on battlefields outside Mathura and Dwaraka, this wedding is to be a slap in the enemy's face, a victory away from the field of war.

But within her father's palace, the bride readies herself not for Sishupala, but for another. She puts on the auspicious gold thread not for the prince of Chedi, but another. She anoints her virgin body of sixteen summers with sandalwood paste, hangs precious jewels around her reed-slim waist, sets a glowing ruby in her deep navel, drapes herself in the finest silk—not for the jackal, but the lion!

She decks her fingers with rare rings, invaluable heirlooms, and turns herself into a perfect bride for the master of Dwaraka. For dark Krishna she comes to Parvati's temple on the eve of her wedding, carrying incense, long grains of rice and garlands, to have the Devi's blessing.

When they see her, the common people of Vidarbha say to each other, "She is fit only for Krishna."

And against the designs of their king Bhismaka and prince Rukmi, out of a simpler, greater love, the people of Vidarbha shower her with rose petals—to bless her marriage to the Blue God!

Nonchalant as ever, Krishna arrives in Kundina with Balarama and his army, just as if to attend his cousin Sishupala's wedding. Bhismaka receives him with honour, but accommodates him on the outskirts of the city, because Jarasandha and his allies have already occupied the mansions closest to the lavish mantapa within Bhismaka's own palace.

But the people of Vidarbha flock to the edge of town to see the Avatara.

Surrounded by guards, eunuch chamberlains, hundreds of courtesans, family elders, friends, brahmanas, bards, singers and clowns, Rukmini comes on the eve of her wedding to worship Parvati. Kings and princes follow her to the temple to catch a glimpse of her beauty, and stand bewitched when she emerges after her prayers, her long eyes shining.

Later, in the confusion, nobody remembers from where the golden chariot appears, it may well have been out of thin air. Nor do they recall which way it flies, in a thunder of hooves, Krishna a flame in it as he sweeps his bride up from under the noses of Jarasandha and his friends and storms away, waving to them in mockery.

Jarasandha bellows, "Shame on us. We are all kshatriyas here, the masters of the age. And a cowherd snatches what is ours from under our eyes, like a deer from a tiger. To arms!"

The warriors scramble to don mail. Clambering into their chariots, each followed by an army, they give Krishna chase. Paundraka is there, Dantavakra, Viduratha and Salva the black. But they get no farther than the outskirts of Kundina, where the Yadava army looms in their path with Balarama cool and menacing at its head.

Once again Jarasandha tastes swift defeat. Unlike his forces, which have been drunk and debauched in Kundina, Balarama's Vrishni army out of Dwaraka is fresh and sober, and has come here just for battle.

Horses fall, and elephants; chariots are smashed by storms of Vrishni arrows. Krishna's subtle plans turn even his abduction of the lovely Rukmini into another bloodbath. Jarasandha's routed legions turn tail but not before a great number of their men have been cut down by the army from Dwaraka.

With a small, fleet force, Rukmi dodges this battle and, weaving through the alleys of Kundina, goes after Krishna. Before he rides he swears an impetuous oath to his friends, to salvage some honour from the disgrace.

"I swear I will not enter Kundinapura again without killing the cowherd and bringing Rukmini back."

Like the north wind he goes after the Dark One. Leagues fly past, and then, far away on the banks of the Narmada, Krishna allows Rukmi to catch up with him. He turns suddenly on his pursuer.

An astra, in complex, eerie flight, cuts down Rukmi's bravado in a flash. His sarathy's throat is pierced, his horses lie twitching, his contingent is slain. He himself has his bow and his sword, his spear and mace shattered into fragments by that missile.

Rukmi finds himself flung from his broken chariot, and lying in the slush of the river-side. Krishna stands over him, eyes glittering, his foot planted across Rukmi's chest, and a short sword in his hand.

Rukmini clutches his arm, wailing, "You can't kill my brother today."

But the spirit of battle is roused in the lion. He won't so easily be done out of his prey, especially Rukmi who taunted him. Rukmini falls at his feet on the banks of the Narmada. Her mouth is parched; her voice comes in a sob. Her golden chain snaps and falls into the silt.

But Krishna is far away from her, wrapt in his rage. He only laughs fiercely. Growling, his movements abrupt and deranged, he rips away Rukmi's clothes and ties him naked and sobbing to his chariot-wheel.

Rukmini wails to someone, anyone, to please save her brother. But Krishna still growls softly in his throat, truly a beast of prey that has scented fresh blood. He laughs again, dementedly, uttering no coherent word.

He lunges at Rukmi with his sword. Rukmini shrieks. But Krishna doesn't kill the scion of Vidarbha, he begins to *shave* him. Bending over the helpless prince, he shaves some of Rukmi's head and half his haughty moustaches. He begins to shave below Rukmi's neck and, eyes shut tight in terror, that kshatriya sullies himself. Rukmi whimpers like a whipped dog, and his filth trickles down his legs; while Rukmini screams on.

Balarama arrives on that scene at the head of the triumphant Yadava force. Leaping down from his chariot with a cry, he pulls his brother away, admonishing him loudly, mainly for Rukmini's benefit. Krishna comes away, choking with laughter.

"To dishonour a relative is like killing him," says Balarama. "It is only an arrogant man, blinded with prosperity, who will offend a kinsman like this."

He holds his own mirth, bubbling dangerously near the surface, in firm check. Gently he helps Rukmini to her feet. He cuts Rukmi free from the chariot-wheel. He helps him wash himself in the river, and offers him fresh clothes. After which, he allows the prince to ride away, speechless, still sobbing; his shame unwashed, unwashable, a stain on his soul.

Balarama scolds Krishna again, very much the elder brother, and the only one Krishna ever allows this liberty. All this is for Rukmini's mollification, just as Krishna has planned.

Until, Krishna himself seems to come back to his senses. He stops laughing, and gravely asks Rukmini's pardon. He tells her it is over now, his bit of fun.

"But you are my bride taken in rakshasa vivaha, and I had to behave like a rakshasa today. Don't cry. I haven't killed your brother, have I?"

He takes her behind a chariot. He kisses her for the first time, and is rewarded with a wan smile. But Krishna wonders if the lesson he meant to impart has been brought home to her proud spirit. Somehow, he doubts it.

All wonderful Dwaraka waits for them, athrob and decked out for the occasion. If Rukmini's father would not celebrate her marriage to Krishna, the Yadavas certainly will. At last, their queen has come, and what a welcome she gets. Loyal kshatriyas from other lands are here, all Krishna's allies and Jarasandha's enemies, as splendid in their finery as are the Vrishnis of Dwaraka and as Devaki and Vasudeva are, today.

Flags for Indra, who is the day's deity, flutter in the ocean breeze. Archways of celebration have been made from fine crystal and studded with jewels. Auspicious incense, aguru, hangs piquant in the sea-swept streets, sprinkled with ichor from the temples of elephants. Dwaraka is alive with the heady tale of Krishna's dashing abduction of the lovely Rukmini.

For seven days and nights, the festivities never pause in the sea-city, and there is singing and dancing in the streets till dawn. But every night, fiercely as his blood is moved, Krishna makes love to his young, young wife, her body hardly full-grown, but her passion so mature.

Only once during all those nights, when she screams long in abandon, another face floats up before Krishna's eyes in their moonlit room, where the song of waves echoes—a face as lovely as Rukmini's, a face woven into memories of a brooding jungle, a midnight-blue river, a magic flute-song, and a faraway green pasture: all from another life.

THIRTY-FIVE

Purusha *Sarvendriya gunaa bhasam...*

"He seems to have *the qualities of all the senses*, but is beyond them. He is perfectly unattached, yet supports the universe. He is free of the gunas of nature, but enjoys them. He is within every creature and past them all, ever working, always still, subtle beyond the mind's grasp; so near us, so utterly remote.

"He is one, and with every creature at once: creating them, nourishing them, destroying them, creating them afresh. He is the light of lights, beyond darkness. He is knowledge, all knowing's only object and its sole purpose, innate in every heart.

"Nature and Soul, Prakriti and Purusha, both have no beginning. The soul in nature enjoys the infinite essences in nature. It is attachment that causes the soul to incarnate in wombs of good and evil.

"The witness is the Brahman in the body. He is the atman, the last self, the final experiencer. No matter how a man has lived, if he once experiences the Brahman directly, beyond the gunas, he will not be reborn.

"By meditation some reach the atman, some by knowledge and others by the way of deeds. Yet others are ignorant of these three paths and resort to worship. They too cross over the sea of death by their devotion to what they have heard."

Prakriti

War and women. Women and war. *Women.*

The old fire still sears him. Only one thing helps at all—women. And none of his women ever complain of neglect; nor do we hear of envy, at least not openly, not yet.

Satrajita of Dwaraka is a devotee of the sun, of coruscating Surya Deva who is his friend as well; strange are the ways of destiny. Surya gives Satrajita the wondrous Syamantaka jewel to be a sign of their friendship and an emblem of their covenant as Deva and bhakta. Wearing the brilliant thing around his neck Satrajita goes about proudly, as dazzling as the Sun God himself.

Krishna sits at dice one day, when some Yadavas who have seen Satrajita in the street come running in to him, "Krishna, Surya Deva has come to see you."

Krishna laughs, "It's only Satrajita with the Syamantaka round his neck."

Satrajita installs the jewel in the temple of his kula devatas, dominated by an idol of the Sun God. Even at night, the shrine shines as if the star has set in it instead of the sea. Each morning Satrajita finds the jewel, which is a tiny piece of cooled sun, resting on a bed of fresh gold.

Krishna knows that the occult thing keeps away famine and illness. He also knows its curse. One day he comes to visit Satrajita, who has quickly become a wealthy and influential man in Dwaraka.

"Satrajita, my friend, I have been looking for a gift for Ugrasena. He is our king, and I thought the Syamantaka might please his heart. Of course, he is past the age when the gold from the jewel would tempt him. And I know you don't care for it yourself. So I thought..."

"I am sorry, Krishna," says Satrajita. "It is a gift from Surya Deva, and I cannot give it away. Not to anyone."

"Of course," says the Dark One. "How thoughtless of me."

Smiling to himself, Krishna goes back to his palace.

The next day, Satrajita's brother Prasena picks up the Syamantaka from its bed of gold, wears it round his neck and goes hunting in the forest looking like a star loosed among the trees. A lion sees him, gives chase to the unearthly dazzle, knocks the witless Prasena from his horse and kills him with a blow of its paw.

Taking the jewel up in his teeth the lion climbs to a cave high on the mountainside, to hide it from the rest of the forest. But Jambavan, ancient king of changeling bears, catches its sparkle from the cave-mouth where he lies basking. He climbs down to the lion's den and kills the beast for the charmed stone. Jambavan gives the Syamantaka, its heart glowing with candescent visions, as a plaything to his small son.

But in Dwaraka, when Prasena doesn't return, Satrajita declares, "Krishna has killed my brother in the forest. He wanted the Syamantaka, he begged me for it."

Within the hour, whispers of this reach Krishna. Taking some prominent Yadus with him, because there are those in the ocean-city who will say he is envious of Satrajita, he sets out on Prasena's trail.

In the forest, they see from hoof-print and pug-mark how Satrajita's brother was killed by a lion. They track the lion down and find him in his lair with his neck broken. Another trail of prints, half-human, half those of a great beast, leads away higher up the mountain.

Someone whispers, "What footmarks are these? Who could have broken a lion's neck as if it were a twig?"

"Only someone from another age, the creatures of this one are too feeble," replies Krishna tartly.

Near the very summit is Jambavan's cool dark cave. From inside, the Syamantaka shines like a bit of the sun. But within is also Jambavan, king of bears from the time of Sri Rama. The wild warrior had fought at that Avatara's side in Lanka, an age ago, when heroes were far greater than in this lesser time.

Telling his companions to wait for him outside, Krishna walks into the cave.

A battle erupts, as Krishna tries to take the Syamantaka from Jambavan's son and, not knowing him, Jambavan attacks, roaring. They fight like titans of a lost age, inside the cave and across a hidden maze of tunnels deep in the mountain. How dare a mortal of this dwarfish time intrude into the home of Jambavan, king of bears, friend and ally of Sugriva?

The battle recedes into the belly of the mountain, and out of hearing. Shortly, when Krishna doesn't appear, the shocked Yadus turn home. They believe he has fallen victim to another yuga. They are convinced the Syamantaka has been the death of Krishna. It was the accursed gift of Surya Deva who, after all, is no mortal man but always and unambiguously a God.

Rukmini and Devaki mourn, Vasudeva mourns; all of Dwaraka is stricken. The very foundations of the city seem to have dissolved in insecure tides.

Within the mountain, unused to such powerful fighting as Jambavan offers, Krishna takes a while to summon his other strength. Once he does, he knocks Jambavan breathless with a flurry of blows that has the king of bears kneeling at his feet crying, "Rama! You are the ancient one. Lord, you have returned."

Other memories stir to bemuse Krishna, memories from a life when he was another man, and this world was a nobler place. He lays a hand in benediction on Jambavan's head.

"I came for the Syamantaka, lord of the jungle, for in Dwaraka they say I stole it."

But old eyes shining, a gleeful Jambavan recalls a promise made to him when the earth was newer—that in return for the inestimable service the king of bears had rendered during the battle of Lanka, his precious Rama would come again, one day, to marry a daughter of his! And when Krishna sees the lissom Jambavati, the old fire surges in him.

So, for a month, he gladly remains in Jambavan's home of labyrinthine caves and the hidden valley beyond, making love to Jambavati, dark herself as he is. Some times they are both human at their torrid sport, but on the night of the full moon they are wild bears in season. Krishna, who can assume any form he wants, transforms himself in lustful caprice; and to her it is natural. And none so pleased as the grizzly Jambavan.

In Dwaraka, despair grips the city of wonder. Satrajita is being blamed for Krishna's death. Even those who took his side once in the matter of the Syamantaka now curse him, and say he should be executed for treason.

All the Yadavas, who had begun to take Krishna for granted, are frantic with remorse. They turn in penitence to Durga, Mother of the Universe, and pray for the return of their Blue God.

He, meanwhile, is blithe in the forest. Jambavan has given his daughter to the Avatara in the unfettered rites of the wise tree and young wildflower, jungle stream, secret cave, and the entrancing moonbeam that falls into it. Krishna remembers Vrindavana's moon-drenched spring nights as he wanders Jambavan's domain, absorbed in his fascinating new bride.

But then, too quickly, it is time to return to Dwaraka. His Yadavas have been punished for long enough, and he remembers how much they need him.

One day, Krishna calls Jambavan. The great reeksha knows that at last his time has come. He embraces his daughter, then kneels at Krishna's feet. Krishna is incandescent when he places his hand on Jambavan's head. The ancient bear's body blazes at the Avatara's touch. As Jambavati stands watching, her father dissolves into that light. With an ecstatic smile on his face, Jambavan melts bodily into Krishna.

The next day, with Jambavati at his side, to Rukmini's consternation, Krishna materializes out of thin air in the sabha of mourning at the palace in Dwaraka: a bit like the risen sun, for he has the Syamantaka round his neck.

With a cry Satrajita falls at his feet, bathing them in tears. Right there he offers his daughter Satyabhama to the Avatara. Krishna accepts her with no hesitation. He is in his prime, and Satyabhama is ravishing.

Though he doesn't protest, Akrura, who is no longer young, and to whom she is betrothed, is deeply hurt by this.

Krishna unfastens the Syamantaka from around his throat, saying, "I am no Surya-bhakta, and you are. So keep this bauble. But since you have no son, and your daughter is now my wife, bring me the gold from the gem. I am its heir now."

He hangs the jewel around Satrajita's throat, knowing that very soon that throat will be slit for the cursed stone of dreams. Since the days when it was first cut by hands not of flesh out of a piece of the sun, the Syamantaka was always a stone of misfortune to whoever owned it with even a trace of attachment.

THIRTY-SIX

Purusha *Kshetra kshetrajna samyoga...*

"All that live do so by *the union between the kshetra and its knower*, nature and soul, Prakriti and Brahman. The man who sees God abiding in all things, all beings, dwelling deathless within the mortal world, he truly sees.

"The man who sees that only the gunas of nature act, not the atman, he surely sees. The atman is actless. When a man sees that manifold, multitudinous existence is centered in just the One, and how from that One it spreads, he attains Brahman.

"The Brahman is without beginning; it is before and beyond the gunas. Arjuna, the Brahman lives in the body, but it does not act nor is it tainted by karma: just as the pervasive ether is always pure, because it is so subtle, immaculate.

"Even as the sun does the world, the Lord of the field illumines every kshetra.

"He who sees the difference between the kshetra and its knower, sees the liberation of man from nature. He becomes free."

Prakriti

War and women. Women!

Then there was dark, dark Kalindi, Surya's daughter, and an unworldly beauty who lived hidden away in a mansion of river-walls and sunbeam-floors built for her by her father under the Yamuna. Until, one day, out hunting with Arjuna near Indraprastha, Krishna saw her, dusky enchantress at her bath, and sent his cousin to ask who she was. She told the Pandava she was waiting just for Vishnu to marry her, that no other would do. Krishna married her when an auspicious constellation was rising, on an auspicious day.

By force, he carried away his exotic cousin Mitravinda.

He won king Nagnajit's tall daughter, Satya, in Ayodhya at her swayamvara. The king challenged him to tame seven frothing bulls loosed into an arena, if he wanted Satya for his wife. Krishna split himself into seven blue warriors, and killed the beasts.

His aunt Srutakriti's daughter, Bhadra, was offered to him honourably by her brother, Santardana, and Krishna took her.

And sixteen thousand women rescued from Narakasura he kept. But the old fire never did cool, until he stood on a star-crossed battlefield on the brink of a momentous war. Only then, did he finally overcome the blaze in his somewhat human flesh, transcend it with a Song.

It is the end of a yuga, and the sinister kali will soon set in. The God in Krishna is *on display,* as if to leave images of magnificence on earth that will survive in the memory of diminished, Godless mankind, even in the heart of the coming age of terror.

Indra, lord of the Devas of light, comes to implore Krishna to do something about Narakasura, son of the Earth and the Varaha, and bane of the worlds. Naraka had usurped Varuna's sovereignty over the oceans. He had stolen the mother of the Devas, Aditi's, golden earrings. He had taken a hundred and sixteen thousand virgins from the three realms as captives to his impregnable city Pragjyotishapura, to fill his harem.

Worse, the asura had cleaned out Indra's stable of four-tusked elephants, all descended from the foam-born Airavata: he whisked them away from celestial Amravati from under the Deva's illustrious nose. He had sorcered away Maniparvata, the jewel mountain, and most recently, he had raped Viswkarman's frail daughter Shanti.

Indra comes to Dwaraka to petition the last Incarnation of the dwapara yuga. He materializes in a form of light, as Krishna sits in his bedchamber with his newest bride Satyabhama.

"He is your son, Lord, born when you lifted Bhumidevi from the waves as the Varaha. He is beyond the rest of us, you must kill him yourself," says Indra.

"But this isn't a burden of the earth, Indra," teases the Blue God, not unhappy that the Deva has come begging to Dwaraka. Krishna hasn't forgotten the incident at Gokula: Govardhana and the thunderstorm. He lets Indra grovel a little.

"Don't you see I am with my wife, Deva? You are disturbing us. You know I haven't come to the earth to settle unearthly disputes."

"He will overrun all three worlds, Krishna, the earth as well!" cries Indra, becoming more agitated.

Krishna says, "You decide this, Satyabhama, I will do as you say."

Satyabhama looks down at her hands; she glances at Indra out of the corner of her eye. She looks away quickly, and whispers, "I don't want you to leave me now."

No, their loving is such a flame.

"Naraka lives high upon the Himalaya, on the borders of Devaloka. I have heard it is an exotic land; perhaps we should visit it," muses Krishna.

"We, my lord?"

"You and I." He adds thoughtfully, "And another, as well, for no one else can take us there. Seeing him, perhaps my people in Dwaraka will believe in me a little more. The Yadavas, Satyabhama, would rather believe in your father's Syamantaka than in Krishna."

He says to Indra, "My lord, not even when you grace this city of mine are my people convinced of who I am. But seeing the one of whom I speak, they may believe. Return to Amravati now, and leave Naraka to me. He has molested Viswakarman's daughter; he has broken every law of heaven and earth. He will not live."

Indra bows, as he is unused to doing, and vanishes. Krishna rises and steps on to his balcony. Throwing back his head, he whistles piercingly into the sky. He comes back to Satyabhama, and picks up the ardent thread where they left it.

A few moments pass, then, high above the world there is an ominous sound, spring thunder. The sky grows dark, as if the sun has been eclipsed.

People in the streets scream, "Krishna! It's a demon in the sky, swallowing the sun."

A flapping of mighty wings, and gusts of wind like small tornadoes swirl down Dwaraka's streets. The ocean lashes the city's marble walls. Fearing an earthquake on the seabed, the people of Dwaraka spill out into the wind-buffeted avenues. "Krishna, save us!"

Above the rumbling of sea and sky, the screaming women and the whistling gale, they hear a shrill, ululating cry—the call of a great eagle!

Vishnu's timeless mount Garuda descends like a vision on Dwaraka.

Folding wings wide as the palace, the awesome kingbird glides down from the sun and settles on Krishna's roof. White feathers on his crown and around his haughty throat, he darts his fierce head this way and that, at times crying that ringing cry of love again: because Garuda is near his Lord.

The Yadavas in the streets fall down and worship the sacred avian perched above them like a cosmic warning. For it is true they have grown arrogant and forgetful, basking as they do in Krishna's grace.

Krishna appears with Satyabhama on the roof, and after a long time, and as much in fear as with love, all Dwaraka cries up to him, "Sadhu Krishna!"

Shaking his head, but smiling too, he tells Satyabhama, "Only because Garuda frightens them, not because they know me truly, or love me. One day..." He sighs, shakes his head again, not saying what would happen one day.

At first, Satyabhama is terribly disturbed by the gigantic bird. She wonders if he is not a dream. He certainly has all the qualities of one; not only his size, but something else, something in his eyes. Not just bird eyes, but more than human eyes, alight to see Krishna.

Quaintly, Garuda bends forward, crouching over his talons, and rests his head at Krishna's feet. And now Krishna is a junglefull of whistles and warbles, as if all the birds in the world roosted in his blue throat to greet their king flown down from heaven. He chats busily to Garuda in his high, mysterious tongue, passing his hands in a snatching rhythm through the white plumage above those piercing eyes, around the curved beak. The great bird lifts his head and rubs it against Krishna.

Then, to Satyabhama's alarm, Garuda turns to her and sets his head down at her feet. She almost turns away in fright, but Krishna restrains her with an arm like a band of steel.

He forces her to stroke the eagle's head, to bless him as he wants. And when she does this, her trembling hands touching sacred feathers, she feels it clearly—a new tide in her blood, Garuda's devotion coursing through her!

Krishna helps Satyabhama on to the neck of his mount, and climbs on behind her. Garuda's power secures them and, launching itself like any eagle, first crouching, then springing up, the golden bird unfolds his immense wings and bears them up and away on a giddy trajectory.

A bird himself once more, Krishna cries gleeful instructions. With a flick of his tail and wing pinions, Garuda changes course with the wind. A little amazed to hear where Krishna tells him to go, he flies north towards Pragjyotishapura set among the most resplendent, most enigmatic, Himalayas.

Satyabhama is terrified by flight, terrified she will fall as the wind rushes around them like a sea in the sky; and the palace, Dwaraka, and then rapidly all land falls away in a whirl. She clutches Krishna's wrists as he sits pressed close behind her, holding her to him tightly as if to share every breath of her fear.

Pirouetting gracefully, banking in widening, ever rising spirals, they fly higher and higher through fleecy clouds of dark and light; and then even higher, through skyscapes like a God's dawn dreams. Gradually Satyabhama stops trembling and shuts her eyes as he whispers soothingly to her. She settles back against him, her body beginning to accept vertiginous, miraculous flight.

Just as she grows calm, just as the exhilaration of flying grips her, and with a soft cry she exults at it, she feels Krishna's hands on her. Calmly, he begins to loosen her clothes, as they arrow through unexplored cloud kingdoms.

THIRTY-SEVEN

Purusha *Param bhuyah pravakshyami...*

Arjuna was awash on that sea of calm, the song of God. Krishna's Gita sang everyday words into a million mystic meanings, shafts of light. They pierced the marmasthanas, the fine portals of the Pandava's soul, and through him entered unborn men of distant times, on extraordinary battlefields. Arjuna heard Krishna under his skin now, *inside his heart*. A smile was always in his voice, as he spoke to those multitudes, beginning again his eternal mission of salvation.

"*Listen to the wisdom of the ages.* The sages on whom it dawned became perfect; they were freed from the bonds of the body. They became like me. They are not born at creation, they are not moved at the dissolution.

"Nature is my womb. I cast the seed of all things into myself.

"Of any being born in any world, Arjuna, I am the Purusha, the father who casts the seed, and Prakriti is the mother. Sattva, rajas and tamas, the three gunas of nature, bring the deathless dweller into the body.

"Sattva is pure, and reveals the atman by light. Yet, sattva binds by attachment to goodness and to knowledge.

"Rajas is attraction, passion sprung from desire and attachment. It binds the soul to the body with hunger for action.

"Tamas is dullness born of ignorance, blind delusion. It enslaves with darkness, sloth, and stupor.

"From age to age, from time to time, sattva dominates, then rajas, and tamas too, prevailing over the other two gunas.

"When the lustre of knowledge shines at all the body's gates, sattva prevails. Unrest and greed are the signs of rajas, and complete delusion when tamas rules.

"If death come when sattva reigns, the soul attains to the higher world of beings who know God.

"If death comes when rajas prevails, the soul is reborn among those who live the life of power and action. And if a man dies when tamas is sovereign, he is born among the deluded once more.

"The good rise up, the passionate remain in the middle regions, and the tamasic sink. They devolve down to the realms of darkness."

Prakriti

Mura is the demon of the moat around Pragjyotishapura, city of sorcery on the loftiest borders of the world, where the earth verges on the Devas' sacred zones. He is five-headed, mountainous, shining like a brown sun so it is impossible to look at him for long. And he is full of snares.

High above the moat, above Mura sleeping submerged in it, Garuda bears Krishna and Satyabhama dreamy with the Dark One's aerial loving. But as the golden eagle begins his descent on Narakasura's black crystal stronghold, his way through the sky is barred by sword-sharp mountains risen out of nowhere: mountains above them, mountains surround them, closing in to crush them, slice them into slivers.

Krishna wields the Kaumodaki, his mace of light. He shatters the razor hills back into the particles of delusion from which Mura has made them.

Garuda flies on, but a fantastic barrage of weaponry from past and future—arrows, maces, clubs, swords, bullets, rockets, serpentine tracers of light and fear, mythic and deadly—comes screaming at them.

Krishna strings the Saringa and, quick as thought, shoots everything into dust.

But then there is water, tidal waves risen in the sky—pralaya, the deluge come to drown them. Satyabhama screams. The Sudarshana appears at Krishna's fingertip, spinning at such speed that it is a wafer of light. He flicks his wrist forward sinuously. A sunbeam at darkness the Chakra sets upon the waves, turning them into gentle rain that falls healing on the Himalaya below.

They fly on, and are beset by fire and wind: mountain-melting tongues of flame, and howling tempests that fan the flames. But the Sudarshana parts both, and quells them, puts them out.

At last, with fine manipulations of his mighty pinions Garuda hangs still above sinister Pragjyotishapura and Mura, only his five hideous heads visible out of the green and slimy moat the monster finds so comfortable. Satyabhama shivers on looking down at him.

The weird lustre around Mura glows and fades with his sleeping breath, his slope-shaking snores. Some of his heads smile, others grimace and frown as different dreams visit them.

Krishna raises the Panchajanya. He blows down a blast like age-ending thunder at the asura, who jumps up with a cry. He is tall as a turret, rubbing thirteen eyes on five faces, snorting in surprise that anyone has arrived here past his snares and dares to disturb his nap. When he stands, his heads are not much lower than the hovering Garuda.

An angry growl begins in the mouth at one end; passing across four others, it grows into a roar that returns to the mouth where it began. Krishna laughs at the performance, but Sathyabhama quakes with fright, clinging to him.

With a curve of his arm that is surprisingly graceful for such an ugly devil, Mura scoops his glinting trident from the ground, where his heads had rested on five pillows, each a different colour. Whirling the talonned thing above his head the demon casts it like lightning at the intruders.

Satyabhama screams again, certain at every moment that death has come. But between the beginning of her scream and its end, with two golden arrows Krishna cuts down the trisula and it falls away tamely. He fills each of Mura's roaring mouths with another clutch of light swift shafts.

Mura screams. The sky trembles at the dreadful noise from five throats, muted though it is by the arrows in his mouths. Even as he plucks out the burning barbs with one hand, he flings a dark mace at the intruders with the other. Krishna pulverizes it with the Kaumodaki.

Mura rushes at Garuda, interminable arms outstretched, six-fingered hands clawing the air to pluck them out of the sky. In a flash the humming Sudarshana severs five heads, and they fall still screaming into the moat. The trunk sways for a long moment, headless, then swivels and drops with a splash, bubbling red geysers at the naked necks. The deep moat turns crimson.

Mura's bizarre sons come roaring out of the gates of Pragjyotishapura, each more grotesque than the others: seven demon commandos, their leader Pitha before them. They are Naraka's crack guard, wearing green fatigues, armed to the fangs. Six-armed Taruna, three-eyed Antariksha, four-faced Sravana, twin-bodied Vibhavasu, tailed and winged Vasu, Nabhasvar and Aruna, who are both one devil and two.

Even as they spill over the drawbridge, they fall to Krishna's wishlike arrows, armour pierced, heads, chests, thighs, arms shredded. Satyabhama sees Krishna four-armed, as he always becomes in the heat of battle, a bow, a conch, a mace, and the Sudarshana in each of four hands.

The thought flares across her mind, even then, that she wishes him four-handed at another heat. He reads her thought, and flashes her a smile, promising.

Mounted on a four-tusked elephant descended from pristine Airavata, churned to life in the Milky Way, awesome Narakasura himself rides out from his sky-scraping fortress. He comes like a thundercloud, twice as big as Mura, twice as terrible. He flies up into the sky to meet Krishna. Around him are other elephants that tread on air, carrying an army on their backs.

As she grew accustomed to flying earlier, Satyabhama now accepts battle. She begins to cry encouragement to Krishna, clapping her hands in excitement at his sizzling archery.

Narakasura is the greatest of the asuras of the air. Flaunting his monstrous body, half-human half dragon, he faces them with fire spewing from his tusked mouth. With a cry that echoes among icy gorges, he hurls a shatagni at them, a weapon of a hundred flames.

Krishna cuts it down with two incendiary arrows, and a roar to shake the peaks. Like gold in the sky Krishna's shafts gleam, quick as thoughts, piercing demon-flesh through Naraka's ranks in astonishing flights.

With a keening battlecry of his own, Garuda swoops on the elephants with curved claw and beak, hunting with fear. Airavatha's children turn tail and, trumpeting shrilly, blunder back into the fastness of the city of night. Naraka faces Krishna, Garuda, and Satyabhama, alone.

Satyabhama cries, "Look, Krishna, he is as blue as you are."

Naraka, son of Vishnu and the Earth, casts at Garuda a shakti which once beat back Indra's vajra. It takes the eagle in the throat, erupting there, but harmlessly as a garland striking an elephant.

Having gazed for a long moment at Naraka, who in some remote and mysterious way is his son, at least the human part of him, Krishna flicks his wrist forward once more, and the battle is over. Naraka's dragon's head is neatly removed from its gargantuan trunk by the calid Chakra which is the very wheel of time. And from above, a shower of barely tangible flowers falls from Indra's grateful Devas.

Dead Naraka's mother, fabulous Bhumidevi appears—the lovely ancient-young Earth, fragrant with ocean girdles, leaf hands, sky eyes, forest and petal breasts. She brings Aditi's earrings blazing with rare jewels, the starry necklace, the Vaijayanti, Varuna's white sovereign parasol and Maniparvata, diamond-mountain in the sky, all of which her son had taken at his arrogant whim.

"All hail," says Mother Earth solemnly, but also with primitive intimacy, of an old lover. "Padmanabha, with the lotus in your navel in which Brahma was born. Hail to you, Murari!"

She ushers him, blue conqueror, into Pragjyothishapura and presents her grandson to him. Naraka's son Bhagadatta has not inherited his father's monstrous features, but is a handsome human youth. "He is afraid," she says. "I have brought him to you for your blessing."

Krishna promptly blesses Bhagadatta, places him under his protection, and sets him on Naraka's throne to be lord of the frontiers between heaven and earth. In a cool show of political expediency, he reappoints all Naraka's ministers to their old positions and influence, as young Bhagadatta's guardians.

For himself he takes sixty-four elephants of Airavata's pedigree to Dwaraka, and untold treasure—jewels, chariots, horses and chests full of gold plundered over the ages: the spoils of war. Krishna leaves Bhagadatta one elephant called Supratika, and sends the rest back to Indra.

But in Naraka's harem are sixteen thousand and a hundred women— lovely, sullied daughters of kings, siddhas, Devas, gandharvas, rakshasas; the asura took them without any criterion save for beauty. Sixteen thousand women from across the universe with nowhere to go, all suddenly focused upon Krishna himself. Who else will have them now, who else can be husband to them all?

He sends them back to Dwaraka in palanquins, along with the gold, the chariots, the elephants and the horses. And he keeps them, each in a mansion of her own, those sixteen thousand rays of the moon.

He marries them all, the Parabrahman in him assuming sixteen thousand bodies, so each woman can have her own dark lover. And as if to leave a memory of matchless grandeur for the trivial age to come, Dwaraka is the uncommonest of cities.

But the wise say, that for the Avatara of great Vishnu, who rests on eternal waters, who is the Lord of galaxies, dimensions, and fathomless time, indweller in everything, what was   truly remarkable in being husband to sixteen thousand women upon one small world?

On their way home, Garuda flies Krishna and Satyabhama to Amravati, Indra's capital, city of light, where they return mother Aditi's earrings, Varuna's parasol and Indra's elephants; where both Satyabhama and he are worshipped by the Devas. Where Satyabhama becomes enamoured of the Parijata, and begs Krishna to bring it to Dwaraka for her. He uproots the tree of wishes and carries it home to adorn her garden.

But typically, led by Indra who laid his crown at Krishna's feet when he wanted Naraka killed, the Devas bar Garuda's way down from Amravati when Krishna takes the magical tree. Surya, Vayu, Agni and the rest, elemental and tremendous, combine against the Avatara.

Smashing his way disdainfully through the gods of light, crying angrily to Satyabhama, "This is why they aren't worthy of men's worship," Krishna comes home to Dwaraka in triumph, bringing the lambent Parijata with him.

THIRTY-EIGHT

Purusha *Janma mrityu jara dukhe...*

Arjuna felt a seismic disturbance in his soul. He could not fathom it; it was the labour of the ending of an age, and the birth of another. Krishna, who saw it clearly, who had caused it, sang on to his bhakta, the lucid ripples of enlightenment on his lips. And his depths were like those of the ocean, unmoving.

The Dark One calmed Arjuna, whose heart was churned by the spirits of the two yugas, at whose very edge they stood on Kurukshetra.

"When the dweller in the body transcends the gunas that cause the body, he is liberated *from life and death, from decay and pain.* He becomes immortal."

Prakriti

After his humiliation on the banks of the Narmada the day Krishna carried his sister away, Rukmi of Vidarbha builds a city called Bhojataka and begins living there. This is because of his boast before the other kings, "I will not enter Kundinapura again, until I have killed Krishna and brought Rukmini home."

History is to repeat itself painfully for Rukmi. Years later, chosen by Rukmi's daughter Rukmavati at her swayamvara, Pradyumna carries her away, defeating, like Krishna at Kundina, a force of hostile kings at Bhojataka, the bride's father among them.

But there is some recompense for Rukmi in the rankling grudge he nurses against the Dark One. He performs a tapasya to Siva who appears in glory and tells Rukmi to ask for his boon. Rukmi asks for a bow, a divine weapon that will make him invincible.

"So be it," says Siva. He adds, "But no boon can be without its condition. So when you confront Vishnu the bow will leave you and return to me."

Armed with Siva's bow, Rukmi goes about conquering vassals for himself. War after triumphant war he wages, until he becomes a power second to none save Jarasandha and Krishna. As ever Rukmi is Jarasandha's staunchest ally, and he hates Krishna obsessively.

Pradyumna and Rukmavati have a son called Aniruddha, as brilliant as his father and grandfather. Rukmi himself offers his grand-daughter Rochana to be Aniruddha's wife. Rukmini, Balarama, Krishna, Jambavati's son Samba and Pradyumna leave for Bhojataka for the wedding, Rukmini delighted by her brother's initiative to placate her husband.

But in private Krishna scoffs to Balarama, "Rukmi is afraid his granddaughter will also be carried away by a Yadava. He has decided to give her to us before that happens."

But Rukmini is thinking and speaking of nothing but peace and an alliance with Rukmi. Many years have passed since her own wedding. Krishna of Dwaraka is reputed to be more sombre these days. And even when she insists that Rukmi genuinely wants peace, Krishna does not argue. He only tells Balarama, "If anyone hates me more than Jarasandha, it is Rukmi."

All through the journey to Bhojataka, he fills his brother's ears with flaming animosity for Rukmi. So at the wedding, the smallest inadvertent word or gesture of Rukmi's appears to Balarama like a slap in Krishna's face.

And Krishna whispers, "If you hadn't stopped me that day beside the river, we would not have to endure such treatment today."

Of course, when Rukmini is nowhere near, Rukmi does actually slight Krishna once or twice. He has never forgotten the day beside the Narmada. Balarama is conveniently at hand to witness these insults to his precious brother. But the wedding is concluded without mishap and everyone agrees that Rochana and Aniruddha make a radiant couple.

After the feast at night, with 'crooked-teeth' Dantavakra of Kalinga at his side, Rukmi challenges Balarama to a game of dice.

"He is as addicted to dice as Krishna is," whispers Dantavakra. "The only difference is this great fool couldn't play to save his life."

Meanwhile, Krishna has gone to bed early with a glowing Rukmini. She is certain a new bond has been forged between her brother and husband, one that will strengthen her position as first queen of Dwaraka, where there has been much lovely competition recently.

Krishna excuses himself, saying the journey to Bhojataka has tired him, he is not as young as he used to be. But just before he leaves the other kings, he takes Balarama aside to breathe in his ear, "Be careful of that serpent, he is a cheat."

The game begins with a thousand gold coins wagered. Rukmi wins. The excellent wine flows. With a hundred toasts to the newly-weds, Dantavakra fills Balarama's goblet the moment it is empty. Strangely, before Krishna left, he had done exactly the same, though he knew that his brother cannot hold his drink.

When Balarama loses the first round of dice against Rukmi, Dantavakra laughs at him, baring huge, entwined teeth in the Yadava's face so the other kshatriyas also laugh.

Balarama boils silently, his face crimson. He promptly wagers a lakh of gold coins. The ivory dice roll, and again, and Balarama has won.

But Rukmi does not agree. "You aren't watching the dice. I won. Ask the others."

They, Rukmi's own, smoothly confirm that the king of Bhojataka is the winner. There are some loud whispers about too much wine, even some about shameless cheating. Dantavakra bares his teeth again, taunting Balarama, and once more the kings laugh.

Balarama swallows another three goblets of wine. Red-eyed now, he thickly wagers a crore of gold coins and sits glowering over the board like a great hawk.

The dice roll: a seven for Rukmi, and another for Balarama; then two eights, then a nine for Rukmi. Balarama throws an eleven, gives a triumphant grunt and sits back. But Dantavakra scoops the dice up almost before they stop rolling, crying, "A seven. Rukmi wins!"

All the others cry, "Rukmi has won a crore of gold coins."

Dantavakra splits another bizarre grin at Balarama; the kings laugh again. Suddenly, a disembodied, but strangely familiar, voice says out of the air, "Balarama has won the wager. Rukmi is cheating."

Balarama sits swaying slightly and drunk by now. Rukmi ignores the voice and, at his cue, the others do as well. Dantavakra cackles, bringing his face still closer to Balarama, provoking him dangerously.

Rukmi says, "After all, what do cowherds know of dice or war? You should go back to your beasts and pastures, that is how you were raised."

With a roar, Balarama seizes the dice-board and fells Rukmi with a blow that cleaves his head down to his eyes, blood spurting on to the silk carpet and covering the ivory dice.

The board cracked in two his weapon, the big Yadava sets about the others. He smashes arms, heads, faces, legs, splattering scarlet everywhere. Shrill cries ring out. Balarama roars above the screams of the others.

He catches Dantavakra by his hair as he flees up the marble stairs, and knocks his teeth out, one by one, on the white steps.

Krishna and Rukmini burst in with some others. Krishna holds Balarama in a clinch, restraining him, rather as Balarama had done once by the Narmada.

Rukmini is hysterical when she sees her brother with his skull split, his blood and brains spilt. She screams at her brother-in-law, "Why did you save his life, Balarama? Was it so you could kill him yourself?"

Both of them turn to Krishna for support. Gambler-faced, he refuses to be drawn into this unseemly squabble between his brother and his wife. He will say nothing, except that they should return to Dwaraka at once. And they do.

Later, Rukmi, shocked, sees that the precious alcove beside his throne is mysteriously empty of the bow that Siva once gave him.

THIRTY-NINE

Purusha *Kair lingais gunaan etaan...*

His terror quietened again, Arjuna said, *"How do we know the man who is beyond the gunas?* How does he live? How does he transcend nature?" Krishna said, "He does not despise illumination, restless activity or dark delusion, when they prevail; nor does he long for them when they cease.

"For him pain and pleasure are alike; he never wavers. For him a clod of earth, a stone and a bar of gold are the same. For him blame and praise are one, because he is established in the atman's inmost calm.

"He who has relinquished the initiative of action, but lives in perfect harmony with his own nature, he has grown beyond the conflicting gunas.

"The man who is devoted to me transcends nature. He becomes the Brahman, for I am that abode of eternal bliss."

Prakriti

Dwaraka is not just the most beautiful city in the world, says Suka, it is much more. Sharing the mystery of its master, like him it is inscrutable; and Krishna lives here with all his wives.

When Narada hears that Narakasura has been killed and Krishna has taken sixteen thousand women home to be his wives, the wanderer cannot contain his curiosity. He doubts what he has heard and arrives in the sea-city to discover how Krishna keeps all those women.

The gardens of Dwaraka are in bloom; birds and insects swarm over the flower-beds in the parks. A picture is Dwaraka of the ocean, of nine hundred thousand crystal mansions.

Come morning, friendly dolphins swim into the city through clever channels that lead into pools where they frolic, chirruping, all day long with human swimmers; and then swim back to the open sea again at dusk, to their fervent rituals under the stars.

The pools in the sprawling parks of Dwaraka are festive with swans and geese, pelican and cormorant, scarlet ibis and awkward crane, burnished teal, pink flamingo and painted stork. Some pools are covered with a profusion of lilies and kalaharas in echoing colours. Wooded parklands are rich with deer, troupes of langur and ring-tailed lemurs with knowing orange eyes.

Narada arrives in Dwaraka, city of dreams, to investigate the Blue God's incredible love-life.

Viswakarman created the palaces of Krishna's harem, and they are the cynosure of the Devas, the envy of Amravati. The Dark One's harem has more than sixteen thousand palatial mansions; it is a city within a city.

Only the love of so many women can somewhat cool the other fire that burns unquenched in him, often fiercer with the passing years.

Arriving by flashing skyway, rishi patha, Narada walks unobserved into one of these edifices. This prominent palace is supported on columns of coral, and has a roof full of purple vaidurya while the outer walls are encrusted with sapphires. Even the floors are paved with slabs of turquoise.

The apartments within are furnished with canopies of pearls and equipped with chairs and beds of ivory inlay. Light shines softly from clusters of other nameless jewels embedded in the walls and the ceiling. Peacocks wander through the airy passages.

Narada walks out on to a verandah, and pauses at a window. He hears Krishna's voice above the tinkling of Rukmini's bracelets. She sits on her bed, fanning him with a golden-hafted fan. Her hair, untied for her husband's pleasure, streams in a silken river below her waist.

Krishna is saying, "I never understand you, Princess. You were sought after by kshatriyas whose power and wealth equal those of the Devas. Splendid kings, famed for their pedigree and valour. But you chose me over Sishupala and the rest: Sishupala, to whom you were already given by your brother. You chose cowardly Krishna who is afraid of these great men, and hides out here in the sea."

"Rukmini of the beautiful face," says the Darkling, teasing her or testing her. Narada, eavesdropping, stands still as stone.

Krishna runs his finger over her cheek. "Women who follow obscure men usually come to grief, O my reed-waisted queen." He drops his hand down to her waist. Not divining the drift of what he is saying, she grows tense as a bowstring.

"Women like rich men, even if they are not handsome. But I am a poor fellow, and loved only by those who have nothing themselves, the wretched of the earth. Marriage should be between equals in wealth, not between a superior and an inferior like you and me.

"Rukmini of Vidarbhha, today I feel that you chose me only because you were young. You were foolishly romantic, you lacked foresight."

"He goes on without mercy now," thinks Narada, who sees Rukmini's eyes fill.

"Even now, Rukmini of the lovely thighs," she shudders as his wicked hand wanders down her body. Narada can feel Rukmini's humiliation through the jasmine-laden sea air. "Even now, you could find some great kshatriya for yourself. Any of them would still have you. And with a proper husband, you could enjoy a blessed life, now and in the future.

"As for me, let me confess to you, Rukmini, I brought you here only to humiliate my enemies: Salva, Sishupala, Jarasandha, Dantavakra and your brother. You saw what I did to him. I brought you here to crush their vanity.

"In truth, I don't hanker after women, children or wealth. I am not concerned about my family or kingdom. I am indifferent to the world, content in myself. I am just a lamp, a witness; I work for nothing."

His tone is ambiguous and insulting. A moan or two has already spilt from Rukmini's lips, and now she begins to cry. She springs up from the couch, trying to blurt out an incoherent sorrow. The fan drops from her hand and she swoons.

Krishna had set out to curb her pride a little, especially after her outburst at Balarama in Bhojataka. He is taken aback by the vehemence of her grief. He jumps up from the bed and gathers her in his arms, whispering to her, kissing her.

She opens her teary eyes and, clasping his neck, begins to laugh herself in great relief that her love is not betrayed. It is night now. Krishna's kisses grow ardent, and she returns them, their faces shining with her tears.

Narada melts back into the street outside, shaking his head in some admiration for the Avatara's technique with his women, even the most royal, most spirited, most beautiful one.

Brahma's son, the peripatetic rishi, ambles through the moonlight, a sea-breeze plucking at his jata. He arrives at another mansion above the waves, as splendid as Rukmini's. Now he walks in through the front door. Inside Krishna sits at dice with Satyabhama and Uddhava.

Brahmanya-Deva, the God of brahmanas, the nurturer of peace who protects those who bear no arms, sees Narada, and jumps up with a cry of welcome. Calling for holy water, he washes the muni's feet. Then he takes him to his own throne, making a great fuss over him.

When Narada sits, he is ill at ease. Krishna says, smiling, "Brahmarishi, what can I do for you?"

Many years ago, when Brahma himself abducted some gopa boys and their calves, Narada had not been in Vrindavana. Though he had heard that story from his heavenly father, he is overwhelmed now by this sight of twin Krishnas in separate palaces at the same time. Surely, the Blue One has not run here before him, leaving Rukmini.

Narada mumbles, "Lord, let me always see your lotus feet before my eyes."

Rising abruptly, his face red, he walks out of Satyabhama's palace, while Uddhava and the queen stare after him. Krishna smiles but makes no attempt to restrain him.

Narada comes out again into the moonlight, but sweating now, mopping his brow though the night has grown cool. Gathering up his loincloth, that rishi—Brahma's son, born from his divine thought before the world was made—abandons dignity altogether. He runs headlong towards the next palace.

Arriving at a window, he sees Krishna playing with Kalindi's children.

Beside himself, Narada scampers from palace to palace. In Satya's, he sees the Blue God bathing with her in a warm pool; in Jambavati's bedchamber he sees Krishna weaving jasmine garlands into that wife's hair, and in Kubja's palace he sees the Dark One enjoying a languorous oil massage.

Narada comes out in disarray into a silvery quadrangle of the harem and, as if in mystic response to the disbelief that brought him here, he is inundated by a vision. He sees into sixteen thousand palaces at once. With miraculous sight, he sees Krishna in every one of them with a different wife and family. The night waves' deep wash echoing in his ears like thunder, Narada stands dazzled. He sees...

Krishna pouring oblations into sacred fires, Krishna performing mahayagnas, Krishna at a feast, Krishna eating alone, Krishna at dice, Krishna in every posture of love, Krishna at sandhya worship, Krishna playing with his many children, Krishna with musicians and poets, Krishna swimming with his women, Krishna meditating on the Parabrahman, Krishna planning a war in a martial queen's company, Krishna with Bhadra, Krishna with Balarama, ah, Krishna with all Creation!

Narada faints, and Krishna appears from everywhere to carry him indoors like a babe in his arms. And smiling to himself in rapture, the rishi whispers on and on, and altogether more sincerely, about lotus-feet, blue, blue lotus feet.

In magical Dwaraka, diamond of the ocean, Krishna lies in sixteen thousand lovely women's arms. But still the old fire burns him. Those that know, like Suka, say that in the curse of being man and God together he shares the anguish of all men through the ages of the earth. Not sixteen thousand women's beds can quench that fire, and the chasmal solitariness that torments the Incarnation.

But they surely comfort him with their love, his numerous wives, in Dwaraka of mysteries.

BOOK FOUR

FORTY

Purusha *Urdhvamulam adhasaakham...*

"The giant, everlasting aswattha is said to have *its roots in heaven and its branches down in the earth below*. Its leaves are the Vedas," said Krishna. At the end of his lonely anguish, sublime calm washed into him.

"Like the pipal, the branches of the tree of life extend above and below; nourished by the gunas, they even reach down into this world of men.

"Its true form is never seen in this world: not its beginning or its end, nor its real nature. The devoted cut down the tree with the sword of detachment, saying, 'I seek refuge not in the tree, but in the Primal One from whom this current of the world flows.'

"He who is free from pride and delusion, who has conquered the evil of attachment, whose lusts are stilled, who is devoted to me, who is free from the tyranny of pleasure and pain, he comes to the changeless state.

"Not fire, not the moon, nor the sun illumine the refulgent Being who is my abode. He who attains me will never be reborn."

Prakriti

Longing to see his old friends and roam the haunts of his childhood, longing to see Yasodha and Nanda after so many years, Balarama goes back to Gokula. The sun is setting behind the great jungle when he arrives in his chariot.

Shot through with the last beams of daylight, a familiar cloud of dust hangs in the air, as the herd returns from pasture along the dirt tracks. The lowing of bulls, the bleating of white calves and all the other sights and sounds are to him redolent of his dreams while he was away.

Like a dream appears the moon-crescent of dwellings where the Sun God is worshipped every morning with fresh flowers, earthen lamps, and incense; like a dream, the dusk-gathering trees with their armfuls of birds settling for the night, singing a chorus to the sunset; like a dream, the velvet fields, the river, and the looming forest: a dream in which time has stood still.

In the dream, memories flood Balarama in a tender rush. His eyes full of them, and tears, he arrives at Nanda's house. That dwelling has now been made solid, with wooden pillars and steps, ceiling and floor.

The once itinerant cowherds have decided to settle where the one they now know is the Avatara grew amongst them. Although he vanished so abruptly from their lives, leaving them only haunting memories of himself, while he became a legend and a saviour in the world.

Nanda comes out and, tears flowing down his face, embraces Balarama; and keeps him thus as if to insinuate him into his flesh with that embrace.

Yasodha comes out on to the wooden steps. He sees her hair is all white now, and her gracious face is lined. And when he touches her feet, she also begins to cry as she clasps him.

Then, all of Gokula is at Nanda's door, hugging Balarama, slapping him on the back as if nothing has changed in their lives or in his since they last saw one another. Except that everyone wears an older face, and the bright, wide-eyed children have never seen him before.

After he has bathed and lounges on a rope cot, Yasodha feeds him with her hands, laughing, just as she used to when he was a boy. Now the questions begin, inevitably about he who hasn't come.

"Is Vasudeva well?" asks Nanda, tentatively, in the crowded yard. Balarama answers that his father is in good health, and Rohini and Devaki also.

A silence, then, someone from the back of the crowd who can't contain herself pipes up, "Is the darling of the city women happy?"

Balarama frowns, pretending not to know whom she means. "Who?"

"Is the blue lover of the clever city women well? Does he ever remember the friends of his youth? Will he deign to visit his mother?"

Another cries, "We abandoned everything for him, our fathers, husbands and children. To meet him on the Yamuna, to dance with him in the forest. He made such sweet promises, saying he would return in a week. Where is he now? He has never come back."

"Do the shrewd women of the city trust that fickle, ungrateful person?"

Another concludes dryly, "Oh, he can win any woman's love with his charm."

Their eyes glimmer, tear-laden in the lamplight. One of the gopis clustered around Balarama says rebelliously, "What have we to do with this talk of Krishna? Let us speak of other things. If his time passes happily without us, why can't we do without him?"

Balarama asks after Radha then, but nobody tells him anything. She is not among the gathering and neither is her husband Ayyan; and Balarama doesn't see her during his stay in Gokula. She has vanished like an illusion, as if she never existed.

Balarama stays in Vrindavana for two months. The gopis attach themselves to him. They follow him to the forest's heart, range with him to the bend in the midnight river, to the pool where Krishna once danced on Kaliya's hood. From the hollows of the kadamba, Balarama and the gopis drink heavenly, potent varuni together, varuni that intoxicates the jungle with its heady scent.

At midnight, Balarama sits beside the moonlit Yamuna with his bevy of women, singing old songs on the white sand-banks, the wind redolent with the scent of lotuses.

The return to Vrindavana is bliss for Balarama. He wears a vanamala of five colours round his neck, trailing the earth, one lily earring, and staggers through the jungle, drunk out of his wits on varuni, and on memories.

He makes love to his old sweethearts, the cowherd women, beside the river and unashamedly out on the pastures under the trees fanned by familiar breezes that seem to blow out of his boyhood. Yet, he is in the grip of sorrow; possibly that too soon he must leave this place he loves, and return to the city that he has come to abhor.

In deep Vrindavana, Balarama's childlike heart turns finally against the opulent, hollow life of sovereignty and power. Wandering alone under the old trees of the precious forest, and missing Krishna as much as the gopis do, with tears in his eyes and dizzy varuni in his veins and tired of this incarnation, Balarama realises he hates war and bloodshed more than anything else.

He decides to go on a pilgrimage of expiation once he leaves Gokula, a tirtha-yatra across the length and breadth of the holy land. For he can feel them clearly in his blood, even here in Vrindavana: Krishna's incessant machinations to begin more murderous wars to rid the Earth of her burden, and to leave no power of this age able to dominate the coming, lesser one.

One moonlit night, after some heavy drinking and love-making on the banks of the Yamuna, Balarama lies naked on damp grass with three gopis, as drunk as himself. Suddenly, he calls out to the river, "Yamuna, I am drunk! Change your course for me and flow nearer. I feel like swimming in your scented water."

Slumbering in fluid dreams, the Yamuna pays him no heed. Up jumps Balarama with a roar, that he, Vishnu's rest, has been insulted by a mere river, and before his women.

He seizes up his Halayudha, the plough-like weapon he carries everywhere, massive, occult thing. With a curse he attacks the Yamuna, dragging her right out of her banks on just one of his ayudha's glinting blades.

"You dare ignore me like some common drunk?" he bellows. "I will split you in a hundred rillets!"

The river-goddess materializes—she that took Vasudeva across her swollen tides one squally, fateful night—and falls at his feet.

"O Ananta! Feeling your strength, I realise how you support the universe."

Bathing his feet with her tears, which the softhearted Balarama cannot bear, the Goddess begs him to release her. Stupefied with varuni, swaying stark naked, he holds her aloft with his plough-weapon, so a wide stream of her flows through night air and moonbeams, and little else.

When she pleads with him like that, he drops the Yamuna back to earth with a grunt. At once she flows for him along a new bed, and much nearer.

"Come, Mighty One, come into my water," she calls seductively.

His point made before the women, the gopis and he wade in. The river wraps herself around them, making their hearts go fast again. Again, Balarama begins to fondle the womens' dusky skins, to kiss their full lips glistening in the mad light of the moon.

He takes them one after the other, Suka says, like a bull-elephant his cows, like Airavata himself in musth. And for all his bulk and vigour, he is entirely gentle.

FORTY-ONE

Purusha *Sariram yad avaapnoti...*

"In this world, the Avatara dons the five senses of nature, and the sixth the mind: the garment of Prakriti!

"*When I take a body and leave it,* these come and go like the scent of flowers on the wind.

"I enjoy the senses, Arjuna, as you do, and suffer by them as well. But they do not delude me. The splendour of the sun, the moon, and the fire are my own.

"I nourish the earth, while I am in it. Then as the moon, as precious soma, I bring sap and water to the living world of plant and herb. And as the fire of life I nurture the bodies of animals. All this world's foods I consume and they become my breathing out and my breathing in.

"I am in the heart of every man who lives. I am the source of memory and knowledge, and of their loss as well. I am the Vedas, the Vedanta, and the knower of the Vedas too.

"Arjuna, there are just two beings in this world: the mortal and the immortal. The one who dies is all these changing lives, and the undying one is changeless.

"But beyond both these, the supreme spirit, the Lord, enters the three worlds and sustains them.

"I transcend the dying and the undying beings. I am the supreme person in the world and in the Veda.

"Blameless Arjuna, he who knows me becomes truly wise," said Krishna.

Prakriti

Dvivida the monkey was a friend of Narakasura. They had both been in the world for countless generations of men; in fact, since before Sri Rama's time. The earth was a purer place then, and monkeys, men and rakshasas were all grander than in Krishna's lesser time, at dark yuganta.

Dvivida was once a counsellor to Sugriva who was a contemporary of Jambavan. He had fought heroically for Rama of Ayodhya on the shores of Lanka against the sinister Ravana. But now, he couldn't believe that Krishna was an Avatara, as Rama had been, not even when Narakasura was killed.

"How could Vishnu kill his own son?" cried Dvivida. And, enraged at Naraka's death, he began to avenge his friend. At dead of night, he would set fire to towns and cowherds' camps in Krishna's lands.

The vanara was old now, the last of his kind left on earth. He had been alive for a long, long time, and he was tired of his life. Krishna's country, Anarta, felt Dvivida's wrath, and the monkey was still as strong as a thousand elephants.

Dvivida belonged to an ancient race; he was a master of the occult siddhis, mahima and anima. In an instant he could grow tiny as a kitten or mountainous. Now he would grow gigantic and swagger into the sea. With hands big as plateaux he beat up tidal waves that smashed ashore, devastating the villages on the coast and killing hundreds of fisher-folk in Krishna's land.

Dvividha attacked rishis' asramas, desecrating their sacrificial food and fires with his excrement.

With boulders he sealed honey-gatherers and lovers into mountain-caves, to die slowly of hunger. How he scoffed at this age grown so puny that men couldn't even roll a little stone away from a cavemouth. What would these pygmies have done on Lanka, just to see that battle of battles? They would have died of fright.

Dvivida became a highway rapist, attacking queens and princesses along Krishna's roads. He would easily dispatch their guards and lay hands on the royal women. Otherwise, cow-girls and gypsies were enough for him; although, at his age the rape itself was perfunctory.

On the whole, he was a great vanara in a hurry to die.

One day, while he is in Gokula with a group of gopis, Balarama climbs the Raivataka hill that overlooks the sea. Lurking nearby, hoping to ambush unwary lovers, Dvivida hears sweet songs and comes at once to investigate, scenting a chance to create some havoc.

Drunk on varuni, Balarama is singing too. Dvivida appears as a tiny monkey, small as a marmoset in the trees, chattering down at them. Looking up into the branches the gopi women find the little creature utterly fetching. He makes monkey faces, wizened old funny faces down at them, and they laugh at him.

Colouring swiftly, Balarama roars, "Doesn't this monkey know who I am?"

But encouraged by the women's laughter, Dvivida grows bolder. He waves his red bottom at them from his branch, baring long fangs in his simian grin. He skins a pink erection for them and, drunk as they are, the unsuspecting gopis shriek with laughter.

In mounting rage Balarama flings a stone at the little vanara, which he nimbly dodges. Dvivida makes a thin stream down from his cackling perch, narrowly missing the Yadava's head. The women are shrill with delight as Balarama leaps out of the way, nearly falling.

Swooping down, Dvivida snatches a wineskin right out of his hands and dashes it on the ground, gibbering in glee. Bold as brass he lifts a young gopi's clothes, strokes her with shiny fingers and scampers away.

Suddenly, Balarama realises who this monkey is, and even as he raises his Halayudha to attack it, the little creature is transformed before their eyes. In a flash Dvivida is as tall as a tree. The women run screaming to Balarama. Dvivida snarls at them in senile viciousness.

In a blur he pulls up a sala tree by its roots and hurls it like lightning at Balarama's head as he had once done to Ravana's demons. The tree shatters, rocking the Yadava back on his heels.

Unharmed, if a little sobered by the blow, Balarama blasts Dvivida with a bolt of light from his plough weapon, cutting his skull open. Blood streams down the golden fur on his face and chest.

Screeching, the vanara pulls up another tree, which Balarama brushes aside like a straw. Dvivida rushes at the Yadava. Who is this mere man, who resists him so disdainfully?

Dropping his weapon, Balarama strikes the monkey two blows with his fists, thunder and lightning. Vomitting blood, rheumy eyes glazing over, Dvivida falls twitching at his feet. Soon, he lies still, the wrath drained from his face, and a peaceful smile curves his wrinkled lips.

And the earth is rid of another ancient burden: a good vanara who once fought at Sri Rama's side, but turned to evil ways in the shrunken time where he was so out of place.

FORTY-TWO

Purusha *Abhayam sattvasamsuddhir...*

"*Pure, fearless,* wise, generous, restrained and sacrificing; learned in the Shastras, austere and honest; non-violent,truthful, relinquishing, serene, never finding fault; compassionate to all the living, free from greed, gentle, humble, and steady; energetic, forgiving, of great fortitude, free from arrogance and malice: this is the man with the divine nature.

"Ostentation, vanity, rage, harshness and ignorance: Arjuna, these are the qualities of the demonic man.

"The man with the divine nature finds deliverance and the demoniacal man is bound in darkness."

Arjuna looked up anxiously at Krishna, who laid a gentle hand on him, reading his thought. "Don't worry, Pandava, your nature is divine, and so is your destiny. But let me tell you about the demonic ones. They know nothing of the paths of karma or of renunciation. They know nothing of purity, truth, or dharma.

"They say the world is unreal, without a basis, without a Creator. These ruthless men of feeble understanding rise up as the enemies of the earth for its destruction. They are full of hypocrisy, arrogance and delusion, and abandon themselves to insatiable desire.

"They live lives of greed and foolish cares, and these end only when they die. Bound with a million fetters by their desires, devoted to lust and rage, their only aim is to amass all the wealth they can, by the vilest means.

" 'I am the lord, the great one,' they think. 'This is mine and the other shall be mine as well. Mighty am I, successful and happy. I am rich and well-born; who is there like me? I will sacrifice, I will be bounteous, joyful will I be.' Yes, thus they think, being deluded.

"Bewildered by a wild jungle of thoughts, helplessly entangled, they fall into hell. Conceited, obstinate and arrogant with wealth and power, they perform hollow sacrifices with great ostentation and no regard to the inner content. Bound over to vanity, anger and violence, they hate me in others and in themselves too.

"These ruthless, hate-filled ones I hurl back again and again into evil wombs, in the great cycle of births and deaths. Fallen into demon wombs, life after life, the malignant ones never rise to me, but devolve to the lowest, bestial state.

"Arjuna, three-fold is the gateway to hell, three-fold the road to the ruin of the soul: lust, greed, and anger. The man who is freed from these naturally does what is best for his soul and attains perfect bliss, the changeless condition.

"But he who discards the scriptures and follows his baser nature's call, he doesn't come to perfection or joy, or the highest goal. In this world, let the scripture be your guide. For it is sacred, it comes from me."

Prakriti

When provoked, Balarama does more than drag rivers from their courses.

Samba, Krishna's son by Jambavati, carries away the Kaurava prince Duryodhana's daughter, Lakshana, during her swayamvara. Karna, Duryodhana, Dusasana and some others give hot chase. After a run in his chariot, Samba turns on them like a lion at bay, and takes their breath away with his valour at the longbow.

But at last their numbers, and all of them great kshatriyas, prove too much for Krishna's son. He is taken with his bride, back to Hastinapura.

Narada promptly brings news of this to Dwaraka. But Krishna is away from his city. In the Sudharma, Narada recounts what Bheeshma, the Kuru patriarch, said: "What can the Yadavas do anyway? They enjoy Anarta that we have given them in our generosity. Confine the upstart boy."

Ugrasena is incensed, and wants to take an army against the Kauravas. But after his sojourn in Gokula, Balarama is full of peace and goodwill. He says, "They are related to us through our aunt Kunti. We shouldn't do anything that will jeopardize her position. We have enough enmity with Jarasandha and his friends without making war on our own people now."

Balarama is respected, even liked, by the Kauravas. It was he who taught both Duryodhana and his cousin Bheema to fight with the mace. Duryodhana had been a favourite pupil. So, though many in Dwaraka protest against this pacific course, Balarama sets out for Hastinapura with Uddhava and a token, insignificant force.

Camping outside the Kuru city, Balarama sends Uddhava to Dhritarashtra, Drona, Bheeshma, Duryodhana, Karna and the others, to inform them of the arrival of a well-loved cousin and master.

The Kaurava princes come to the gates of their capital to receive the great Yadava, for they are indeed his affectionate disciples. Gifts are exchanged as well as formal and filial embraces and the usual greetings and inquiries after those who aren't present.

Duryodhana knows what Balarama has come for. And he is quite prepared to set Samba free with a warning, when he sees his old master has come without an army.

But all at once the big Yadava draws himself up and declaims, "Our king Ugrasena has heard that a number of you combined to defeat Samba, who fought single-handed, and you hold Krishna's son captive. Ugrasena orders you to bring Samba to us immediately, and to release him and his fairly taken bride into my custody."

"How grand this is," retorts Duryodhana icily. "A low shoe tries to ride upon the head that wears a crown."

He turns his back on Balarama and, laughing, cries to the other Kauravas, "These Yadavas are related to us now because Kunti married into our family. By our indulgence these, whom Kamsa once scattered like straws in the wind, now enjoy a kingdom again, a throne, and even a bed to sleep in.

"But like serpents given nectar, they turn on the hand that fed them. They dare come to order us at our own doorstep. We should take away our favour from these upstarts, and leave them begging again."

Balarama's face is a picture. He howls, "I came here to keep peace between the angry Yadavas and the foolish Kurus. But the stick is the only language a witless beast understands. You are so drunk with power and wealth you forget whose son it is that you dare hold prisoner."

But even as he rages, Duryodhana walks away into Hastinapura, followed by Karna, Drona, and the others. Deprived rudely of his audience, Balarama is left stuttering.

His roar shakes Hastinapura. Rushing forward, he locks his Halayudha under the walls of that city, much as he did to the Yamuna. He knits his brows, the muscles on his back stand out like tree-roots. Before the eyes and under the feet of the amazed Yadavas, who had begun to mutter about the insult they had to swallow because they came here without a proper army, the earth begins to quake.

Hastinapura is tossed about like a skiff in a gale, as Balarama's weapon hums in his hands with the sound of a valley full of black bees. Stones and masonry come clattering down into the streets; in places, entire walls crumble.

In moments the Kauravas bring Samba and Lakshana and stand them free outside the gates. Their memories powerfully restored to them, the Kurus beg Balarama on their knees to stop his earthquake.

"O Ananta!" Duryodhana begs him, "Supporter of everything, we seek refuge in you."

His purpose accomplished, and easily pacified these days, Balarama shoulders his weapon. Duryodhana comes out with twelve hundred elephants, ten thousand horses, six thousand golden chariots, and a thousand sakhis, as his daughter's dowry. He falls at Balarama's feet, and solemnly begs his master's protection for ever, protection that the fond Yadava grants him.

Which is why Balarama takes no part at Kurukshetra, in the Mahabharata yuddha that was fought on the crack of the ages; except at the very end, when most of the Kaurava heroes were killed and Bheema and Duryodhana faced each other in single combat. Then

Balarama tried, in vain, to stop his two pupils from fighting to the death.

Shrewdly, presciently, Duryodhana elicits the promise at the gates of Hastinapura. For if Balarama had fought for the Pandavas, by himself he would have razed the Kauravas in a day, and the mettle of Yudhishtira and his brothers would never have been tested.

Since that day, Hastinapura stands slightly askew on her southern side, and sloping towards the river, to show where the great Yadava dragged the city of elephants.

FORTY-THREE

Purusha *Ye shastravidhim utsrijya...*

Arjuna asked, "*Those who do not regard the scripture* but sacrifice to God in faith, what place have they in sattva, rajas or tamas?"

Krishna said, "Each man believes according to his nature, Arjuna, and he is what he believes. Sattvic men worship the Gods. Rajasic men worship wealth and power. And men of tamas worship the spirits of the dead, make gods of their ancestors' ghosts.

"Because vanity and lust fill them with egotism, demonic men mortify their bodies with violent austerities, which the scriptures do not ordain. These fools weaken their organs of sense and outrage me, dwelling in their bodies.

"The sattvic sacrifice is scriptural; it seeks no reward. The rajasic yagna is all for show and gain. And the sacrifice of tamas distributes no food, no hymns are sung, and it is faithless.

"The worship of the Gods, of the wise and of teachers; purity, uprightness, continence, and non-violence: this is the tapasya of the body. Sweet words that offend no one, but are truthful, kind and beneficial, and the charity of the Veda: this is the tapasya of speech. Serenity of mind, gentleness, integrity of purpose, self-control, and silence: this is the tapasya of mind. Together, these are the three-fold tapasya of sattva.

"The rajasic tapasya is done from pride, seeking fame for the sake of exhibition. The obstinate tapasya, done from a lust for pain, or to hurt another, is the tamasic one.

"The sattvic charity is dutiful, made to the deserving at an auspicious moment and place, and seeks nothing in return. The rajasic gift is always made with a selfish purpose, for some gain. The tamasic gift is a contemptuous one, made without regard for time and place, nor for the one who receives it."

Prakriti

Pundra is a vassal state of Jarasandha's and part of the alliance of Evil. Advised by cunning courtiers, Paundraka, the unhinged king of Pundra, declares himself the true Avatara, and Krishna an impostor. Urged by Jarasandha, the courtiers spread the rumour among the people of Pundra, and when Paundraka sees them prostrate themselves in the streets to worship him, he begins to believe in the lie himself.

He sports three peacock feathers in his crown, carries ludicrous replicas of the Panchajanya, the Kaumodaki, the Saringa and the Sudarshana. He wears an imitation of the Kaustubha, and has himself adorned with a counterfeit Srivatsa, stuck on hair by hair in his harem. He wears a vanamala too; though, unlike Krishna's wildflower garland, which stays fresh for months because it touches him, Paundraka's fades in a day.

Pundra's deluded sovereign dresses in bright yellow silk, like Krishna, wears golden alligator earrings, like the Dark One, and flies the emblem of Garuda on his chariot.

Once Paundraka goes to visit the king of Kasi, and from there, instigated by his friend, he sends a messenger to Krishna in Dwaraka.

The kings of Jarasandha's alliance are pleased with Paundraka's mania. Any way, however trivial, to get back at Krishna is welcome for all the defeat he has inflicted on them.

These days Jarasandha is hard-pressed to raise another army, the greatest yet, against Krishna, and he is glad to see the demented Paundraka taunting him.

Paundraka's messenger arrives bravely in Krishna's sabha. After presenting his credentials the man begins, his eyes always averted, to read Paundraka's message aloud.

"I am the true Avatara, who has come to this world out of compassion for created beings. Give up your pretensions, Krishna of Dwaraka. Give up the Chakra, the Vanamala, the Kaustubha, the Saringa and the Panchajanya. Come to me for refuge, if you value your life."

A stunned silence, then raucous laughter rings through the court. Krishna sends his reply. "Tell your master, messenger, that Krishna of Dwaraka says—I come straightaway to Kasi to seek refuge. Prepare to become meat for kites and vultures."

Time again for killing. Krishna summons Garuda once more, and flies to Kasi where Paundraka and Kasiraja meet him with three aksauhinis. He sees Paundraka ride against him, wearing brilliant yellow, flying an eagle-banner on his chariot, clumsily carrying the signs of the Avatara. And he is as fair as a ghost.

Krishna's laughter rocks the field, sends shafts of fear among his enemies.

"I have brought your weapons to you, Paundraka!" sings the Blue God, four-armed suddenly. With a snarl, he looses the Sudarshana Chakra. No army fights for Krishna today; he fights as a God, alone and more awesome than any army.

The wheeling Chakra is quicker than thought, more final than time. In moments, a headless, dismembered enemy lies in a crimsoned field. Elephants, horses, and men have been cut down in an eyeflash, as if in another dimension of experience: a nightmare.

On the edge of grace themselves, Paundraka and Kasiraja stand open-mouthed. *What had happened?*

Krishna still offers his weapons to the giggling Paundraka, "I have brought these for you. *Here!*"

Languidly, mace, wheel and arrows from the Saringa fly at the interloper. Paundraka believes so completely in his delusion, he stretches his arms out to receive them.

"I seek refuge," smiles Krishna blandly, as Paundraka dies of mace, disk and arrows, at once: his chest smashed, his head struck off, his delusions undone.

Like a flower bud in a tornado, Kasiraja's head, bizarre trophy, is carried off his neck by a shaft from the Saringa, up over the walls of the city of Kasi and into the palace and the presence of his son Sudakshina, who jumps up with a scream when the grisly thing falls staring at his feet.

Paundraka's long obsession with Krishna began during the abduction of Rukmini. At last, it liberates the mad king of Pundra, and he attains moksha when the Avatara kills him. His battle won with terrifying ease, Krishna flies home to Dwaraka on Garuda, while in Kasi there is great lament.

"Dwaraka can't be threatened with armies," decides Sudakshina, yuvaraja of Kasi. He prays to Siva, God of his ancient city, from whose ear the pristine place first fell to the earth. Sudakshina worships Siva to help him avenge his father's death.

Siva appears before the prince of Kasi and his family priest.

"Summon the dakshinagni," advises the glorious Mahadeva. "The witchfire will consume any enemy of the brahmanas."

Sudakshina undertakes an occult sacrifice, the abhichara-prayoga. As soon as it is completed, Agni springs up with a howl from the pit as an incendiary female, fire leaping from her mouth and eyes, her waving tresses aflame. She is tusked, licking bloody lips, naked and immense, a trident in her hand, and surrounded by burning goblins.

At Sudakshina's command, the mindless abhichara, tall as a palm-tree, flies roaring towards Dwaraka.

Krishna sits at dice in his sabha. The people in the streets cry out to him to save them from the apocalypse blazing down from the air. Calmly intoning an **AUM**, Krishna looses the Sudarshana at the spirit of fire.

Chakra and abhichara lock five thousand hands above Dwaraka and there seem to be two suns risen in the sky. For a while they are fused in a single fireball. After an explosive trial, the abhichara flees the Chakra, which pursues it like a meteor chasing another.

The demoness flashes back towards the pit from which she rose, the Sudarshana flaring after her. The abhichara falls on prince Sudakshina who summoned her. In rage at her humiliation, she burns him up in an instant, before subsiding into the pit of sacrifice with an echoing ululation like a forest-fire dying.

The Chakra burns down Kasi, palaces and stables, markets, homes and streets, killing everyone in sacred Manikarnika, reducing Siva's city to ashes.

Finally sated, the disk turns back to Dwaraka, to blue Krishna who has just won his game of dice against the brilliant Uddhava.

FORTY-FOUR

Purusha *AUM TAT SAT...*

Krishna said, "**AUM TAT SAT** is the three-fold emblem of Brahman. The brahmanas, the Vedas, and the yagnas were ordained by this, of old.

"**AUM**, say the worshippers of Brahman at sacrifice, penance and charity.

"**TAT**, they say at sacrifice, penance and charity.

"**SAT** means the absolute, Arjuna, everything that is auspicious, good and true. All tapasya, yagna and daana are called **SAT**.

"But if a man performs any of these without faith in Brahman, it is asat, unreal, of no account here or hereafter."

Prakriti

The Blue God sits on a crystal throne in Dwaraka, in the splendid Sudharma. He is surrounded by his Yadavas, brave and strong as lions. They are like the full moon and the stars in a clear night sky.

There arrives in that court a dishevelled, hard-travelled stranger with a missive from ninety-eight kings who did not submit to the might of Magadha, to the empire of Jarasandha. He has imprisoned them in his capital, Girivraja, in an underground catacomb, and means to sacrifice them to Siva, when he has a hundred of them.

"Incomprehensible Krishna, conqueror of fear, Lord of the universe! Liberate us from the bondage of karma called Jarasandha. Mighty with vassals, strong as a thousand elephants, he holds us prisoner. He means to sacrifice us to Siva when we are a hundred. Only you can save us; we consign ourselves to your grace."

No sooner has the captive kings' envoy finished delivering his message, than the sabha in the Sudharma hears a golden song in the passage outside. His face lambent, his jata bright, a contrast to the kings' messenger, Narada arrives there singing a paean of Vishnu.

Krishna and his court rise and, twinkling at the wanderer, the Dark One says, "Are the worlds free from fear that your worship ranges over them? To be sure, nothing anywhere is unknown to you. So if I might ask, divine Narada, what do our cousins the Pandavas now intend?"

Smiling himself, Narada bows low, "Inscrutable, pervasive, Krishna, you always pretend to be ignorant and merely human. But I know better and I seek asylum in your grace. Yet, since you ask, your cousin Yudhishtira aspires to be an emperor of all kshatriyas. He means to perform a Rajasuya yagna. It is you he wants to worship with the sacrifice, and he wishes you would attend his yagna, O God whose presence in the world is so auspicious!"

There are loud murmurs among the Yadavas, all afire to ride against the old enemy Jarasandha. Krishna raises a hand for silence. Turning to Uddhava, he says, "No one knows politics as well as you do, most intelligent, far-seeing friend. You tell us what we should do."

After a moment's thought, Uddhava says, "You must be with the Pandavas at their Rajasuya. But you cannot ignore the message from the captive kings."

Uddhava turns to the other Yadavas, "Jarasandha has been given a boon that only a mortal man can kill him. There is only one man who can match his strength—our cousin Bheemasena the Pandava. Jarasandha has amassed an army of a hundred aksauhinis. He cannot be vanquished in battle without great loss to ourselves. But by Bheema in single combat, yes."

He pauses, then adds softly, "Let the way to Magadha lead through Indraprastha. And you might remember that Jarasandha can refuse a brahmana nothing."

Narada claps; he approves. And the Yadavas are possibly better persuaded by Uddhava than even by Krishna. They decide to go first to Yudhishtira's capital, Indraprastha.

In a week, Krishna sets out with an army of countless chariots and elephants, horses and foot-soldiers. The Avatara goes forth from Dwaraka to the beating of tabors, gongs, kettledrums, and the auspicious sounding of conches, horns and trumpets.

His wives follow him in golden palanquins. Like a sea that army marches, flags waving, voices and spirits lifted to the sky, armour and weapons flowing in a tide across the earth, gleaming in the sun.

The Blue God passes through his own country, Anarta, then through Sauvira, Marus, Vinasana, over dark hills, through emerald forests and across scented, lotus-laden rivers. Through the Panchala country and the Matsya, resplendent he marches on Indraprastha. When he arrives, Yudhishtira comes out of his city in the wilderness with his priests and his family to receive his divine cousin.

Gentle Yudhishtira, usually so calm, unmoved even by bloody war, stands overwhelmed before Krishna, with tears in his eyes. With a cry he embraces the Avatara. A glowing Bheema comes forward and hugs Krishna in his mighty arms.

Then, Arjuna bends to touch his feet. But Krishna, who knows the two of them are the same age exactly, lifts him up quickly and clasps him instead. The twins, Nakula and Sahadeva, touch the Dark One's feet, and Krishna blesses them fondly.

Yudhishtira climbs into Krishna's chariot and drives him himself through his city.

Set out in silver archways, Indraprastha welcomes Krishna, with ecstatic singers and dancers going before his train. Pitchers of water adorn every doorstep, a symbolic offering of man's soul to God; and every man, woman and child has turned out in colourful new clothes to receive him. The air is laced with incense, musky attar, other rare perfumes, and the scents of a million flowers.

The women of the city, who have dreamt of him since they heard he was coming, abandon whatever they are doing, some leave their husbands in bed, and they flock to the royal road for a glimpse of the dark and precious One.

The younger women climb on to their roofs for a clearer view. They shower petals down on him and his queens and favour him with amorous smiles when he waves up at them.

The city reaches out a sea of hands to touch Krishna along his way. At the palace Kunti receives him lovingly, her great blue nephew.

Krishna stays three months in Indraprastha, while Yudhishtira prepares for his Rajasuya yagna. And now, one cousin who is the same age as Krishna—they were born on the same night, like two halves of the same soul—grows as close to him as a twin, or even closer.

In Indraprastha, Arjuna and Krishna become inseparable. They are together from morning until late at night, and often on into the next morning—hunting, at dice, or just content in each other's silent company: locked in the mysterious covenant of a God and his devotee. At times, it seems Krishna has come to Indraprastha just for Arjuna.

One day, when Yudhishtira sits in his sabha among his brothers, his gurus, and his family, he says solemnly to Krishna, "Lord, I want to worship you with a Rajasuya yagna."

Krishna approves at once. "I am happy, cousin. Conquer the corners of the earth in my name. But then, not only in mine but in the names of your ancestors.

"Your brothers are all Devaputras, they are the guardians of the earth. Send them forth and they will prevail. For in all the world, no one can vanquish any bhakta of mine, let alone one as steadfast and as true as yourself, Yudhisthtira, who have conquered me with your love."

How Yudhishtira glows to hear him.

Sahadeva is sent to the south with Srinjayas, Nakula to the west, Arjuna to the north, and Bheema to the east. Weeks go by, and months. While the seasons change, Krishna stays in Indraprastha: the unmoving eye of the storm he has set in motion.

One by one, the conquering Pandavas return to their city, laden with the tribute of vassals acquired either in peace or often, in fierce war. Blood spilt on far-flung fields throughout the holy land darkens the grateful earth, for whose sake the Avatara has come. Her burden grows lighter still by all the killing the Pandava brothers do; and she can, more easily, cross the threshold of the new age that flies near along the mazes of time.

The four quarters of Bharatavarsha are subdued in Yudhishtira's name and Krishna's. Kings through the length and breadth of the land are bound in fealty. But Jarasandha does not submit in Magadha, and the promise Krishna sent to the kshatriyas held in Girivraja remains unredeemed. Yudhishtira is shaken.

"Krishna, what power is this that withstands your grace?" he asks. He knows the implications of his brother's failure outside the gates of Jara's mighty son. Yudhishtira feels vanquished.

Musingly, Krishna recalls Uddhava's words in Dwaraka: "Jarasandha cannot refuse a brahmana anything, because he was born by a brahmana's blessing."

FORTY-FIVE

Purusha *Sannyasasya mahaabaho...*

Near the end of the dwapara yuga, the Pandava warrior Arjuna said to his cousin, the incarnate Lord, "Krishna, *tell me about renunciation* and relinquishment, and the difference between the two."

The kali yawning plain before him, the Blue Lotus of the dwapara yuga said, "Renunciation is when you abandon karma out of desire. Relinquishment is when you act, but abandon the fruits of what you do.

"Yagna, tapasya and daana must be done; they are the purifiers of the wise. But this karma should be performed without attachment to its results. A man should never abandon his dharma.

"The tamasic renunciation is because of ignorance, the rajasic is through fear. But if a man does his duty abandoning its fruit to me, his relinquishment is sattvic.

"The sage of relinquishment does not doubt. He does not shrink from unpleasant action, nor is he drawn to the pleasant. No embodied being can renounce karma completely. But he who relinquishes the fruit of his work is enlightened."

Prakriti

Arjuna, Bheema and Krishna journey to Jarasandha's palace in hilly Girivraja, and arrive in his opulent court at the hour of audience for strangers. They come disguised as three brahmanas, with bodies bare of ornaments, carrying no weapons, their faces masked with holy ashes.

"Great Emperor," says Krishna, "lord of the four quarters, grant a wish to three wandering mendicants."

Jarasandha sees the muscled forearms of these 'brahmanas' marked with the abrasions of bowstrings. He sees the nobility of their proud features beneath the ash. He hears their voices of habitual authority, and he knows they are kshatriya warriors. Moreover, he is certain he has seen them before, specially the dark, lithe one who is their leader.

But then, didn't Mahabali welcome Vishnu when He came disguised as a brahmana Dwarf, asking for three paces of land? Mahabali of old was Jarasandha's hero. The master of Magadha reveres the ancient king of Kerala, the virtuous demon fabled as the archetypal sovereign.

Mahabali stood up to Vishnu and prevailed morally, in legend, though Vishnu slew him by deceit. Jarasandha likes to see himself as a modern Bali, standing up heroically to the vagaries of God, now born as Krishna.

Of course, there is no place in this reckoning for the ninety-nine kings imprisoned in darkness and filth below his city, whom he intends to offer as human sacrifice at Siva's altar, to make a rill of their blood.

But seeing these palpably fake brahmanas before him, the lord of Magadha thinks, irrationally, "I will give them even my life, if they want it."

A man tired of his power and his life, a king anxious to be released from himself, he senses that his chance of escape has come to him. Jarasandha cries impulsively, "Brahmanas, ask anything you like of me. You can have my head if you want."

Krishna says quietly, "We didn't come to beg for food; we are kshatriyas seeking battle. I am Krishna, your enemy, and these are the Pandavas, Arjuna and Bheema. We want single combat with you. Choose any of us for your opponent, if you dare."

Jarasandha begins to laugh; a silent shaking of his enormous body, which turns quickly to echoing peals.

His deep eyes smouldering, the monarch of Magadha says, "Cowherd, I will not fight a coward who abandoned Mathura and fled into the sea. Your puny Arjuna is not my equal in age or strength.

Bheema, too, is no match for me; but since you have come at the hour of alms, and since you insist, I will fight him." He holds up a warning finger, "Let both your kingdoms be forfeit when he dies."

Krishna nods assent. Jarasandha claps his hands and calls for maces, huge gadas. He gives one to Bheema and hefting another, leads the way outside his city gates to an arena of grass shaved close for combat.

Jarasandha and Bheema circle each other slowly at first, manoeuvering carefully, and smashing out with skill and power. Soon they fight like two bull-elephants in the heart of the jungle, with weird cries, earthshaking roars, and reverberant laughter.

The first maces are quickly smashed. Another pair is fetched, as the people gather thickly around the immense duellists. These weapons are shattered in just two blows. And another set, and another, and five more; until, with a yell, Bheema rushes at the Magadhan with his bare hands.

"It is a better fight than I thought it would be!" cries Jarasandha, matching the Pandava's stunning blows.

Then, the three hours stipulated for the duel are over. Conches blare, the warriors and their attendants embrace each other and return to the city and the king's palace—for nightlong revelry, and the civil and drunken exchange of pleasantries and insults.

Later that night, awash on Jarasandha's hospitality, Arjuna says wryly to Krishna, "This enemy is a better host than many kinsmen."

Full of the best wine, cosseted by lovely women from Jarasandha's harem, Krishna agrees with a laugh, "I hope Bheema kills him slowly, over many days."

So it turns out. For twenty-six days, the two titans set on each other for three hours every day. Come evening they return to the palace, bruised and bloody, and more exhilarated than ever: to dice, wine, song, dancing, uninhibited gaiety, and luscious women all vying with each other, especially for Krishna's favours.

He confesses to Arjuna, "I now see how this demon commands such loyalty. Twenty-six days, and still this great generosity. He is a kshatriya!"

But on the twenty-seventh day, Krishna calls Bheema to him at the crack of dawn. Bheema has grown strangely close to Jarasandha, as if they are tied together with invisible bonds by the fight to the death they wage, day after day.

"Today it must end," says Krishna to his cousin. "Watch me when I signal you, because there is only one way to kill Jarasandha. Tomorrow is the day of the new moon, when his kind is at their strongest. He will kill you tomorrow, if you don't kill him today. I know how his foster-mother Jara gave him life, and I know how he can be killed. It is time the earth was relieved of this burden."

That morning, five sets of maces are soon shattered. The king and the Pandava circle each other, more wary now, ever slower to make a move, each conserving his waning energy. Then, unaccountably, Bheema begins to feel stronger, as if someone outside himself were transferring great strength to him.

From the corner of his eye he glances at Krishna, who stands languidly by, picking his teeth with the tip of a long blade of grass. Krishna smiles and winks. Just before he passes out of Bheema's vision, Krishna holds the blade of grass up in front of him and tears it in two along its length.

Jarasandha's name meant 'joined by Jara'. King Brihadratha of Magadha once had a son born in two halves. He was abandoned by his twin mothers, both the king's wives, who ate two halves of an apple that a rishi gave them to cure their barrenness.

Jara the rakshasi found the two parts, joined them together with sorcery, creating Jarasandha. The rishi's potent blessing ensured that no Deva or Asura, or even Avatara, could kill him. He could only be slain by a mortal man and that too, most unusually.

The extraordinary strength in Bheema's arms grows. Jarasandha glares at him, suspicious that the Pandava has been hiding his best strength all this while; but the emperor is confident of wearing Bheema down, if not today then tomorrow, when the new moon would swell his own strength a hundred-fold. Meanwhile, he is inexhaustible, and he is certain Bheema will never discover his secret, the only way he can be killed.

Jarasandha does not see Krishna's signal to Bheema with the blade of grass. Bheema himself takes a moment to understand. Then, the

Pandava darts low and seizes the Magadhan's ankles. Now with so much more speed than the king believes he has, Bheema trips Jarasandha to the ground. Before he can recover, Vayu's Pandava son jumps on to his chest.

In a blur, Bheema rips the demon in two from the fork of his legs, just the way Krishna tore the blade of grass. Jarasandha's faeces, heart, liver, spleen, all his innards, spill bloody and steaming on to the trampled green arena. There is not even time for the Magadhan to scream, so swiftly does Bheema kill him.

Krishna cries out wildly in triumph, even as he had when Kamsa died. He runs forward to hug Bheema. The mysterious strength of the day deserts the Pandava and he collapses on to the ground out of Krishna's embrace, unsure whether he is happy or sad that he has killed Jarasandha. Bheema sleeps for a week.

With no fuss, Krishna installs Jarasandha's eldest son, another Sahadeva, on the throne of Magadha. At last his most implacable enemy is dead, and the alliance of Evil is headless again. Krishna knows his own time is drawing near. He will fight no more great battles himself, but others will in his place and in his name.

A hundred kshatriyas, who were to have been sacrificed on the night of the new moon, are freed from the foetid dungeons of Girivraja. They see Krishna resplendent and four-armed, fall at his feet, overwhelmed, and vow their allegiance for ever, to him and to Yudhishtira.

Back at the gates of Indraprastha, Bheema, Arjuna and Krishna sound their war conches together in ringing triumph that shakes the city walls. Yudhishtira comes out exultantly to welcome them, knowing that Jarasandha, emperor of Evil, is no more in the world.

FORTY-SIX

Purusha *Anishtam ishtam mishram...*

"*Pleasant, unpleasant and mixed* are the fruits of action, each in its season. But those who are detached reap no fruit at all, in this world or the next.

"The Vedanta says there are five participants in any deed: the body, the ego, the senses, the motions of life in the body, and providence the fifth. Any karma, of speech, of deed, or of mind, good or evil, is caused by these five.

"He who thinks that he is the one who acts is deluded. But the man who is detached, untainted by egoism, who acts naturally, perfectly, no deed binds him with any bond. Though he kill thousands, he is no killer."

Prakriti

Headless once more with the killing of Jarasandha, as it was after Kamsa's death, the alliance of Evil is in disarray. Its heroes like Sishupala, Salva, and Dantavakra are in a panic.

Pale Sishupala, the 'Bull of Chedi', is the cousin of Krishna and the Pandavas as his mother Srutadevi is Vasudeva's youngest sister.

Sishupala was born an unnatural, outsized infant, white as a sheet, and with four arms and three eyes. He made no remotely human sound when he was a baby. Instead, he brayed like a little donkey.

When the priests in his court told his father that the birth of the freak was an evil omen, king Damagosha thought of doing away with the monstrous child.

But one night a heavenly voice spoke to him and his queen, "This child brings you no harm. Even if you abandon him, he will not die. For he is destined to die only at the hands of the one born to kill him."

Sishupala's mother cried, "How will I know my son's killer?"

The voice said, "The child's third eye will vanish when it sees him; and its superfluous arms will disapper when it sits on his lap."

Krishna remembers going to visit his freakish cousin in Chedi, soon after he was born. He remembers how Sishupala's third eye had disappeared as soon as he saw the Dark One; and how two of his thick, uncouth arms vanished when Krishna took him onto his lap.

For the first time, as if his cousin's very touch made him less bestial, little Sishupala cried in a human child's voice.

Sishupala's mother was as anxious as she was delighted. She wept that day, and said, "Krishna, promise me that if my son gives you any offence, you will forgive him for my sake."

Putting his arm around his aunt, laughing, Krishna promised, "For your sake, I will pardon him a hundred times. He is my little cousin, after all."

But when Damagosha heard what had happened, he thought the promise of a hundred pardons was facile. Next to Krishna, Jarasandha was the most powerful kshatriya on earth, and he was Krishna's mortal enemy. When Sishupala was twelve, Damaghosha sent him to Jarasandha in Magadha to be his protege.

Jarasandha welcomed the fierce-looking youth with a great embrace. "A fine boy!" he roared. "I will make you into a lion among men."

In Magadha, Sishupala first met Rukmi of Vidarbha. The two became like brothers at archery lessons and during Jarasandha's masterly instructions on the subversive secrets of statecraft and kingship.

In Magadha, Rukmi offered his sister Rukmini's hand, uncontested, to his friend Sishupala, who was smitten by her, loving her to distraction at first sight. Unwittingly, Rukmi sowed the seed of a life-long, obsessive hatred, which sprouted when Krishna abducted Rukmini on her wedding day.

In every battle Jarasandha fought against Krishna, Sishupala, once he was a man, fought at the Magadhan's side. Time after time, Krishna spared his cousin's life.

On countless occasions, Sishupala was in the eye of the Avatara's arrow and, remembering his aunt and his promise to her, Krishna turned his hand away. Countless times, Sishupala was at Balarama's mercy. Each time, Krishna persuaded his brother to spare their cousin, despite the filthy, hate-filled abuse he hurled at them.

Confident, cocky even, that his cousins would not harm him, no matter what, Sishupala used up most of the hundred pardons Krishna had promised his mother. He bragged that Krishna was afraid of him, but Krishna kept count of the number of times he spared Sishupala.

When Bheema arrived at the gates of Chedi after killing Jarasandha, he was taken aback at the reception he received. His notoriously recalcitrant cousin welcomed him, crying, "Great Bheema, my kingdom is yours!"

Bheema was surprised that Krishna's fiercest surviving enemy submitted so easily to Yudhishtira's sovereignty. For a month Bheema stayed in Chedi, enjoying Sishupala's lavish hospitality.

Finally, when he was leaving he insisted that, as such a fond cousin, Sishupala must attend Yudhishtira's Rajasuya yagna. Sishupala, now ostensibly part of the Padavas' new empire, said how could he not?

Vyasa's enlightened son, Suka, says the time draws near when the old forces of Evil on earth passed on, and the mantle of night fell on the shoulders of Duryodhana, the Kaurava. But men are blind to destiny. Neither Sishupala nor Salva, not Dantavakra, not even Duryodhana himself gauges what is afoot—the spirit of the times.

It is a period of profound turbulence and change, the time of Yudhishtira's Rajasuya yagna.

FORTY-SEVEN

Purusha *Buddher bhedam dhriteshchava...*

"*There are three kinds of conscience*, and three kinds of happiness. "The sattvic intellect knows right from wrong, what is safe and what is dangerous. It knows discrimination and relinquishment, what binds the spirit, and what frees it. The rajasic intellect cannot clearly tell wrong from right, what to do and what not to. And when a man's conscience tells him wrong is right, that evil is goodness, and distorts the world, it is tamasic.

"So too with happiness, Partha. The man who knows the atman has the joy of pure knowledge, like poison at first, and then ambrosial at the end: the joy of sattva, the end of sorrow. The joy of rajas is of the senses that unite with the things of sense: sweet in the beginning, deadly at last. The warped pleasure, which deludes the soul at both beginning and end, bestial satisfaction born of stupor and sloth, is tamasic, always fatal.

"Arjuna, there is no being on earth, none among the Devas of heaven, who is free of the gunas of Prakriti."

Prakriti

Spring comes to Indraprastha, the season for the imperial sacrifice. All the kings subdued by the Pandavas have arrived in that city, where the most illustrious rishis will conduct Yudhishtira's Rajasuya yagna.

Vyasa is here, Bharadavaja, Narada, Sumantu, Gautama, Asita, Vasishta, Chyvana, Kanva, Maitreya, Kavasa, Trita, Vishvamitra, Parasara, Kashyapa, Virasena and a hundred others out of Devaloka, not yet sealed from the earth by the kali yuga.

The people have turned out in crowds: brahmanas, kshatriyas, vaisyas and sudras, from every station and walk of life.

With golden ploughs, the munis turn the earth where they will worship the Gods with oblations, and then consecrate Yudhishtira as emperor and sacrificer. The Devas of light grace the yagna. Indra is here, Agni and Vayu, awesome and splendid. Besides them, siddhas and gandharvas, vidyadharas, holy nagas, rishis, yakshas, rakshasas, Garuda and his eagles, kinnaras, charanas and all the immortal ones have come.

The vessels used at the sacrifice are of gold: the very ones Varuna used during his Rajasuya of antiquity, in the pristine krita yuga now no more than the shadow of a sacred memory on earth.

The yagna unfolds solemnly and with order, until the day arrives for the extraction of the Soma rasa. Today, they must decide who in that congregation should receive first worship. Yudhishtira is silent. As the sacrificer he doesn't want to be the one who proposes the name he longs to speak.

At last, it is the youngest Pandava, Sahadeva, who jumps up and cries, "Who but Krishna? He is the yagna, the agni and the yoga!"

To Yudhishtira's surprise, all the assembled support this suggestion. "Sadhu, Krishna!" they chant, even Indra and the Devas, and, "Jaya, Krishna!"

Yudhishtira washes Krishna's feet with holy water, and sprinkles the sanctified water over his head and the heads of his queens, his brothers, ministers and his family. Ceremonially, he offers Krishna yellow silken robes, and priceless ornaments. As he does this, his eyes are so blinded by tears that he can't see the Blue One clearly. Iridescent flowers fall out of Devaloka, the spirit realm.

Despite himself, even the bull-like Sishupala has been deeply moved by the great sacrifice. He notices that Salva and Dantavakra are conspicuously absent from the sabha of kings.

But when Krishna is chosen to receive the purodasa, Sishupala begins to quiver with resentment. When Yudhishtira kneels before Krishna and worships him, the lord of Chedi can't bear it any more.

"Stop!" he cries, springing to his feet.

"It seems the elders of this sabha have lost their wits. How else could they heed the prating of an ignorant boy like Sahadeva? How in this company of rishis established in Brahman, in this sabha graced by the Devas, can a cowherd and a disgrace to his clan, have such honour?"

He loses all restraint, and insult after insult flares hotly off his tongue.

"He belongs to no varna of society or asrama of life. He isn't nobly born. He is an outcast from every dharma. He is wanton and a drunkard. His family has been cursed by Yayati. How does he merit this worship? How can any Yadava deserve such reverence? They fled Mathura, and cower in a citadel at sea—Dwaraka."

He hawks in contempt.

"Dwaraka where no Vedas are read, where no brahmanas live; but from where these cowards terrorize the kshatriyas of the earth."

Sishupala is shaking. Krishna sits very quiet, a thin smile playing on his lips. The Pandavas spring up to stop the Bull of Chedi. But with the fearlessness of the unhinged, he cries at them, "Shame on you, Kshatriyas! You draw your swords against your own blood for the sake of an upstart cowboy."

His voice has turned strange. It is a bray once more, as when he was born. But at this last taunt, Krishna rises as if to a signal, with the Sudarshana burning over his finger.

"You have wasted a hundred pardons, Sishupala."

The Dark One flicks his wrist, and in a blur and a scream, the nitid Chakra takes off Sishupala's head pale as lilies. His blood, startling red against his fair skin, gushes on to sanctified ground in the midst of Yudhishtira's Rajasuya yagna. Deafening thunder, peal after peal, rends the sky.

A handful of kings from Jarasandha's old alliance slips away hastily, terrified by the Avatara's cool justice. As soon as they have gone, as if miracles will not happen before the cursed, a light, of a soul, issues from dead Sishupala's chest. Like a comet, it flashes into Krishna.

Krishna laughs softly. Urbane as ever, he says, "He thought of me so much while he lived, that my cousin Sishupala is now with me for ever."

FORTY-EIGHT

Purusha *Karmaani. pravibhaktaani...*

"Arjuna, *each man's inner nature ordains* his dharma, his duty. Brahmana and kshatriya, vaisya and sudra, each has his innate prakritic dharma.

"The brahmana's dharma is to know the atman, to be serene, self-controlled and pure; the kshatriya's to be battle-skilled, fearless, generous and resolute; the vaisya's to breed cattle, to till the earth, to trade; and to serve other men, the dharma of the sudra.

"But all men are born equal, and equally for perfection. And each shall find it if he follows his nature's dharma.

"A man worships God when he respects the call of his own nature, and so reaches perfection. It is better to live by one's own dharma, however imperfectly, than in the dharma of another, even immaculately. For, there is no sin in following one's own true nature.

"As to imperfection, all action is clouded with imperfection, as fire is with smoke. But that isn't cause to give up one's natural duty, nor reason to stop worshipping God or to stop seeking Him."

Prakriti

For the avabhritha-snana, the closing ceremonial bath of the Rajasuya yagna, Krishna goes alone to the Ganga. The old conspiracy of Evil is shattered beyond repair; and maddened by the news of Sishupala's death, a desperate Dantavakra confronts Krishna at the river's side, mace in hand, eyes slitted with hatred.

"Traitor! You've killed Paundraka and Sishupala. You are a disease in our family, and I will finish you now."

As Krishna turns his back to lift his own weapon from his chariot, Dantavakra swings his mace down on his head. But the heavy thing smashes to dust against the peacock feathers that deck Krishna's crown.

Krishna strikes Dantavakra with the Kaumodaki, shattering his chest, blood spurting richly through his mouth and nose. Dantavakra falls with a sigh. From his body too, by the undulating Ganga, a dazzling light courses into the Blue God.

Krishna bathes, and returns to the yagnashala.

All the other guests follow the Pandava emperor and his empress to the river, all the kings and queens, the common people and the rishis, to bathe together ritually. All save Sishupala, who is dead, and another in whose heart a seed is sown that fateful day.

Duryodhana is not happy. He cannot bear to see the opulence and power of his cousin, Pandu's son Yudhishtira, whom he had once exiled from Hastinapura into a wilderness. The treasure that Duryodhana secretly covets most is the wife of the five Pandavas: the dark and peerless Draupadi.

After the Rajasuya, even as he swaggers into the Mayaa sabha in Indraprastha, making a grand entrance, his eyes stray towards her whom his devious heart can never resist. Before he came, he swore to himself he wouldn't so much as look at her. But in her presence, he is helpless.

Krishna smiles to himself. The subtle Lotus hidden in every heart, he stokes that fire with deep magic.

Because his eyes never leave Draupadi's face, Duryodhana trips over his own feet when he mistakes the crystal floor of the court of marvels for a pool of water. Then, he falls headlong into a real and cunning pool that he takes for the shining floor.

Bheema roars with laughter, and the women of the court titter with him. Yudhishtira raises a hand to stop them, but the dark and divine guest of honour also begins to laugh infectiously. The other kings gather round and laugh as well.

Duryodhana clambers out of the pool, red-faced and dripping, and no one comes forward to help him. Most of all, Draupadi's clear laughter burns him like smoking oil in his ears.

Trembling with shame, Duryodhana stalks out from Indraprastha. Appalled, the gentle Yudhishtira turns to Krishna. But Krishna looks away.

On that day, when he was humiliated, Duryodhana, though he doesn't realise it at once, inherits an ancient mantle of Evil, one worn by Kamsa and Jarasandha before him.

And Krishna smiles. He knows he has pushed the Kaurava over the edge of hatred, and sown the seed of the war of Kurukshetra. More than any other, that war will lighten the burden of the earth, spinning dizzily now into the kali yuga.

The Mahabharata yuddha will destroy the power of the race of kshatriyas for ever, and let in the new age.

FORTY-NINE

Purusha *Siddhim prapto yatha Brahmam...*

"Listen, Arjuna, *to how the perfect man is one with Brahman.*
"His mind and heart are free of delusion, full of compassion. His
senses are subdued, naturally, by the steady exercise of will and without
regret. He seeks solitude, eats little, speaks less, and is always meditating
on the Brahman, the truth.

"Vanity has gone from him. He has abandoned violence, lust, anger,
and all his possessions, which once possessed him. Serene, he is fit to
be with Brahman.

"He who is with Brahman, quiescent, past sorrow, past craving, all
beings the same to him, he loves me dearly.

"To love me is to know the inmost truth that I am; knowing me is to enter
into my being. Everything that man does is offered to me in total surrender,
and my grace is upon him. He finds the eternal, the place unchanging."

Prakriti

After the Rajasuya yagna, Yudhishtira was loth to let Krishna return to
Dwaraka; and, when the other Pandavas also implored him to stay, the
Dark One agreed to spend some more time in Indraprastha. For they
would be his standard-bearers, his warriors of truth during the war upon
the turn of the ages.

While Krishna was away, Salva, sorcerer of the old conspiracy, laid siege to Dwaraka. When he heard that the last of his friends, Sishupala and Dantavakra, were dead, Salva swore he would annihilate the Yadava clan, and Krishna and Dwaraka with it.

He prayed to Siva, and the Lord gave this old bhakta a rare gift. When he was still a young man, Salva had once actually renounced his kingdom and worshipped Sankara for many years as a solitary hermit in a jungle's heart. Now Siva gave Salva a glittering, silver and black flying disk, big as a town, swift as light, with which he could attack Dwaraka from the sky.

Siva gave Salva the Saubha, a vimana armed with every kind of weapon. Shrouded in its own darkness, flying obedient to Salva's every thought, invincible against Devas, Asuras, men, gandharvas, nagas and rakshasas, the Saubha negotiated land, air and water with equal ease.

With an army for support, Salva laid siege to the citadel in the ocean. Hovering low in the Saubha like a malefic planet over Dwaraka, he razed parks and gardens, towers, gates, mansions and palaces with occult thunderbolts and twisting gales.

Pradyumna led a Yadava force out to face Salva's army by land. A savage battle was joined. The intrepid Yadavas quickly established their supremacy on the ground.

But Siva's flying disk was another matter. It had a magical structure, so that at times it appeared as one giant craft, while at others as many smaller ones; and it was not always visible.

Gada, Satyaki, Akrura, Samba, Suka, Ugrasena and the other Yadus decimated Salva's land army in rage. But Salva ruled the air from the Saubha. He rained down fiery narachas and screaming shaktis on the ocean-city. Flaming missiles swallowed whole mansions in a moment, leaving no stone of which they had been made.

Other unseen beams dried up Dwaraka's lotus pools, and blazed holes in the city's foundations so the sea surged into her streets from below. Salva was determined to fight to the end; and even with most of his army destroyed, he himself seemed invincible.

Meanwhile, bidding farewell to the Pandavas, Krishna has finally left Indraprastha. Halfway along the road to Dwaraka he sees evil omens all around him.

"Dwaraka is besieged," he cries to his sarathy. "Daruka, fly!"

Krishna finds his precious city devastated. Eerie serpents lie hissing in his lily-pools. Towers and domes of crystal have been smashed down; palaces have vanished. In the streets flow lava streams.

His son Samba rides out to tell him of Salva's aerial assault, and remnants of the land-battle still smoulder outside the city-gates. Dazzled by Pradyumna in a chariot by land and in the air as well, Salva has hidden his ship of war under the sea. He is saving himself for Krishna. It is the Blue God he has come to kill.

Hiding submerged, he sees Krishna take to the sky in his own chariot. Parting the waves, Salva rises from the deeps. He looses a macabre shakti at Daruka. But unmoved by the thought-like speed of the Saubha, Krishna shatters the recondite missile in flight. He covers the Saubha with a storm of golden tracers from the Saringa, that darken the sky with their trails.

But from the gleaming body of the flying disk flares another shakti, howling like a devil. It plucks the Saringa out of Krishna's hand and carries the divine longbow to the sea below, down below the waves, into deep vaults.

"Stupid cowherd!" screams Salva across the sky. "You stole his bride on his wedding day, and now you've murdered Sishupala. I mean to send you straight to hell."

Salva swoops on Krishna out of the sun. But Krishna flings a mace at him, striking him on his chest. The asura is now revealed in an inhuman form, yellow eyes burning among fiendish features. He screeches and spits up dark blood. Suddenly he disappears from the sky, disk and all.

Krishna brings his own chariot down outside Dwaraka. There he sees a messenger come hotfoot and panting out of the city.

"Your mother sent me, Krishna!" Krishna sees the man is in tears. "Salva has taken your father captive."

Krishna cries out. "Where is Balarama? Where are Pradyumna and Samba?" He hangs his head in swift despair. "Ah, Providence is stronger than I am."

Salva descends on that beach in the Saubha. Tall and lean, he steps down from the shining craft. He is half-human, half a sulphurous beast. He wears black silk from head to foot, and comes dragging Vasudeva behind him, with a curved blade glinting at his throat.

Before Krishna can say a word, Salva cries in his harsh whisper of a voice, "Save your father now if you can, cowherd."

With a clean stroke of his sword, he hews off Vasudeva's head. He holds it aloft, spouting blood at the neck, while the body tumbles twitching on to damp sand.

Krishna runs forward with a cry, but Salva scrambles back into the Saubha. He flies up, carrying Vasudeva's head with him and laughing maniacally.

Krishna bends sobbing over his father's headless trunk. He tries to take the torso, still spasming on scarlet sands, in his arms. He gives a cry of surprise; his father's body vanishes when he touches it. The messenger from his mother is mysteriously gone as well. They were both unreal, made only of Salva's formidable maya. From above, wafts down another howl of laughter.

"God himself are you?" mocks Salva.

"Human as well, Salva!" roars Krishna, climbing back into his chariot.

Up he flies, after the sorcerer-king in his flashing disk. Krishna materializes the Sudarshana over his finger, and charges it with an agneyastra. With a sky-shaking God's roar, he looses it at the vimana. The Chakra cuts the Saubha in half and it falls away into the sea.

Cursing and spluttering, but still charged by hatred, Salva swims ashore. Mounting a chariot on the ground, he rides at Krishna again. But the Dark One stands implacable before him, his hand raised above his head as if he carried a lamp on a dark night. The Sudarshana is rutilant over his finger. Krishna stands on that twilight beach like the eastern mountain with the sun rising on its summit.

The Blue God flicks his wrist forward, and the last of Jarasandha's kings of Evil falls headless on to the waiting earth.

FIFTY

Purusha *Drashtum icchaami te rupam...*

Krishna felt a great war already won within himself. He knew he had not been abandoned, only tested: his humanity tried against inhuman evil. He felt fulfilled, whole again, man and God at once, with no conflict between the two. Suddenly, his old burning was gone for good.

He drew in the cool, rain-washed air deeply. Most of what he had come for was accomplished. The ocean swelled in him again, but now with no torment cresting its tide.

Radiant with faith, Arjuna said, "You have dispelled my confusion. I feel my battles already fought and won. I know that whatever you have said to me is true, but Krishna, *I want to see your Viswarupa.* Lord, if you think I deserve that revelation, show me your immortal Self."

The armies vanished from Kurukshetra; the world vanished from Kurukshetra. Only the Blue God stood smiling before Arjuna.

"You cannot see me with your human eyes, but I will give you divine sight. See my forms a hundred-fold, a thousand-fold, endless. See the adityas, the vasus, the rudras, the asvins, the maruts. Here, today, see the universe. *Arjuna, behold Me!"*

And Krishna stood forth, transformed before his devotee: speaking from many mouths, seeing with numberless eyes, of endless visions and marvels, with countless jewels and weapons, wearing divine garments and garlands, unearthly perfumes, relucent, boundless. His face was turned everywhere, the nebulae were his ornaments. If a thousand suns rose together into the sky, their light might approach the splendour of that Being.

Arjuna saw all the universe with his gifted sight, its eternity gathered in One, in the body of the God of Gods. His hair stood on end, the Pandava fell on his knees.

"Lord, I see all the Gods and all the hosts in your body. I see Brahma on his lotus throne, the rishis and the heavenly nagas. I see you with numberless arms, bellies, mouths and eyes. But I don't see your end, your middle, or your beginning, O cosmic, infinite One!

"I see you with your crown, mace and wheel. You are the light of lights, incomparable," cried Arjuna in ecstasy and, also, terror verging on death. "The moon and sun are your eyes, your face is an eternal fire whose brilliance burns up the universe.

"The void of space between the stars is full of you. The three worlds are in awe of this form of yours, and I tremble seeing you shouldering the sky, blazing in more colours than I had dreamt could be.

"O, Vishnu, this vision of you fills me with fear. I see your mouths, terrible with tusks, full of Time's consuming flames, and I quail. Be gracious, Lord of Gods, sanctuary of the galaxies.

"I see not just my enemies and my friends, but all men, all mankind, fly helplessly like moths into your flaming jaws. Lord, I see the worlds, the deep constellations, spinning into your yawning mouths, and you licking them up.

"Have mercy, O Godhead, I know nothing of thee."

God said in thunder, "Time am I, waster of worlds. Fight or stay your hand, no matter: all these kshatriyas shall die in me. For that I am come. So, take up your weapons. Win glory by vanquishing your enemies; enjoy a kingdom, Savyasachin, ambidextrous bowman.

"I have already slain your foes; now you must be my instrument. Kill Drona, Bheeshma, Jayadratha, Karna, and the rest, whom I have already condemned. Fear nothing. Fight, and you will conquer."

Laying his face in the grass, Arjuna prostrated himself at the Vision's feet. He breathed, "O Krishna, it is well that the world worships you. I understand it now. Hail, hail to you. A thousand times hail. I have spoken rashly to you in the past, thinking of you as only my cousin. Not knowing who you really are, I called you Krishna, Yadava, or friend.

"Father of worlds, I beg your forgiveness. Dear God, bear with me as a father with his son, as a friend with a friend, as a lover with his love. I can't bear this vision of you. Be as you were before, just four-armed, O thousand-membered!"

God said, "My love has shown you this primal form of fire that no one else in the world has ever seen before. Not by the Vedas, not by sacrifice or study, not by the greatest penance will my Viswarupa be seen in the world of men by anyone but you. But look, and don't be afraid."

Again, Krishna, his friend, stood smiling and gracious before Arjuna, and gently pulled the Pandava to his feet.

Red-faced, hands still folded, Arjuna panted, "O, Lord! I am quiet again."

The panic drained out of his body and his soul, though he still shook where he stood. And Krishna himself knew again the final purpose of the tormented incarnation—*that it was to allay the terror of man faced with pure and absolute Godhead.*

He said, "Even the Devas, Arjuna, are always eager to see me as you just did. Only by bhakti can I be seen like that."

He embraced the shaking warrior. "He who worships me, he who has no enmity with any creature, he comes to me, O Prince."

The sun broke from behind clouds over the field of Kurukshetra. Once more, Arjuna heard the clamour of the two armies, impatient for battle.

Prakriti

Krishna is lonely, as his end draws near. He is deeply tired. The moonlit and the dark nights all burn him; though he lies with sixteen thousand lovely women in the uncanny dimension of Dwaraka that is his antapura.

Balarama has gone away on a pilgrimage to the ancient tirthas, to the corners of the holy land. Krishna knows his brother is also exhausted by this incarnation, sick of the life of war, and blood spilt on a hundred battlefields.

Balarama is unhappy about Krishna's subtle machinations that are bringing relations between their cousins, the Pandavas and the Kauravas, to a head.

Blind Dhritarashtra banished the Pandavas, who were the rightful heirs to the throne of Hastinapura. He gave them a desolate place in the wilderness for their patrimony. And there Krishna raised fabulous Indraprastha for them with his power.

Then, at a loaded game of dice, the sons of Pandu were exiled to the forest for thirteen years. Now they have returned after their long travail, and mean to have their kingdom back.

Balarama senses the greatest war of the age, the final one, drawing near. In deference to his promise to Duryodhana, he goes away on his tirtha-yatra, leaving Krishna alone and restless in Dwaraka.

Thirteen years have passed after Yudhishtra's Rajasuya yagna. Duryodhana is entrenched at the head of Evil on earth. All Jarasandha's lesser allies—those left alive and the sons of the dead ones—have come together under the ruthless Kaurava's lead.

The time is ripe for the last war of the age, the apocalyptic Mahabharata yuddha. After this war, the world will close in darkness and be as an island of sin in the universe.

Left alone in Dwaraka by his brother, Krishna falls into an unprecedented dejection. He takes to stealing from his bed at nights. He haunts the deserted passages and balconies of his palace, abandoning his wives till dawn.

Tormented, he sits out in the dark, listening to the crested waves that dash against the city walls. He gazes up at the night stars and the moon, as if for a sign. But they are mute. Savage doubt has its way with him. The anguish of his unresolved humanness burns him with hellfire.

He knows he has not yet fought his fiercest battle on earth, the purest one: of only the spirit. It lies in wait for him like a beast of prey, always round the corner of the next day.

Perhaps on Kurukshetra, he thinks; but that vision is opaque. He sees nothing with any clarity of the final war, out on the cleft between the yugas; the one he must fight as just a man, the one he must fight in his own soul. Yet, he knows it is nearer than he dares believe: the war on the cusp of the ages, which will destroy kshatriya kind.

Then, Arjuna and Duryodhana come to Dwaraka to ask on whose side he will fight. The Pandavas and the Kauravas are determined to have war between them.

Krishna says, "One of you can have my army and the other can have me, but just as your charioteer. I will not carry arms or strike a blow during the war."

Without hesitation, Arjuna asks the Dark One to be his sarathy. Duryodhana is pleased to have the Yadava army. Krishna knows beyond doubt that his last war, for which he must become just a man, will indeed be fought on the field of the Kurus.

He walks out under the canopy of fateful stars, out on to the empty streets of Dwaraka. At daybreak, the people find him asleep in one of the parks or gardens, curled up against the cold night and the dew.

He drinks more wine than ever, insisting his queens stay up and drink with him, as much as they can. But they soon fall asleep, and he is left to his own devices, his raging insomnia, his yawning visions of darkness and light, blinding him, searing him until the blue of his skin is burned almost black.

Like a dark sun risen from the sea by night, Krishna haunts his city. He fears the maya that is the secret of his human form may dissolve with his monstrous pain, and kill him before his time has come. Before Kurukshetra, before … ah, the pain is intolerable, even for him. It tears into him like the deaths of a hundred generations.

Alone at night, he abandons himself to agony, out on the terraces and among the lily-pools of Dwaraka, twisting on the ground like an epileptic. His cries are wafted out to sea between midnight and dawn, cries of the ravaged Incarnation; while, by his grace, the city sleeps.

What can they do for him, anyway? Except watch him, themselves helpless and terrified, watch him naked-souled like this, their invincible Krishna, so human, so bereft.

FIFTY-ONE

Purusha *Chetasaa sarvakarmaani...*

"*Consecrate whatever you do to me*; think of me as your dearest loved one. Know that I am your only refuge, be united with me in your heart. When you are with me, I will take you past all sorrow. But if your mind is full of conceit, and you don't listen to me, you will be lost.

"It is your vanity that says 'I will not fight'. You will fight, Arjuna, your own nature will compel you to. You yourself create the karma that binds you. And caught helpless in its web, you will do even what you want to avoid.

"God abides in the hearts of all creatures. He turns them round on the wheel of his maya. Surrender to him, Arjuna. By his grace you will find supreme peace, and the place beyond change."

Prakriti

Then, one day, as if to console Krishna in his most fractured time, fate brings a quaint visitor to the gates of Dwaraka. His hair unkempt, his feet dirty, his body so emaciated his veins stand out like blue grass snakes, he arrives at the city-gates and is stopped by the guards.

He has been sent by his wife, who said to him, "Isn't it true the lord of Dwaraka studied with you in Guru Sandipani's asrama? You are forever talking about your precious Krishna. We are so poor our little girl goes about in rags, and all of us hungry. Why don't you go to Krishna now, in your time of need? They say he is generous to a fault."

At first her husband Sudama, the poor brahmana, was mortified, "Go to a friend for alms?"

Then he heard his daughter crying softly from hunger, and he thought, "Perhaps Krishna himself is calling me."

But then an old anxiety recurred to him, "Suppose Krishna doesn't remember me? He is a great king now."

"That you will have to discover for yourself," said his wife firmly.

"But I have nothing to take for Krishna," said Sudama. "I can't go empty-handed to Dwaraka."

"I have four handfuls of aval, the puffed rice you always marvelled he was so fond of. I'll wrap it in a cloth for you to take."

Sudama set out for Dwaraka, with the aval for his friend tied in a square of cloth, and tucked into his waist. On the long way to the ocean-city, hunger overcame him and he ate two fistfuls of the puffed rice. Then he stopped himself.

"I can't go empty-handed to Krishna."

And the bedraggled brahmana who arrives at last at Dwaraka's gates is also a starving man and faint from his journey.

He staggers up to the guard's post, and tells the soldier weakly, "Please tell Krishna that Sudama has come to see him. I won't take much of his time, I assure you. Just a few moments."

No matter how he tries, the guard cannot send the wretched brahmana away. The fellow squats down on the road at his feet, to wait for him to take his message to the master of Dwaraka. Finally, the exasperated soldier goes to Krishna.

"Did you say Sudama?" the Dark One shouts, seizing the man by his shoulders. "Where? Where?"

Krishna runs through the interminable passages, crying "Sudama! Sudama!" as if he might forget the name, or as if it were nectar in his mouth. At the guard's post, he finds Sudama keeled over on the ground, unconscious.

Tears springing in his eyes, Krishna picks up the brahmana in his arms and carries him, all skin and bones, into the palace. He lays him on his own bed, waving away the other guardsmen who now spring forward to help. Lovingly he washes Sudama's feet, and sprinkles his own head with the water! He wants this story told among the arrogant.

"Oh, Sudama, Sudama, what have you done to yourself?" croons Krishna.

Rukmini knows all about his friend from her husband. Chowrie in hand, she fans the half-naked brahmana.

The women of the harem whisper to one another, "He rose and ran from Rukmini's side, when he heard the beggar's name."

"Cast aside as worthless by the world, but Krishna welcomes him as if he is his elder brother."

Finally, Sudama opens his eyes, smiles wanly at Krishna and whispers, "So you did remember me, after all," and promptly falls asleep again.

What reminiscing they do when Sudama wakes! About being stranded all night in a thunderstorm when they were out in the forest gathering firewood for Sandipani's wife. About their friends at the asrama and Krishna's flute, of which the brahmana could never hear enough; and of all, all those fine old days. And soon Sudama makes Krishna play again on his flute, which he hasn't touched for years.

So, on the eve of Kurukshetra, it seems Krishna is granted a reprieve from his anguish by Sudama's arrival. Once the brahmana comes to Dwaraka, the Blue God's harrowing insomnia, his lone vigils in the small hours, are all forgotten. He sleeps unperturbed in the arms of his queens; not even nightmares trouble him now.

Adrift on the sea of memories, and upon Sudama's friendship, Krishna is free of the painful present and its constant, fearful reminder of the thing still to be accomplished—*the war on the split of the ages, the reason he was born.*

It is as if Sudama saves Krishna from himself by coming to Dwaraka. Krishna becomes so absorbed in his friend that he forgets himself, and his own agony.

Those first few days, Sudama eats at Krishna's table as only a man well acquainted with hunger can. Glowing to watch him, Krishna once says jovially, "Brahmana, what have you brought for me from home?"

Involuntarily, Sudama's hand moves to his waist, where the mean parcel of puffed rice nestles like a guilty secret amidst the splendour of Dwaraka. In a flash Krishna wrests the square of cloth from hiding. As he opens it, his eyes grow round.

"Look, Rukmini! Who ever brought me such a gift? Sudama, you almost died of hunger, but you didn't eat the aval you carried for me. O, for every grain of this rarest rice, I will give you a treasure the Devas will envy. You came to me in my time of pain; and make no mistake, your love brought you here. I must reward you for your love, *for you came to me when I was most forsaken.*"

Greedily, Krishna eats the first handful of dry rice, shutting his eyes as if he has never tasted anything to match those parched grains. But when he reaches into the parcel for the second handful, Rukmini seizes his wrist.

Scooping up the remaining rice, she thrusts it into her own mouth, crying, "Don't be so selfish, let me also taste Sudama's aval."

Krishna laughs delightedly, as happy as he has ever been, with one arm around his beloved, the other around his old friend. But Sudama doesn't fail to notice Rukmini's keen taste for aval. Later, when they are alone, he asks Krishna about it. Krishna just laughs and says, perhaps she liked puffed rice as well.

Then, all too soon, it is time for Sudama to go back. Without ever mentioning his plight at home, he tells Krishna one day, "My wife and daughter must miss me. Being with you, I've all but forgotten them. I must not stay any longer, you must let me go."

Krishna calls for his chariot to drive his friend home, and he will not hear any protest from Sudama. A tearful Rukmini asks for the brahmana's blessing, touching his feet. Sudama gives it shyly, blushing, telling Krishna with his look how unnecessary this was.

Krishna embraces Sudama, holds him tightly for a long time, as if to imprint his friend's frail form on his heart. When he releases him, the Avatara's black eyes are full.

Sudama climbs into the chariot, and Daruka drives him out of Dwaraka. The brahmana looks back and keeps waving until they are out of sight, while the wind blows the streaming tears out of his eyes.

On the way, sitting uneasily behind the sarathy in the unaccustomed seat, Sudama thinks, "Like a brother, an elder brother, he treated me. And I wondered if Krishna would remember me. He had Rukmini herself fan me. He washed my feet with his own hands. And, ah, such memories!

"Of course, in his wisdom he knew that if he gave any wealth to an impoverished fellow like me, it would turn my head and ruin me. How gently he avoided the subject of money or gifts, how adroitly, thinking only of how not to hurt me. Truly, there is only one Krishna."

"Sadhu Krishna!" he says aloud, and Daruka the sarathy turns and smiles at him.

Soon enough, they arrive in the small town where Sudama lives. The brahmana is embarrassed at the thought of being seen riding in a royal chariot. He does his best to persuade Daruka to set him down at the edge of the town. But Daruka will have none of it. He says Krishna had told him to see Sudama to his doorstep, and so he would.

Sudama sits crouched as low as he can in Krishna's Jaitra, whispering directions, while Daruka walks his fine horses through the streets, and people stop to stare. But it soon becomes plain that they are, in fact, going round in circles.

"Are you so shy, Brahmana," Daruka says, reining in his horses and laughing, "that you won't show me the way to your home? Are you ashamed of your house?"

"No!" protests Sudama, flustered. "It's around the next corner."

"But we have already driven that way three times."

"I can't understand it," says Sudama, shaking his head. He points, "My hut stood right there."

"Where the palace is now?"

"Yes. The crystal palace."

"Perhaps, you should ask at the palace about your hut?"

"I am nervous of palaces."

"Come now, we can't keep going round in circles. I'll go in with you."

Attended by a score of servants, a lady opens the door of the palace that looks rather like Krishna's in Dwaraka. She wears finery from head to foot, and flashes gold and diamonds, rubies and emeralds, at throat, wrist, and finger. And she is Sudama's wife—mistress of this mansion of a hundred rooms in which she awoke one morning while her husband was away with his friend.

The previous night she had gone to sleep with her daughter in their old mud hut. It was the night Krishna ate the aval.

The wealth of Sudama, the impoverished brahmana, now rivals that of the greatest kings of the earth.

He, of course, is more than a little alarmed by his sudden riches. But when he sees his wife so happy, and nagging him no more, and his daughter delighted with her new clothes and toys, he is mollified.

He remembers how laconically, but with that fathomless look in his eye, Krishna once asked him in Dwaraka, "So have you tied the knot yet, Sudama?"

Only that, but it had meant everything.

In Dwaraka, Krishna chuckles, thinking of Sudama in the lap of all that wealth.

"Like a fish out of water, Sudama out of poverty. But he will grow used to his discomfort, he may even learn to enjoy it for his family's sake."

Rukmini says sharply, "And you were going to eat the second handful also."

Krishna laughs again. He muses, "Yes, so I was. And if I had, you would have become Sudama's too, wouldn't you, my love?"

FIFTY-TWO

Mahabharata *Sarvaguhyataman bhuyah...*

"Now you know the wisdom that is *the secret of secrets*. Think carefully on it, and then do as you decide. These are my last words to you for now, the deepest of truths. You are the friend I chose and love, and I speak for your good," said Krishna, infinite tenderness welling in him.

"Give me your heart, love me, worship me always, and you shall find me. This I promise, who love you more than you can imagine. Abandon all your karma to me; I am your sanctuary. And fear no more, I will save you from sin and from bondage.

"Arjuna, you must never tell this holy truth to anyone who has no restraint or devotion, who hates his guru, or mocks me. But the man who loves me, and teaches my bhaktas this supreme secret of the Gita, will surely come to me. If any man meditates on this song of ours, I will know he has worshipped me in spirit. Why, the man who just listens to it with faith and without contempt, will be set free from his sins and reach the heaven of the just."

His deep hour over, his battle of the spirit won, Krishna embraced his cousin. Kurukshetra resounded again with conches, kettle-drums and tabors. The river of light, the song of God, swollen like a sea in his heart, enfolded in his cousin's vast calm, Arjuna stood forth at peace with himself.

Krishna said, "Have you heard with your soul what I have said, Arjuna? Have I put out your darkness?"

The Pandava replied serenely, "By your grace my doubts have ended. I will do as you say."

Krishna looked at Arjuna, and wondered.

Krishna's own song was sung, for now and ever. He himself was delivered of his burden by it. He was made human and whole, his lonely hour fulfilled. But he wondered if, when faced with his kin, Arjuna would truly aim to kill; and the eyes of the Blue Lotus of the world twinkled at his cousin.

Krishna turned his chariot back to the armies. He bore Arjuna into the greatest war of the age, the one that would ruin kshatriya kind.

The battle of Kurukshetra began with a deafening clash of weapons, and men fell in their thousands, while death danced there horrific and celebrant. The chariot of Arjuna the Pandava flew at the Kaurava army like a wrathful wind.

His sarathy, the Avatara, drove his white horses in a quiet frenzy of perfection. They rained arrows on him, and some pierced his blue skin like fire. But never stopping the chariot, which flew a banner of Hanuman, Krishna plucked the shafts out with one hand, holding his reins in the other.

Just as he had expected, Arjuna's hand faltered at his bowstring whenever he faced a kinsman. Bheeshma cut down their chariot in a hail of arrows from his bow of deep genius, while Arjuna made no reply.

Cursing, Krishna jumped down from his ruined ratha. He wrenched a wheel from its shattered axle, and strode grimly towards the enemy.

But at that moment an old and habitual resistance within Arjuna gave way. Leaping down after his incarnate sarathy, he cried, "Stop, Krishna!"

"If you won't do your dharma, cousin," said the Dark One, his brow stormy, "I will do it for you, vow or no vow. Moreover, this chariot-wheel is hardly a weapon. Though I swear I will make it work as well as the Sudarshana today."

"Don't break your oath, Krishna. Come back, I will fight."

And Krishna, master of stratagems, master of minds, turned reluctantly back, a bloodthirsty look still in his eye.

Another chariot was fetched for the Pandava warrior and the pale horses yoked to it. Krishna took his place at the chariot-head, and Arjuna climbed in behind him. From then on, Arjuna's bow was death itself on Kurukshetra, picking souls off that field at will, his every shaft a killer. He no longer cared who stood before him, kinsman or not; each enemy was just a target. The Kaurava army shrank from his ambidextrous archery.

Arrows flowed from his bow like the notes of a fatal song. The Kaurava morale, which had soared in the brief hour that Arjuna had lost his nerve, now collapsed.

"You never know how brave a kshatriya really is, until he is faced with a war," Kaurava foot-soldiers had said dismissively to each other.

"Arjuna is afraid to kill his kinsmen."

"He is just afraid. He knows our numbers will win the war. Bheeshma for victory!" they had shouted. And Krishna had listened to them silently.

But now the Pandavas rallied round Arjuna, and the enemy fled before his cool fury.

The battle raged for fourteen days, and millions died, while Balarama was a pilgrim far from Kurukshetra. One evening, while the Pandavas sat around their campfire after the day's fighting, Arjuna had his heart broken.

"Your son Abhimanyu has been murdered in the chakravyuha by Jayadratha and his men."

As brave and gifted as his father, the youth of sixteen had been a scourge on Kurukshetra. Arjuna roared like a tiger shot with an arrow. Again and again, he roared his grief into the hearkening night.

Across the chasmal battlefield the Kaurava generals heard him, and Duryodhana smiled. "Arjuna has news of Abhimanyu's death. He is noble and soft-hearted; he will do something rash."

Across the lake of death which was that field, his arm a band of iron around Arjuna, Krishna said calmly, "The cowards hunted Abhimanyu down to destroy Arjuna. You mustn't let them conquer you so easily. Let anger be your truth and revenge ride with you."

Arjuna's eyes shone with of the shock of his son's death.

"I will kill Jayadratha," he said softly. "I will kill him before the sun sets tomorrow, or I will take my own life."

He sat quiet as a grave, staring into the flames of the campfire.

The Pandavas were dismayed. The night had ears; news of Arjuna's impetuous oath would reach Duryodhana, and he would keep Jayadratha at the rear of his whole army, to have Arjuna's life for his word. Next to Krishna, nobody knew better than Duryodhana that Arjuna was the key to this war: its living heart, the warrior who would decide who won or lost.

But Krishna knew this as well. He had always known this cousin of his would dictate the outcome of the war of the ages. For Arjuna was a man who lived this final life of his at the edge of salvation. He was the bhakta in whose soul an older, more secret battle must also be fought before he was saved. And Krishna had nurtured Kunti's third son carefully.

Now, to the surprise of the other Pandavas, Krishna clapped his hands in approval, taking even Arjuna a little unawares.

"You shall indeed kill Jayadratha!" announced the Avatara, as if the thing was already done. "Before the sun sets tomorrow, we will break Duryodhana's last hope, and his spirit with it. He is desperate now, he smells defeat. The murder of Abhimanyu is the deed of a desperate man."

All day, from dawn the next morning, Arjuna and his dark sarathy hunted Jayadratha. But in vain, because Duryodhana kept him safe at the back of his army, at the tip of an impenetrable suchimukha vyuha.

Today, all the Kaurava army served just to shield Jayadratha. They fought only to keep that kshatriya alive, and so at sunset to force Arjuna to take his own life. Ring on ring of the finest Kaurava warriors barred Arjuna's way.

Try as Krishna would to break past, there were too many of them arrayed against him. Even he, unarmed, couldn't pass those shifting mazes of heroes, and find his way to the eye of the needle.

Then Krishna thought of another way. Late in the afternoon, heavy clouds began to drift into that sky, and twilight seemed to set in before time.

Night wasn't far. Suddenly, Krishna reined in his horses. He unyoked them, as if in despair. Time flew swifter than light for the Pandavas, and appeared to creep along agonizingly for the Kauravas; it even seemed to move backwards.

Duryodhana saw the Blue God whisper to Arjuna, and shake his head as if in resignation. Then, darkness fell over Kurukshetra. Duryodhana roared, "Come out, Jayadratha! The sun has set, and Arjuna must kill himself."

There was lusty cheering in the Kaurava ranks. Jayadratha came forward slowly in the fallen darkness, towards where Krishna was rubbing his horses down. Arjuna stood downcast.

Krishna hissed, "Kill him, the sun hasn't set. Don't hesitate!"

In a dream, Arjuna raised his bow. A shaft of crimson light, the last ray of the setting sun, flashed across Kuruskshetra like Death's pointing finger. As Krishna withdrew his illusion of night, the Sudarshana Chakra spun away from across the final sliver of the fiery star.

A brilliant beam illumined Jayadratha's astonished face, and Arjuna shot him dead with a humming arrow of fate. The paasupatastra sloughed his head off in a flash of blood and bore it far from the field. As the Kaurava army stood rooted in shock, Krishna drove his warrior back to the Pandava camp erupting in jubilation.

When Arjuna killed Jayadratha, the morale of the Kaurava army was destroyed for a time. Then Drona died, and there were whispers in the ranks of desertion. The foot-soldiers complained that the Kaurava cause was an evil one, and could never be won, not by any superiority of numbers.

But there was one man among the Kaurava horde who shone like the noonday sun on Kurukshetra. His archery rivalled Arjuna's; no, his archery excelled Arjuna's. His spirit was not cowed, and he seemed to grow stronger whenever the rest of his legions were demoralized.

He was a man who carried within him a secret of blood of which he himself was not aware—he was Karna, bane of the Pandavas.

Karna was also Kunti's son, her child by the Sun God, Surya Deva whom she once invoked innocently with a rishi's mantra, when she was just a girl living in her father's palace.

She had floated her baby down a river in a wooden box. Around his neck she tied a golden locket that his blazing father had given her.

A common charioteer, a suta, found the box floating on the river with the brilliant child inside. It was he who raised Karna as his own son. Karna had lived a tortured life. He never knew who he really was, and dreams of his mother, whom he had never seen, haunted him.

Though he was a great archer, Karna had no honour among the kshatriyas because he was a sutaputra, a charioteer's son; until, realizing how invaluable he would be to him one day against Arjuna, Duryodhana shrewdly crowned him king of Anga. Karna was absolutely loyal to the Kaurava, prepared even to die for him.

The Pandava army fled from Karna, even as the Kauravas did before Arjuna. Like Yama himself, Karna straddled Kurukshetra, unafraid, apparently invincible; which in fact he was, owing to the golden locket he wore around his neck, the blessing of his father, the Deva.

But Arjuna's sarathy, who knew so much that no one else did, knew the secret by which Karna could be killed.

After Bheeshma fell, and Jayadratha, Karna and Arjuna divided Kurukshetra equally between them, each presiding over the killing on half the field. After Drona was slain, after Duryodhana's slide into a manic dejection, Karna was made senapati of the Kauravas. Under his ferocious lead, they recovered heart.

Veda Vyasa says Karna went among the Pandava army with shafts of fire and his burning sword, as if he was harvesting a field of ripe corn. Soon, Yudhishtira's soldiers fled at just the sight of him.

Then, one day, ignoring the battle around him, Krishna piloted Arjuna's chariot straight to where Karna brought death to the Pandava army in a storm. Arjuna hailed him, "Karna, not both of us will see the sun set tonight."

Raising an imperious hand Karna stopped the battle around them. He leapt down impulsively from his chariot, and ran to Arjuna, who stood taken aback. Tears springing in his eyes, he embraced Arjuna.

Karna said wistfully, "It is too late to turn back."

And did Arjuna imagine he heard his old and sworn enemy whisper the words 'my brother', as well; or was it the hot wind of death murmuring on Kurukshetra? Karna kissed Arjuna, too stunned to respond, on both cheeks, on his lips.

He darted Krishna a brief, hate-filled glare. Then he smiled and strode back to his chariot with the cry, "Either you or I must die today. So, fight. Let us be done with it."

Arjuna didn't hear him tell himself softly, "And I will die for you, my brother."

The previous night in his tent, when the stars were hidden by clouds, Karna received the visitor he least expected: the mother he had never known, Kunti sent to him at the midnight hour by Krishna. Alone with him, she told him whose son and brother he really was.

When she broke down and wept, he knew that this was no cunning fiction of Krishna's, but the truth, savage and inescapable. A moment's disbelief, then a cry of anguish tore itself out of Karna. But he waved his men away, when they came running to hear him cry out like that.

Somehow, he stilled the trembling that had broken out over his body. Karna said coldly to his mother, "You gave me life and, for that, you can ask me for one boon. But don't ask me to abandon this battle against your other sons, whom you love so much, for whose sake you have come to me like a beggar in the night. For my honour, I am a Kaurava and I will die one. I think you know that.

"All these men you see depend on me. They will gladly die for me, and I won't abandon them. Most of all, the only man who has ever loved me depends on me. I will never betray Duryodhana."

Krishna had warned her to expect as much. Her voice unsteady, Kunti said, "Give me the talismán you wear around your neck, to remember you by."

Karna breathed, "I have always worn this next to my body. But here!" He drew the chain of the golden locket over his head, and handed it to her. "Now go. Because I want to be as I always have—alone. Except that I did not realise it so completely until now."

With the locket clutched cold in her mother's hand, Kunti rose silently and went out of the tent. But a sob from him called her back.

Despite herself, she ran into the tent again. He knelt in the lamplight before her, and clasped her feet. His face was twisted with the truth with which she had pierced him, more terrible than any arrow.

"Mother!" he cried, and prostrated himself before her. "Mother, save me, I can't bear this pain."

Kunti touched his head, blessing him distantly. Quietly, she told him, "You have to."

She went out again, though he wanted her never to leave him, now that he had finally found her.

But a great and inscrutable war for a kingdom came between them, a war between legions of darkness and light. And Kunti left him, her first-born, desolate; shaking in every limb, she went back to her other sons, the ones she had raised.

The battle of Kurukshetra was still everywhere; an immense silence reached into the sky. In the space between the two hushed, spectator armies, both dwindled to a fraction of their original teeming numbers, Arjuna and Karna fought.

Karna appeared to have the edge. He was perhaps a shade, or a shade of a shade, quicker than Arjuna. But Krishna's dazzling manoeuvers in the Pandava's chariot tipped the balance back in Arjuna's favour. Karna's sarathy Salya was no match for the Avatara, whose horses obeyed not merely his masterly hands but his very thought.

And on a steep and swirling turn, Karna's chariot-wheel was mired in a bed of slush into which Krishna's deceitful artistry plunged it.

Forgetting his guru Bhargava's curse, that at the hour of his death his chariot and his astras would fail him, Karna jumped down to lift the wheel out of the mire. Krishna hissed at Arjuna, in a voice that would not be resisted, "Kill him! Or the war is lost."

Arjuna raised his bow, the Gandiva. Defenceless, without a weapon in his hand, or his father's golden talisman around his neck, Karna cried, "Arjuna, a kshatriya never kills an unarmed man. It isn't dharma. Wait till I lift this wheel out, and we will fight again."

But Krishna roared, "Dharma! You dare speak of dharma? Was it dharma when you helped Duryodhana build a house of lac and set it on fire, when the Pandavas and Kunti were asleep inside? Was it dharma when they were banished for thirteen years at a game of loaded dice? Was it dharma when you sat in Duryodhana's sabha and told Dusasana to strip Draupadi naked?"

Then, without looking at Arjuna, "Was it dharma when you hunted Abhimanyu down like a dog?"

There was no mention of the cruelty of Karna's own life, or his nobility in not telling Arjuna who he really was; none from Krishna, not now.

Instead, like an astra from his lips he let fly dead Abhimanyu's name, and roared at Arjuna again, *"Kill him!"*

Arjuna was shaken by this duel. He was certain, as never before, that he would lose if he fought fairly. This adversary, the one he had always feared most, was like no one he had ever fought: not merely his equal, which Karna had always been, but today his brilliant superior, as if the Kaurava hero had tapped a fresh spring of genius within himself.

Arjuna shot Karna down with an astra through his heart, the anjalika. Karna fell without a sound, blood bubbling at his mouth.

Somehow mastering death's twitching throes, he beckoned to Arjuna from the ground, to come close. Krishna tried to restrain him, but, responding to an undeniable instinct, the Pandava leapt down and was at his fallen enemy's side in a moment.

"Send for your mother, I must see her before I die," whispered Karna. Both the armies had gathered round thickly, and the message flew to Kunti. She came at once to the dying warrior's side.

He reached out an imploring hand to her, and gasped, "Look, I have died for you today, just as you wanted. And your son Arjuna has won the day for the Pandavas."

Suddenly he clutched her hair and drew her face close to his bloody lips. "Once," he whispered, so no one else heard, "before I die, I want to hear you call me son. Say it mother, say 'My son' to me, so I can die in peace."

But though she wanted so much to clasp him to her, to lay his head on her lap and cry a hundred times that he was her son, Kunti raised her head

away from him for a moment. She hesitated, as Arjuna and the other
Pandavas stood within hearing.

At that fateful moment, she glanced anxiously at Krishna, who shook
his head, then looked away at the sky as if to divine whether or not it
would rain in the night.

In that moment, Karna died without ever hearing that word from
his mother's lips.

After Karna's death, the last resistance in the spirit of the Kaurava army
was gone. Fired by Arjuna's triumph, the Pandavas made short and brutal
work of those who remained to fight.

And finally, one day, when a lone pilgrim wandered on to bloody
Kurukshetra, after a long journey of penance, a tirtha-yatra that had
taken him from Prabhasa to the source of the Saraswati, to all the holy
fords along the Ganga and the Yamuna, to the Naimisa forest, where
he killed the arrogant Romaharshana with a blade of kusa grass, and
Balavala, the asura who attacked the asramas and put out the yagna fires
of the rishis of the forest, down the Sarayu, to Prayaga, on to bathe in
the waters of the Gomati, Gandaki and Vipasa, to Gaya where he
worshipped his ancestors, to the Mahendra hill where he met the
awesome Parasurama, so peaceful now, on to bathe in the seven
tributaries of the Godavari, the Vena, the Pampa, and the river Bheema,
to the Venkata mountain, to Kanchi, to Kamakoti, to bathe in the Kaveri,
to Srirangam to Agastya's home in the Malaya range of mountains, to
Kanyakumari to worship Durga, the Panchaprana lake, to Kerala, to
Siva's Gokarna, to Parvati's island shrine, to the Dandava forest, and
from there to the Narmada, and back at last to Prabhasa from where
he had set out; one day, when this lone pilgrim, Balarama, arrived at
Kurukshetra, the Kaurava army was decimated, and out on the yawning
field where two ages coalesced, that battle-ground bulging with heaped
corpses, stained scarlet with a small sea of blood, Bheemasena the Pandava
and Duryodhana the Kaurava faced each other grimly, maces in hand.

"Stop!" cried Balarama to them. "The burden of the earth has been
removed. The beasts of the wild say so, the birds that are free sing it,

and the Gods of the sky celebrate it. You will serve no purpose by killing each other, not even to prove who is stronger. You are cousins, and I, your guru, say each of you is as great as the other."

But their eyes were glazed with all the killing they had seen and done, and with the implacable hatred begun when they were boys. The only answer he got from them was the clash of their maces ringing together, throwing showers of sparks in the air.

At long last, the hour of reckoning for Bheema and Duryodhana had come; and not Balarama, not anyone, was going to stop them now.

From Krishna, standing nonchalantly by, Balarama heard a wry chuckle, "No ablutions in tirtha-jala here, my brother, but the bloodbath."

The Dark One shook his head, when Balarama stared at him in another silent, accusing query. Krishna said, "No. I bore no arms at any time during the war. It was difficult, but your prayers have been with me."

He escorted Balarama away from that last combat between Duryodhana and Bheema; as he might a child who was innocent and pure and should see no bloodshed. Balarama went quietly back to Dwaraka.

His pride wouldn't allow Duryodhana to submit to Bheema or beg for his life. What would he do with a life anyway, now that Drona, Bheeshma, Dusasana, all his other brothers, and, most of all, his precious Karna, were dead?

Still brave as a lion, he battled Bheemasena as if some of the shame of defeat could be wiped away by this cousin's death. For it was Bheema that Duryodhana most hated. But the Pandava knew that his war and his brothers' was won. He fought in elation, in faith.

But unknown to Bheema, that morning Duryodhana had received a strange and powerful blessing from his mother Gandhari. She told him to come naked before her, after his bath and worship.

Gandhari was a great bhakta. She had bound her eyes many years ago, when she married the blind Dhritarashtra. And she never saw since, choosing to share her husband's disability. But that day, when everything seemed lost, in despair she decided to unwrap her eyes and bless her son with the vision of the first moment of her seeing the world again.

Clutching at straws, Duryodhana had bargained with Yudhishtira that all the war should be decided on the outcome of the gada-yuddha between Bheema and himself.

But a Dark One accosted Duryodhana at dawn, on his way from the bathing-tank. Krishna laughed at him, crying, "At your age, to go before your own mother like this. What a sight for her to see after her long blindness!"

And Duryodhana, always sensitive to mockery, covered his manhood with a large pipal leaf. So when Gandhari unwrapped her eyes and looked at her eldest son, they only sheathed almost all his body with their virgin vision's protection.

Long and fierce was the duel of maces between Bheema and Duryodhana. Since it was a sacred law of mace-fighting that an opponent may never be struck below the waist, Duryodhana laughed off Bheema's most powerful blows, strokes that would have felled elephants. And Bheema, who knew nothing of Gandhari's blessing, wondered at his cousin's amazing resilience.

Again and again he struck Duryodhana, and the Kaurava shrugged off his blows like a child's. But Bheema had no magical protection himself. Duryodhana's blows knocked him down whenever they landed, and he staggered to his feet, shaking the shock from his body.

As usual, only when Bheema had almost succumbed to Duryodhana's assault, did Krishna, standing coolly by, cry to the Pandava, "His thighs, Bheema, his thighs as you swore!"

The day Yudhishtira lost everything at dice—his kingdom, his brothers, his wife—Duryodhana and his brothers tried to strip Draupadi naked in the Kuru sabha.

Duryodhana bared his thigh lewdly to his very sex, and called the Pandavas' wife, as he might a whore, to come and sit in his lap. He called her saying that as she already enjoyed five men, why not another?

And then, his brother Dusasana had begun to tear away her clothes in that ancient court, where the Kuru elders sat helpless and silent.

But Krishna's grace, which she invoked in despair, had clothed Draupadi in an endless garment, of many colours, that could never be undone.

Bheema had sworn he would drink Dusasana's blood, one day, and promised Draupadi that she would wash her hair in it. This they had already done on Kurukshetra, after Bheema had torn Dusasana's chest open. Bheema had also sworn he would break Duryodhana's thigh, where his cousin called Draupadi to sit.

On Kurukshetra now, Bheema blinked at first to hear Krishna's extraordinary advice. Then, with a roar just to think of that other day's monstrous shame, the Pandava bent low and struck Duryodhana three stupendous blows below his waist. Two of them broke Duryodhana's thighs, and the third smashed his manhood, spilling his seed on to the battleground.

The last great king of evil of the dwapara yuga fell, screaming. At Krishna's word, Bheema and his brothers left Duryodhana there, in agony—to die slowly, to pay for all his crimes. It took half a day of torment before the last, rasping breath went out of him, and he was still.

The earth shuddered a tremor of relief, that at last she was rid of her final burden.

And so ended Krishna's last war against evil in the world, the one during which he bore no weapons. More than ten million kshatriyas perished on Kurukshetra during the Mahabharata yuddha, and the power of the race of kings was broken for ever.

The Avatara's mission was accomplished.

But for his warriors of light, the conquering Pandavas, there was more tragedy in store.

At midnight of the day the war ended, maddened by his father's death, his beloved Duryodhana's brutal death, Drona's son Aswatthama set fire to the tents where the Pandava's sons and the Panchalas lay asleep, and immolated them all in gruesome revenge.

For a month, the Pandavas mourned their dead on the banks of the Ganga; while the holy river washed some peace over their sorrow.

At the month's end, his spirit shriven, Yuddhishtira rode back in triumph to Hastinapura.

There, it was his blue cousin, a smiling Krishna, who welcomed him home, set the ancient crown of the Kurus on his noble head, and marked his brow with the auspicious, vermilion rajatilaka.

ANTAH

The dwapara yuga had almost set. The sinister spirit of the kali crouched just below time's horizon: baleful eyes gleaming, monstrous tail flicking from side to side, impatient to be loosed upon the earth.

But as long as Krishna lived in it, the kali yuga could not come into the world. And Krishna had a final task to fulfil before he left.

"As long as the Yadavas are alive, the world will not be safe. Even I have been hard pressed to contain them, as a shore does the sea. If I leave this power-drunk clan of mine behind, they will overrun the earth. Neither men nor the Devas can curb these, especially my own blood among them."

One day, a group of divine rishis with Viswamitra, Kanva, and Narada himself came to visit the old shrine at Pindaraka. Some Yadava youngsters lounged nearby, recounting the thrills of the battle of Kurukshetra to one another.

Seeing the holy men, and addled by fate and their own arrogance, they decided to have a little joke at the munis' expense. They dressed Jambavati's son Samba in clothes borrowed from a fisherwoman, and led him, his face covered, to the profound ones.

They prostrated themselves at the rishis' feet, and one bold spark said, "This dark-eyed beauty has something to ask you, Brahmanas. But she is too shy to ask herself and bids me speak for her. She is pregnant, and she is anxious to have a son. Rishis, tell her if she will have a boy or a girl."

And all the Yadu boys wore solemn faces.

They expected a mild reproof, at worst, for they carried with them the smugness of being Krishna's invincible clan. But they were taken aback at the ferocity of the rishis' response; those youths were taken unawares by time.

"She will give birth to an iron club," cursed one of the wise, in rage. "And that club will raze the arrogant Yadava clan!"

Pale with fright, the young men ran to Ugrasena. They told him, and not Krishna, what had happened; and there was suddenly something growing in Samba's belly. The same night his stomach had to be incised and yielded an iron club.

Ugrasena had the club ground to powder, and the powder cast into the sea where it floated on green waves. Then, washed landward with the tide, the powder settled on a sacred shore where a great river flowed into the sea, and was transformed into luminous pollen. Under a blazing moon the pollen grew with supernatural swiftness into a bank of silvery eraka reeds.

One perfectly arrowhead-shaped sliver of the club could not be ground. Ugrasena thought, surely, one small sliver couldn't destroy all the Yadavas, and he had that cast into the waves as well; where, as fate would have it, it was swallowed by a large fish.

The next morning the fish swam into the net of some fishermen. While gutting their catch, they discarded the bright iron sliver they found in the creature's belly, and it lay shining on a white beach on the night of a full moon.

An old hunter, Jara abroad at his poaching, spotted the sliver and was attracted by its perfect shape. He picked it up and fixed it to the head of his hunting arrow.

Evil omens gathered in the sky and on the streets of Dwaraka. The astrologers saw cataclysmic aspects in the heavens and tremors of ocean and earth rocked the city.

Krishna said gravely in the Sudharma, "We are cursed. We mustn't stay in Dwaraka a day longer. Perhaps, in Prabhasa we will find expiation for our sins, as did Soma Deva. Let the women and children go ahead to the Sankhodhara island and wait for us there. We men will go to the place from where the Saraswati flows west."

The Yadavas prepared to leave Dwaraka, jewel of the sea. An hour before they went, gentle, visionary Uddhava came to Krishna when he was alone, and fell at his feet.

"Lord, I am afraid!" he whispered. "I see portents of doom everywhere. I believe you mean to kill the Yadavas and to leave this world yourself. Krishna, I can't bear to be separated from you."

Krishna raised Uddhava up and embraced him.

"Go, Uddhava, to Badarikasrama on Mount Gandhamadana. There, at the shrine of Nara Narayana, you will find moksha. The seventh day after I leave Dwaraka, it will submerge. Only my palace will remain above the waves for a time in memory of me."

He spoke to Uddhava, expounding the eternal dharma even as he had done for Arjuna on Kurukshetra. Finally, he gave him his wooden padukas, the ones he himself had worn for years.

Hands folded, Uddhava walked around Krishna in pradakshina. He laid his head at the Avatara's feet, bathing them with tears. And laying a hand on his friend's head, Krishna blessed him to attain moksha.

Uddhava left on his final pilgrimage, alone, and bearing the precious sandals on his head.

When he had gone, Krishna went into the temple that stood in his garden, beside the parijata tree he had once taken from Amravati. He stood in dhyana before the stone idol in the shrine, the image he had made himself for his father Vasudeva.

With a thought, he summoned two lambent beings to that sanctum. They stood before him as soon as he invoked them, their bodies immaterial, made of light. One was Brihaspati, the Devaguru, and the other Vayu, the ancient wind.

Krishna gave the sacred idol of Dwaraka into their hands. He said, "Take this holiest of my icons to Kerala, which is divided from the rest of Bharatavarsha by the western mountains. Establish it there, and there let it remain, safe from the invasions of darkness that will sweep the land in the centuries to come. In Kerala, in a shrine you must fashion yourselves, let this idol stand as a solace to all men: a lamp that will burn in the darkest nights of the kali yuga."

The unearthly ones received the image in reverent hands, of wisdom and air. They knelt at his feet for his blessing. When he had blessed them, they vanished, taking the holy image.

They ranged over the country of Kerala seeking a place to install Krishna's idol, and once they saw the Lord Siva praying beside a pool of clear water. Brihaspati and Vayu established the idol there and created a temple in that place which was called Guruvayoor, after both those Devas.

Krishna called Balarama and, for the last time, embraced him within the sea-walls of Dwaraka. Arm in arm, they came down the palace steps and climbed into the chariot of the air, the Jaitra, which had stayed with Krishna since it appeared in Mathura years ago when Jarasandha first attacked it. Last of all, Krishna rode out from his beloved city.

Only the wind sighed then in the crystal streets. The birds and the animals, even the merry dolphins, had all gone. The crash of waves against the marble walls was woven, clear and lonely, with the wind. The sun set sadly over the ghost city, all its loveliness abandoned.

When they reached Prabhasa the Yadavas bathed at the holy confluence, where river and sea flow together. They performed some rituals, as Krishna asked them to: ostensibly rituals for their redemption and prosperity; but, though they did not know this, in fact their own last rites.

In the forenoon of the day after they arrived, persuaded by subtle fate, they drank huge quantities of the potent, sweet stimulant maireyaka, just before the noonday meal. Krishna himself began the drinking.

A strange mood gripped them all, but they hardly noticed it. Just as they hadn't yet seen the uncommon reeds, formed like jagged thunderbolts, growing at the water's edge.

The quarrel began over nothing: the food. Fate fluttered down and settled invisibly on each Yadava's shoulder, like a dove of death.

"This food isn't clean!" yelled Pradyumna out of the blue, his voice thick with drink.

"Yes it is!" cried Samba, springing to his feet.

In a flash, Pradyumna drew his sword and, kicking over a table and the food on it, leapt at Samba. Like helpless players in a nightmare, the Yadavas enacted the tragedy.

Akrura drew his sword against Bhoja; Aniruddha and Satyaki fought. Son fought father, brother battled brother, all deranged with maireyaka, and by Krishna's maya.

Krishna had hoped the Yadavas might purify themselves and live peacefully on Sankhodhara. He was encouraged when they readily abandoned Dwaraka, as soon as he asked them. Perhaps, he even thought his own life was not yet over. Like any man he had hoped.

Now the Yadavas fought like wild dogs. But they had fought at Kurukshetra as well, and though the side they had fought for was routed, they themselves were immortal because of who they were.

They fought again viciously at Prabhasa. They felled each other with dreadful sword-strokes. But those struck down rose at once, intoxicated and laughing. Their wounds healed miraculously, and death seemed their friend because they were Krishna's own people, his flesh and blood.

Aniruddha saw the eraka reeds in the shallow water and, moved by an irresistible impulse, strode across and grasped at them. Balarama cried out to him not to, but too late. When the youth pulled up a clutch of the reeds made of the rishis' curse, they turned into a sword in his hand. Roaring, helpless in the clutch of destiny, all those kshatriyas began to pull up the uncanny reeds to be their weapons.

When they struck each other with the glittering things, the invincible Yadavas fell dead. And now they did not rise again, even those who were wounded with no more than a scratch. Krishna ran to them in dismay, shouting that they should stop.

But Pradyumna turned on him, growling, and Samba, Charuka, and Charuvarman, all at once. They fell on him: sons who had repressed a lifetime of resentment and envy; sons who hated their father more than they could bear any more, and must kill him at once.

Then, Akrura and Satyaki were at their king in fury beside the river. His own head turned, with a heartbroken roar, Krishna snatched up a handful of the deadly reeds, and set on his murdering kinsmen.

The reeds in his hand turned again into a shining club, and roaring out of control, roaring for fate, roaring in sorrow, he slaughtered his clan with it, smashing their noble heads and splendid bodies.

Blood flew everywhere, bright in the sunlight, splashing into holy water. Heads were broken open like melons, young, handsome torsos shattered, in an orgy of killing. Before there was time to take account of what went on, every last Yadava was dead, and Krishna stood alone among the smouldering ruins of his people, drenched in scarlet, panting.

Still, the bloodlust raged in him.

"Balarama, where are you?" he cried, red-eyed. In a whisper, his heart called him to the sea.

There Balarama sat calmly under a great aswattha tree that grew on the shore-line at the forest's edge. Even as Krishna watched him, his brother began to metamorphose. An immense white serpent slithered slowly from his mouth. It transformed Balarama's body into its own flesh as it came; so when it had emerged fully, nothing was left of the man.

Krishna grew quiet again. The shining Snake paused for a moment, its hood inclined to stare at the Dark One. Then it lowered itself, glided majestically into the ocean, and was gone.

With a sigh, Krishna sat down under that aswattha, and the supreme Brahman, the timeless Spirit, came over him in an infinite tide.

He was four-armed again, unearthly weapons in his hands; a dazzling vanamala appeared for the last time around his neck. The Jaitra drew up before him as, now utterly at peace, everything accomplished, he shut his eyes in dhyana and fused himself with the Brahman, surging oceanic in him.

The Sudarshana, the Kaumodaki, the Saringa and the Panchajanya detached themselves and circled him three times. Then, with the complex chariot, which was both chariot and smooth flying disk, they rose into the sky by the path of the sun, and vanished from the world; until the yawning ages came round again in their deep turning and he, the Blue God, returned.

Krishna sat in padmasana, the posture of the lotus, under the tree of wisdom, abandoned to the bliss of sweet eternity come to claim him.

From afar, around the bole of the tree, Jara the old hunter saw Krishna's foot, bloodstained from the slaughter of the Yadavas. Jara stalked that bright foot, thinking it was the ear of a red deer. When he was within range he raised his rough bow carefully and shot his fateful arrow, humming and true.

Krishna cried out, a last reverberant roar in the world, as the arrowhead made from the sliver of the accursed club pierced the only vulnerable part of his body: the sole of his foot, under his big toe.

Jara came running when he heard that cry. Gasping to see Krishna, knowing him at once from rumour, the hunter fell on his face in the sand before the dying Avatara.

Krishna placed a hand on the wild man's head, and told him, "It was only as I willed it. Go now, your mission in this world of sorrow is over."

A wonderful chariot flew down from heaven, a pushpaka vimana. All his illusions dispelled in that moment of grace, Jara ascended in it.

Now the Devas of light, Indra and his gods, gathered above that tree, anxious to see what would happen to Krishna's blue body when the soul left it. Would he consume it with agneyi, ash it with the fire of yoga? The Devas waited breathlessly to collect those ashes, to battle over them if need be.

But Krishna heard another voice calling him where he sat dying, a voice he had never hoped to hear again in this world.

There she stood between heaven and earth, just as he had left her. But now her form was of light and, her eyes full of love, she held her hands out to him. He shut his own eyes, thinking she was a hallucination of death. And still he saw her smiling; he still heard her calling him.

And even as, with a sigh, he reached down and pulled the arrow from his foot, all at once he vanished before the Devas' astonished eyes. For she came near him and he took her hand, and then Radha drew him across the mystic threshold. She took him, his blue body rich with his fabulous life, and his ancient spirit, into the living Earth's heart of deep legend. His every purpose of incarnation accomplished, she took him back into eternity.

At that moment, like black lightning, into Krishna's great void, the kali yuga flashed into the world.

GLOSSARY

Abhichara	Occult power, dark sorcery. Also a spirit raised by an occult ritual.
Abhimanyu	Arjuna's son.
Aditya	Sun God. Being of light.
Airavata	Indra's four-tusked white, flying elephant.
Akrura	A Yadava nobleman.
Amravati	Indra's heavenly city.
Amrita	Nectar of immortality.
Amsa	Essence, part.
Ananta Sesha	The Cosmic Serpent on which Vishnu rests.
Anarta	Krishna's country.
Antah	The end
Arista	Demon bull bison.
Arjuna	The third Pandava, a great kshatriya archer.
Aryaman	Ancestor, the first man.
Asrama	Hermitage.
Astra	Unearthly weapon.
Asura	Demon.
Asvamedha	Horse sacrifice.
Aswattha	Pipal tree.
Atman	The individual Soul.
AUM	Holy syllable, represents the Ultimate Reality.
Avatara	Incarnation.
Bakasura	Crane demon.
Balarama	Krishna's older brother, an incarnation of Ananta Sesha.
Bhagavad Gita	The Song of God.
Bhakti	Devotion. Worship.
Bhakta	Devotee.
Bheeshma	Kuru patriarch.
Brahma	One of the Hindu Trinity. The Creator.

Brahman	Ultimate, transcendent, Godhead; quite different from Brahma.
Brahmana	The priestly caste of the Hindus, also 'Brahma's people'.
Brahmanirvana	The final liberation, when the Soul is united with Brahman.
Brahma Rishi	Sage of Brahman.
Brighu	An ancient rishi.
Brihaspati	Guru of the Devas. Also the planet Jupiter.
Chakra	Wheel. In the body, a subtle centre of energy along the spinal column and in the brain.
Chakravyuha	A wheel-like battle formation.
Chanura	A demonic wrestler in Mathura.
Charana	An unearthly being.
Chitraratha	King of the Gandharva elves.
Daitya	Demon, son of Diti.
Danava	Demon, son of Danu.
Dantavakra	'Crooked-teeth'. Krishna's cousin and enemy.
Daruka	Krishna's charioteer.
Deva	Celestial; elemental deity. Also 'Being of Light.' 'Divya' is light.
Devaki	Krishna's mother.
Devaloka	Realm of the Devas.
Dharma	Truth, justice.
Dhritarashtra	Blind king of the Kurus.
Dhyana	Meditation.
Drona	Guru to the Kauravas and Pandavas.
Duryodhana	An evil Kaurava. Dhritarashtra's eldest son.
Dusasana	Duryodhana's brother.
Dvividha	An ancient vanara.
Dwapara Yuga	The third great age.
Dwaraka	Krishna's ocean city.
Gandhamadana	Fragrant mountain. Gatekeeper to the heavens.
Gandharva	Unearthly being. Elf. Race of heavenly minstrels.
Garuda	Vishnu's Eagle.
Gokula	Cowherd village.
Gopa	Cowherd.
Gopala	Krishna.
Gopi/Gopika	Cowherd woman.
Govardhana	Holy mountain which Krishna lifts to protect the gopas.

Govinda	Krishna. Vishnu.
Guna	Archetypal essence in Nature.
Guru	Preceptor. Master.
Hari	Vishnu.
Hastinapura	Capital of the Kurus. 'City of elephants.'
Hrishikesha	Krishna. Vishnu.
Ikshvaku	Ancestor. A royal house of the Sun is named after him.
Indra	King of the Devas of light.
Indraprastha	City raised by Indra in the wilderness for the Pandavas, at Krishna's instance.
Jaitra	Krishna's magical chariot.
Jambavan	Ancient king of Bears from Rama's time.
Jambavati	Jambavan's daughter. Krishna's wife.
Janardhana	Krishna. Vishnu.
Japam	Chanting God's names.
Jara	A hunter.
Jarasandha	King of Magadha. Krishna's inveterate enemy.
Jayadratha	A Kaurava warrior.
Kaala	Time.
Kadamba	Krishna's favorite tree.
Kalayavana	The Black Greek.
Kali Yuga	The fourth, and the most evil, of the four ages. (Not the black Goddess, Kaali).
Kama	The God of Love.
Kamadhenu	Sacred Cow of wishes.
Kama Shastras	Sacred arts of loving.
Kamsa	Krishna's evil uncle, the tyrant of Mathura.
Karma	Action, duty, also the fruit of past deeds.
Karna	A hero of the Mahabharata. In fact, he is the Pandavas' eldest brother, but fights for the Kauravas since he does not know who he really is.
Kaumodaki	Krishna's mace.
Kauravas	Dhritarashtra's sons, a hundred of them.
Kesava	Lank-haired, Krishna, Vishnu.
Koyal	Cuckoo.
Krita Yuga	The first of the four ages. The purest, post pristine yuga.
Kshatriya	The warrior caste.
Kubera	Lord of treasures. A Deva.

Kubja	Hunchback whom Krishna heals.
Kunti	Pandavas' mother, Krishna's aunt.
Kuru	Race descended from the ancient king of that name.
Madhusudana	Slayer of the demon Madhu. Vishnu.
Mahabharata	Great war between the Pandavas and the Kauravas. Also, the epic about that war.
Mahamaya	Goddess of Illusion.
Mahavishnu	Second God of Hindu Trinity. The Preserver.
Mandala	Dimension, galaxy.
Mantra, mantram	Sacred chant.
Manu	Ancestor. Lawgiver. Lord of a manvantara.
Margasirsa, mrigasirsha	An auspicious Hindu lunar month.
Mathura	Ancient city of the Yadavas.
Matulan	Uncle.
Matuli	Aunt.
Maya	Illusion, cosmic illusion. As different from the reality of God. Also, the Goddess of illusion.
Moksha	Liberation, salvation.
Muchukunda	A king from an ancient yuga.
Muni	A Seer. A Rishi.
Mustika	A demonic wrestler of Kamsa's.
Naga	Great serpent. Also magical, serpentine race.
Nakshatra	Asterism in lunar Hindu astrology.
Nanda	Krishna's foster father. A gopa chieftain.
Narada	Brahma's son. A wandering Rishi. A great devotee of Vishnu's.
Narasimha	Vishnu's Manticore incarnation.
Narayana	The Sleeper on eternity's Waters, which are called the Naara. Vishnu.
Nirvana	Moksha. Liberation.
OM, Omkara	The Primal, holy, syllable which represents Godhead. AUM. Pranava.
Panchajanya	Krishna's Conch.
Pandavas	The five sons of Pandu: Yudhishtira, Bheema, Arjuna, Nakula and Sahadeva.
Parabrahman	Brahman. The ultimate, undifferentiated Godhead.
Paundraka	The false Vasudeva, king of Pundra.
Pitr	Ancestor. Literally, father.
Pitrloka	Realm of the manes.
Pradyumna	Krishna and Rukmini's son. He is Kama born as a man.

Prakriti	Nature. The female, earthly principle.
Pralaya	The deluge which ends the world.
Pranava	AUM.
Punnaga	A tree.
Purodasa	The main honour at a sacrifice.
Purusha	Soul. The male, transcendent principle.
Pushpaka vimana	Sky chariot.
Putana	A demoness.
Radha	A gopi. Krishna's first and eternal love. She is the great Goddess.
Rajarishi	A royal seer. A king who is a sage.
Rajas	The second guna, essence, in nature.
Rajasuya	A great sacrifice of emperors.
Rajatilaka	The royal mark on a king's brow.
Rakshasa	A demon.
Rakshasi	A demoness.
Rama	A previous incarnation of Vishnu.
Rig Veda	The first Veda.
Rishi	A Sage.
Rudra	Siva. Also a class of fierce beings associated with Siva.
Rukmi	Rukmini's brother, Krishna's enemy.
Rukmini	The princess of Vidarbha, Krishna's wife.
Sakatasura	The cart demon.
Salva	An evil king, Krishna's enemy.
Sama	A Veda.
Samba	Krishna's son by Jambavati.
Samsara	The world. Illusion.
Samvartaka	One of Indra's stormclouds of the deluge.
Sandhi	Conjunction, Cusp.
Sankara	Siva.
Sapta Rishi	The seven original sages, born from Brahma's mind.
Saringa	Krishna's Bow.
Satrajita	A Yadava who had the Syamantaka jewel.
Sattva	The first and purest of Nature's gunas.
Satyabhama	Krishna's wife. Satrajita's daughter.
Senapati	General. Literally, lord of an army.
Siddha	A realised being.
Sish	Pupil. Disciple.
Sishupala	Krishna's cousin and enemy. King of Chedi.
Siva	Third God of Hindu Trinity. The Destroyer.
Skanda	Siva's son. Also called Karttikeya.
Soma	The Moon God. Also, lunar nectar.

Srivatsa	Literally 'beloved of Sri Lakshmi.' The whorl of hair on Vishnu's (and Krishna's) chest.
Sudama	A Brahmana. Krishna's beloved friend.
Sudarshana Chakra	Vishnu's weapon, a blazing wheel.
Sudra	The fourth Hindu caste, the servitors.
Suka	Vyasa's son. Often the narrator of the Purana.
Surya	The Sun God.
Swayamvara	The ceremony at which a princess chooses her own husband.
Syamantaka	Jewel of the Sun.
Tamas	The third and grossest guna in Nature.
Tapasya	Penance. Long meditation or austerity.
Treta Yuga	The second great age.
Trinavarta	Demon who comes as a storm.
Tripura	Three sky cities which Siva brought down with a missile of fire.
Ucchaisravas	The Sun's peerless horse.
Ugrasena	King of Mathura.
Vaikunta	Vishnu's celestial city.
Vaisya	The third Hindu caste. The traders.
Vamana	A Dwarf incarnation of Vishnu, who covered the three worlds in three strides.
Vana	Jungle, forest.
Varuna	Lord of seas.
Vasudeva	Vishnu. Also Krishna's father's name.
Veda	Ancient, sacred book of hymns.
Vrindavana	Literally 'forest of Vrinda'. Vrinda, who was once Vishnu's lover, is born as this magical forest for Krishna to roam in.
Vivasat	An ancestor.
Vyasa	The son of Rishi Parasara and Matsyagandhi the fisher-girl. The greatest poet, and compiler of the Vedas, the Puranas, and the author of the Mahabharata.
Yaga, Yagna	A sacrifice.
Yajus, Yajur Veda	A Veda.
Yama	God of Death.
Yamala	A tree.
Yasodha	Krishna's foster mother, a gopi.
Yoga	Union. Union with the Self, with God.

Yogi, Yogin	One who is united with his higher Self, with God.
Yuga	An Age.
Yugantara	The conjunction of two ages. Time of change.
Yugasandhi	The cusp between two yugas.